Universities in Transition

This book is available as a free fully-searchable ebook from
www.adelaide.edu.au/press

Universities in Transition:

Foregrounding Social Contexts of Knowledge in the First Year Experience

Edited by

Heather Brook, Deane Fergie,
Michael Maeorg and Dee Michell

UNIVERSITY OF
ADELAIDE PRESS

Published in Adelaide by

University of Adelaide Press
The University of Adelaide
Level 14, 115 Grenfell Street
South Australia 5005
press@adelaide.edu.au
www.adelaide.edu.au/press

The University of Adelaide Press publishes externally refereed scholarly books by staff of the University of Adelaide. It aims to maximise access to the University's best research by publishing works through the internet as free downloads and for sale as high quality printed volumes.

© 2014 The Contributors

This work is licenced under the Creative Commons Attribution-NonCommercial-NoDerivatives 4.0 International (CC BY-NC-ND 4.0) License. To view a copy of this licence, visit http://creativecommons.org/licenses/by-nc-nd/4.0 or send a letter to Creative Commons, 444 Castro Street, Suite 900, Mountain View, California, 94041, USA. This licence allows for the copying, distribution, display and performance of this work for non-commercial purposes providing the work is clearly attributed to the copyright holders. Address all inquiries to the Director at the above address.

For the full Cataloguing-in-Publication data please contact the National Library of Australia: cip@nla.gov.au

ISBN (paperback) 978-1-922064-82-0
ISBN (ebook: pdf) 978-1-922064-83-7
ISBN (ebook: epub) 978-1-922064-84-4
ISBN (ebook: kindle) 978-1-922064-85-1

Editor: Rebecca Burton
Editorial support: Julia Keller
Book design: Zoë Stokes
Cover design: Emma Spoehr
Cover image: iStockphoto

Contents

Notes on Contributors	vii
Introduction *Heather Brook, Deane Fergie, Michael Maeorg and Dee Michell*	1

Part 1 — Reconceptualising: transition and universities

1. Navigating student transition in higher education: induction, development, becoming — *Trevor Gale and Stephen Parker* — 13

2. University transitions in practice: research-learning, fields and their communities of practice — *Deane Fergie* — 41

Part 2 — Revaluing: 'non-traditional' student groups in higher education

3. Classism on campus? Exploring and extending understandings of social class in the contemporary higher education debate — *Angelique Bletsas and Dee Michell* — 77

4. Reframing 'the problem': students from low socio-economic status backgrounds transitioning to university — *Marcia Devlin and Jade McKay* — 97

5. Changing social relations in higher education: the first-year international student and the 'Chinese learner' in Australia — *Xianlin Song* — 127

| 6 | Relating experiences: Regional and Remote students in their first year at university
Michael Maeorg | 157 |

Part 3 — Realising: transformations on campus

7	The University of Adelaide Student Learning Hub: a case study of education co-creation *Pascale Quester, Kendra Backstrom and Slavka Kovacevic*	187
8	Thinking critically about critical thinking in the First-Year Experience *Chris Beasley and Benito Cao*	205
9	Knowing students *Heather Brook and Dee Michell*	229

Notes on Contributors

Kendra Backstrom is Associate Director, Infrastructure Engagement, at the University of Adelaide. After graduating from the University of South Australia, she worked as an interior designer before joining the University of Adelaide in 2006. Whilst at the University she has worked on numerous projects and strategic initiatives. She was the Programme Director for the Learning Hub Project and was responsible for the delivery of a new $42 million state-of-the-art collaborative learning facility, as well as engaging with diverse and multiple stakeholders to ensure the success of the project's objectives.

Chris Beasley is Professor in Politics and Co-Director of the Fay Gale Centre for Research on Gender at the University of Adelaide. She has an interdisciplinary background in both humanities and social sciences, has been employed as a teaching and learning academic, and has also coordinated enclave programs for Indigenous students. In 1994 Professor Chris Beasley received the peak teaching prize from the University of Adelaide. Her books include *Heterosexuality in Theory and Practice* (with Heather Brook and Mary Holmes, Routledge, 2012) and *Engaging with Carol Bacchi* (edited with Angelique Bletsas, University of Adelaide Press, 2012). She is currently writing a book on contemporary popular film titled *The Cultural Politics of Popular Film: Power, Culture and Society* (with Heather Brook, Manchester University Press) and preparing another book, *Internet Dating* (with Mary Holmes, Routledge).

Angelique Bletsas has enjoyed appointments as a Research Fellow at both the University of South Australia and the University of Adelaide and has taught undergraduate courses in Australian Social Policy and Honours courses at the

University of Adelaide. She has published in the areas of Australian social policy, gender equality, and more reflectively on the limits of academic discourse. Dr Bletsas is currently employed at the ACT Council of Social Service as a Policy and Advocacy Coordinator. Her research interests continue to reside in exploring the ways conceptualisations of poverty and disadvantage inform policy and impact people's lives.

Heather Brook teaches and researches in the School of Social and Policy Studies at Flinders University. An alumnus of the University of Adelaide and the Australian National University, she is the author of *Conjugal Rites* (Palgrave Macmillan, 2007) and *Conjugality* (Palgrave Manmillan, forthcoming), and a co-author (with Chris Beasley and Mary Holmes) of *Heterosexuality in Theory and Practice* (Routledge, 2012). Outside the ivory tower she likes running, reading novels, and making music.

Benito Cao is Lecturer in Politics at the University of Adelaide. He has received several teaching awards and has published in the fields of pedagogy, political culture, national identity and environmental politics. Dr Benito Cao has recently completed a manuscript on environmental citizenship for the Routledge Introductions to Environment series. The book, titled *Environment and Citizenship*, will be released in 2015. He is currently working on another book, *Mediating Environmental Citizenship*, for the Ashgate series Transforming Environmental Politics and Policy. He holds a doctorate in Politics from the University of Adelaide.

Marcia Devlin is the Deputy Vice Chancellor (Learning and Quality) at Federation University Australia. She is a nationally and internationally recognised expert in tertiary education. Areas of particular expertise and interest include quality, equity, leadership, teaching and learning, student engagement and digital education. Her research incorporates both theoretical and practical investigations into contemporary tertiary education, policy, e-pedagogy and curriculum. Professor Marcia Devlin currently holds an Australian Research Council grant on international student policy and recently led to completion an Office of Learning and Teaching-funded national research project on effective teaching and support of students from low socio-economic status backgrounds. She publishes widely in academic and popular outlets.

Universities in Transition

Deane Fergie is a Senior Lecturer in Anthropology and Manager of LocuSAR (Locus of Social Analysis and Research), a research and consultancy unit based in the School of Social Sciences at the University of Adelaide. She is also Director of ANTS (Australian Native Title Studies) at the University. She has extensive teaching experience in the tertiary environment, and has been awarded for her teaching excellence. Her long-term anthropological research into academic cultures has resulted in innovative transition-to-university pilot educational programs (Pre-O and Re-O) as well as originally conceived and successful undergraduate courses based on a 'community of practice' framework. Her current research interests and activities are particularly focussed on higher education and native title anthropology.

Trevor Gale is Professor of Education Policy and Social Justice at Deakin University (Melbourne), founding editor of the international journal, *Critical Studies in Education*, and co-editor (with Kal Gulson) of the book series, *Education Policy and Social Inequality*, published by Springer. From 2008 to 2011 he was the founding director of Australia's National Centre for Student Equity in Higher Education. Trevor's research focuses on education policy and social justice, particularly in formal education contexts (schooling, vocational and higher education). He is chief investigator on two current Australian Research Council Discovery Grants, one researching the aspirations of secondary school students in Melbourne's western suburbs and the other researching the social justice dispositions of secondary teachers in advantaged and disadvantaged Melbourne and Brisbane schools. He has recently completed major research reports for the Australian Office of Learning and Teaching on higher education student transitions, for the Higher Education Funding Council of England on widening participation in Australian higher education, and for the Australian National VET Equity Advisory Council on TAFE bachelor degrees and disadvantaged learners.

Slavka Kovacevic is a communications and marketing manager with more than twelve years of experience across the education, commercial and government sectors. She is a graduate of the University of South Australia and has a Bachelor of Management degree in Marketing. Slavka has successfully led the development and execution of effective strategic and tactical plans for internal and external communications across a range of organisations, including the Learning Hub

Project at the University of Adelaide. She worked in partnership with key stakeholders across the University and ensured that communication strategies, messages and tactics were strongly aligned with project and University objectives.

Jade McKay is a Research Fellow in the Faculty of Business and Law at Deakin University, Australia. She has a PhD in Literary Studies and works across a range of research projects, including a national study on innovative technologies in teaching and learning funded by CPA Australia. Jade McKay's research is interdisciplinary and she publishes broadly in literary studies, higher education and business. Her research is guided by a focus on minority and disadvantaged groups in both higher education and western culture in general.

Michael Maeorg, an anthropologist by training, is a researcher and educator in LocuSAR (Locus of Social Analysis and Research), a research and consultancy unit at the University of Adelaide. He has conducted ethnographic fieldwork in India and Australia, and his recent research activities have focussed on higher education, native title and cultural heritage. Over the past two decades he has gained rich experience as an educator in a variety of contexts and roles: from teaching ESL in Japan, to co-coordinating the Humanities and Social Sciences Foundation Program for Indigenous students and teaching numerous anthropology courses, often with a focus on ethnographic methods, at the University of Adelaide.

Dee Michell teaches and researches in Gender Studies and Social Analysis at the University of Adelaide. An alumnus of both Adelaide and Flinders Universities, she is the author of *Christian Science: Women, Healing and the Church* (University Press of America, 2009). Dr Dee Michell has also co-edited two anthologies of self-narratives: *Women Journeying with Spirit* (with Jude Noble, Ginninderra Press, 2010) and *Recipes for Survival: Stories of Hope and Healing by survivors of the State 'Care' System in Australia* (with Priscilla Taylor, People's Voice Publishing, 2011). When not working she likes to read and watch drama, spend time with her family and friends, and play in her garden.

Stephen Parker is Research Fellow in the Centre for Educational Futures and Innovation at Deakin University. He has interests in social justice, public policy, social and political theory, and sociology. Stephen has researched and published in higher education policy, student aspirations and student transitions appearing in *Cambridge Journal of Education* and *Studies in Higher Education*. Dr Stephen Parker has recently contributed to a number of research reports including VET providers, associate/bachelor degrees and disadvantaged learners (for the National VET Equity Advisory Council), *Student Aspirations for Higher Education in Central Queensland: A survey of school students' navigational capacities* (for Central Queensland University) and *Widening Participation in Australian Higher Education* (for the Higher Education Funding Council for England). He is currently Research Fellow on the ARC project, *Social Justice Dispositions: Informing the Pedagogic Work of Teachers*, with Trevor Gale, Russell Cross and Carmen Mills. Prior to working at Deakin Stephen was a researcher at Australia's National Centre for Student Equity in Higher Education.

Pascale Quester's qualifications include a Bachelor of Business Administration from her native France, a Master of Arts (Marketing) from Ohio State University and a PhD from Massey University (New Zealand). A researcher in the areas of consumer behaviour and marketing, she is the author of two leading textbooks on Marketing and Consumer Behaviour as well as over 200 international refereed publications. Professor Quester has held the positions of Professor of Marketing, Associate Dean of Research and then Executive Dean of the Faculty of the Professions before her appointment as Deputy Vice-Chancellor and Vice President (Academic) at the University of Adelaide in 2011. Professor Quester has held several appointments as a visiting professor including at La Sorbonne, Paris II, ESSEC and at the University of Nancy. In 2007, she received the highest French academic recognition to become *Professeur des Universités*. In 2009, she was awarded the prestigious title of *Distinguished Fellow of the Australia and New Zealand Marketing Academy*. In September 2012, Professor Quester was awarded the *Ordre national du Mérite* (National Order of Merit) in recognition of her contribution to higher education in both France and Australia.

Xianlin Song is a Senior Lecturer at the Centre for Asian Studies, University of Adelaide. Her research focuses on the current cultural transition and gender issues in contemporary China, and higher education in Australia. Dr Xianlin Song's most recent publication includes a co-edited book with Dr Kate Cadman, *Bridging transcultural divides: Asian languages and cultures in a global higher education* (University of Adelaide Press, 2012), and the co-authored book with Professor Kay Schaffer, *Women Writers in Post Socialist China* (Routledge, 2014).

Introduction

Heather Brook, Deane Fergie, Michael Maeorg and Dee Michell

For some time now the terms 'transition to university' and 'first-year experience' have been at the centre of discussion and discourse at, and about, Australian universities. For those university administrators, researchers and teachers involved, this focus has been framed by a number of interlinked factors ranging from social justice concerns — the moral imperative to foster the participation and success at tertiary level of 'non-traditional' students from socially diverse and educationally disadvantaged backgrounds — to the hard economic realities confronting the contemporary corporatising university. In the midst of changing global economic conditions affecting the international student market, as well as shifting domestic politics surrounding university funding, the equation of dollars with student numbers has remained a constant, and has kept universities' attention on the current 'three Rs' of higher education — recruitment, retention, reward — and, in particular, on the critical phase of students' entry into the tertiary institution environment.

In recent times, reforms launched by the 2009 Federal Labor Government (in office from 2007-13) sharpened the focus on student transition into university and the 'three Rs'. The aim of those reforms was to increase the number of graduates between the ages of 25 and 34 years from 32 per cent of the population to 40 per cent by 2025. In order to meet this ambitious target, universities were offered financial incentives to increase the proportion of students from low socio-economic status (SES) backgrounds from 15 per cent to a more representative 25 per cent of the student population, a key platform in the Government of the day's strategy (Australian Government, 2009: 12-13). Because Australia's drop-out rate was high (28 per cent in 2005) relative to comparable countries, the need for student retention was emphasised. To this end, funds were injected specifically to improve the student learning experience, offer effective student services, and sustain student engagement. Economic and social rewards have been expected to flow from the Government's program to recruit more students from low SES backgrounds and improve the retention of all students, leading to a more globally competitive and 'stronger and fairer Australia' (ibid.: 7).

In the light of such initiatives — and current concerns and debates, as this book goes to press, about the impact of the new government's policy of deregulation and anticipated funding cuts — university campuses and committee rooms have been abuzz with research and comment about students, particularly first-year students. The chapters in this book have been prompted by several ideas in circulation amongst university managers, administrators, professional staff and academics alike — ideas that, in our view, should be debated and challenged. These include the idea that universities are (already) well-equipped and flexible enough to accommodate a more diverse student body; that those new to university culture will experience it as inevitably welcoming and enriching; and that support for first-year students is best conceptualised as something additional to, or separate from, day-to-day teaching and learning activities. Most of all, however, the chapters in this book respond critically to the idea that extending university participation to a more diverse and more disadvantaged student body involves correcting a deficit on the part of those students. Informed by this 'deficit model', university staff strategise ways to equip students for university study, often assuming, for instance, that those who come from poorer backgrounds will be poorer students: less intelligent, less engaged, less able to meet the demands made of them. This model implies that the task of extending access to higher education in ways that accord with a commitment to social justice involves remediation of these 'other' students.

Given the complex social composition of universities and range of views on offer, we note also that many staff reject, as we do, this deficit model of students. Some have in its place a deficit model of universities, meaning that it is the university as a social institution which requires remediation, not students from 'other' backgrounds. While we commend the supportive attitude toward students this approach embraces, we believe (as argued in particular by Marcia Devlin and Jade McKay in Chapter 4) that deficit models per se are insufficient to address the challenges currently confronting Australian universities. Such models, we maintain, are counter-productively one-sided, polarising, and myopic in their failure to recognise the strengths that both students and institutions bring to educational engagement. More fundamentally, such discourses reflect and reproduce overly generalised, distanced, 'top-down' perspectives on higher education processes, and entail assumptions about both 'the student' and 'the university' which fail to take into account the complex and diverse social relations, identities and contexts involved. For instance, the 'non-traditional student' is all too easily constructed as a 'type' with attendant 'typical' issues — the 'typical' low SES student, the 'typical' Asian student, the 'typical' Regional and Remote student — in opposition to an equally 'typified' but often unmarked local high school leaver. Similarly we caution against the tendency, as evidenced in the creeping bureaucratic 'standardisation' of teaching and learning procedures in the name of pedagogic and managerial accountability, to imagine and reify 'the university' as a relatively singular, contained and homogenous entity that can be straightforwardly addressed, and redressed, *en masse*.

In this book we acknowledge that universities are social universes in their own right. Moreover, we note that these institutions are complexly embedded in myriad other social domains, such as global fields of practice, which extend beyond local campuses. We therefore foreground a view of universities as sites of multiple, complex and diverse social relations, identities, communities, knowledges and practices. At the heart of the book are people enrolling at university for the first time and entering into the broad variety of social relations and contexts entailed in their 'coming to know' at, of and through university. By recasting 'the transition to university' as simultaneously and necessarily entailing a transition of university — indeed universities — and of their many and varied constitutive relations, structures and practices, we seek to reconceptualise the 'first-year experience' in terms of multiple and dynamic processes of dialogue and exchange amongst all participants. By carefully and critically examining the social relations involved in the movement of neophytes/new scholars into this complex and shifting ensemble of communities, contexts and worldviews, we interrogate taken-for-granted understandings of what 'the university' is, and consider what universities might yet become. In this way the book lays out challenges for all those involved in contemporary higher education in Australia and beyond.

Our commitment to conversing across institutional divisions in higher education is reflected in the range of contributors to this book. Included here are researchers with key expertise in first-year transition, and/or the first-year university experience; university administrators embracing institutional change in keeping with the needs of twenty-first century students; lecturers and researchers with particular insights relating to power relations; and academics teaching first-year students. Also reflective of our commitment to diversity and interdisciplinarity are the variety of methods contributors have used to explore their areas of concern and interest. Some writers review and critique current teaching and learning practices, models of student transition and higher education policy documents; others have employed social research methods of surveys, interviews and reflexivity.

Outline of the book

The chapters comprising this volume all engage, in varying ways and to varying extents, with questions and issues ranging from the general and theoretical to the particular and substantive. While contributors tack between these two poles even within chapters, we have sought to chart the course of the book in terms of a broad movement from the former towards the latter in three stages: *reconceptualisation*, *revaluation* and *realisation*.

The first section is devoted to broad, deep re-thinking of the very nature of 'transition' and of 'universities', and of processes and practices of 'coming to know' and 'coming to be' in higher education. While grounded in particular pedagogic and research experiences, the two chapters in Part 1 offer especially expansive and critical reconceptualisations of the wider landscape of contemporary higher education, challenging key taken-for-granted assumptions informing approaches to transition in Australian universities. While maintaining this critical attention to the bigger picture, successive parts of the book increasingly focus on the particular and local. The four chapters comprising Part 2 revolve around the revaluation of several 'non-traditional' student groups and their discursive and experiential engagement with universities. Contexts for this revaluation include policy documents as well as classrooms and campuses, figuring students as subjects engaged in relationships with policy-makers, academics, communities, and each other. The third and last section brings the reader close to processes of effecting transformations on campus in the interests of all — in the creation of new learning spaces, the promotion of engagement in classroom contexts, and in prompting shifts in consciousness for students and staff. Together, the three chapters in Part 3 demonstrate a variety of ways the first-year experience of higher education can be made more flexible to the needs of an increasingly diversified student body.

Part 1: Reconceptualising: transition and universities

The book opens with an examination of what Trevor Gale and Stephen Parker see as three primary modes of conceptualising transition to university. Transition as Induction (T_1) researchers conceive of students transitioning to university along a 'pathway' which can be smoothed out by institutions providing appropriate support services and curricular activities, and preferably integrating both social and academic domains to enhance the student experience. Transition as Development (T_2) researchers, however, focus more on transition to university as a crucial stage in the development of an *identity* as a university student on the way to becoming somebody else, for example, a teacher or doctor, and thus the emphasis is more on change at an individual level. The third conception of transition is Transition as Becoming (T_3) which challenges normative accounts of transition to university — and even the concept of transition as a singular event — and argues that the voices of the students themselves are absent from these accounts. Developing an understanding of the students instead of continually privileging institutional processes will require that institutions become more open and flexible, not only to varying pathways through university but also to non-normative epistemologies.

In Chapter 2, Deane Fergie broadens the conceptual frame of inquiry into transition and universities. Taking a practice perspective she argues that there is a core but richly variegated approach to coming to know, which frames universities and university transitions. She names this practice 'research-learning' and explores its richly variegated expression in the different fields of knowledge practice and their constitution in different 'communities of research-learning practice' which transcend any particular university in global trajectories. This reconfigures ideas of transition from a simple view of the ins and outs of undergraduate student transition to a focus on coming to know, and different ways of coming to know, which includes the transitions of all who work in a university. This perspective also reconfigures the research-teaching divide that looms in an academic-centric view of university life, and invites us to consider whether, by thinking about how learning is constituted in and constitutive of communities of practice, we might enrich the educational experiences which academics lead and, in important ways, share with students. In the end she asks us to consider the fruits of our research-learning practice.

Part 2: Revaluing: 'non-traditional' student groups in higher education

Angelique Bletsas and Dee Michell (Chapter 3) take Australian culture as their focus. In a direct challenge to characterisations of low SES students as academically or aspirationally deficient, they suggest the low valuation of low SES students is a cultural assessment and evidence of classism in the academy. While 'classism' is a term rarely used in Australia, it is very much in evidence in the United States, where a number of scholars have called for this discriminatory practice to be added to the equity agenda. Although not suggesting that the authors of the Bradley Review (the comprehensive review of the Australian Higher Education sector and key document sparking changes in Government policy) are classist, Bletsas and Michell do, however, argue that classism remains evident within that document.

In a trenchant critique of 'deficit models' as such, Devlin and McKay (Chapter 4) seek to find a way by which the voices and experiences of students from low SES backgrounds can be valued and used in 'joint ventures' to change the institution. Devlin and McKay begin by arguing that neither low SES students nor universities should be conceived as 'the problem' and suggest the need for a two-way exchange to bridge the 'socio-cultural incongruence' between the two. In this exchange, staff come to know such students and the ways in which their needs might differ from other students, as well as the many strengths they bring to the university. By facilitating and supporting students to learn academic discourse while not devaluing the non-academic discourse students arrive with, low SES students can transition to and through higher education successfully.

In Chapter 5, Xianlin Song looks at the difficulties Chinese international students have in coping at university in Australia and suggests ways to improve this important exchange of knowledge — an exchange which has been ongoing for centuries. First, she critiques a prevailing view of Western education as superior to Chinese, and commensurate imaginings of Chinese students as arriving with an inferior education and inadequate, non-critical study habits. Next, Song challenges any assumption that knowledge exchange in higher education involves only knowledge transmission from Australian educators to Chinese nationals. Finally, she argues for heterogeneous pedagogies that have a respectful regard for all students.

In Chapter 6, Michael Maeorg challenges the deficit model as it applies to Regional and Remote students. Coming to urban universities from culturally 'different' rural areas, and without the support of a network of peers and family members, these students are often characterised as self-evidently disadvantaged and 'deficient' in terms of a number of areas, including peer engagement and social integration. While not wanting to dismiss the particular difficulties and challenges this demographic of students face, Maeorg argues that such students are often well aware of significant socio-cultural competencies they have accrued, thanks to their socialisation in community-oriented rural settings, and practise effective deployment of these competencies in the university environment. Indeed, Maeorg observes that Regional and Remote students themselves note the difficulties that local middle class school-leavers have in coping with the diversity of students at university, with many appearing to manage or even deny this difference by 'closing ranks'.

Part 3: Realising: transformations on campus

In Chapter 7, Pascale Quester, Kendra Backstrom and Slavka Kovacevic describe the co-creation process which informed the building of innovative learning infrastructure at the University of Adelaide. 'The Hub' was designed to accommodate changes in student learning behaviours which had been occurring over a number of years. In a practical manifestation of Devlin and McKay's call for a two-way exchange between institutions and students (in this case the student body as a whole), and T3 researchers' call for universities to become more open and flexible, Hub planners moved away from an autocratic approach and consulted with students, reflecting a desire on the part of key administrators to become more student-centred and to change the previously wary relationship between the university and its students. The result was the co-creation of a vibrant facility which brings together counselling and academic support services as well as spaces for students to study individually or in groups.

Not only are particular 'non-traditional' subsets of the student population sometimes considered a problem; so, too, is the entire student body, particularly when it comes to general yet sophisticated skills development such as critical thinking. Chris Beasley and Benito Cao (Chapter 8) take issue with this version of the deficit model and its problematisation of students as lacking critical analytical aptitudes and skills. Drawing on a research project conducted with first-year Politics students, Beasley and Cao conclude that, contrary to the literature, novice students do have an understanding of what critical thinking entails, and value it as a skill with applications not only in the study of Politics but to their university studies in general.

Knowing both where students come from (personally, socially and academically) and the skills they bring with them to university is fundamental to navigating easier transition pathways. In each of the previous chapters, understanding epistemology as always/already rooted in social relations is a key element of our collective approach and analysis. In Chapter 9, Heather Brook and Dee Michell explain how an almost incidental classroom exercise in getting to know their students affected them and their teaching practice.

In combination, the essays across all parts of this volume are optimistic about the general and particular challenges associated with broadening and extending access to university. We express confidence in the talents, skills and capabilities that well-supported students bring to their initial experience at university, arguing, in sum, that modelling transition for non-traditional students as an exercise in recuperating a deficient student body is misguided. We suggest, too, that while such characterisations may not always be obvious or direct, they often underpin institutional attitudes and approaches to access and equity in universities. We hope, in the essays presented here, that some alternative conceptions — from the general to the particular — can be identified and championed.

References

Australian Government. 2009. *Transforming Australia's higher education system.* Canberra: Commonwealth of Australia.

Part 1

Reconceptualising: transition and universities

1 Navigating student transition in higher education: induction, development, becoming

Trevor Gale and Stephen Parker

Abstract

Student transition into higher education (HE) has increased in importance in recent times, with the growing trend in OECD nations towards universal HE provision and the concomitant widening of participation to include previously under-represented groups. However, 'transition' as a concept has remained largely uncontested and taken for granted, particularly by practitioners but also by many researchers. Based on an analysis of recent research in the field, the chapter suggests three broad ways in which transition can be conceived and, hence, three approaches to managing and supporting student transition in HE: as (1) induction; (2) development; and (3) becoming. The third — transition as 'becoming' — offers the most theoretically sophisticated and student-sympathetic account, and has the greatest potential for transforming understandings of, and practices that support, transitions in HE. It is also the least prevalent and least well-understood. Apart from being explicit about how transition is defined, this chapter argues that future research in the field needs to foreground students' lived realities and to broaden its theoretical and empirical base if students' capacities to navigate change are to be fully understood and resourced.

Introduction

The focus of this chapter is on 'transition', specifically on how it is conceived in relation to students and higher education (HE). It is premised on the understanding that its different interpretations variously inform policy, research and practice in the field and that despite a growing level of interest in HE, transition remains a largely unconsidered concept. Notwithstanding this, student transition — change navigated by students in their movement through formal education — has a long history of examination in the international research literature (Ecclestone, Biesta and Hughes, 2010), dating back at least to the introduction of compulsory primary schooling and later as increasing numbers of students continued from primary/elementary to secondary school. As an object of research, student transition in HE has similarly grown as more — and a greater proportion of — people have taken up university study.

Drawing on an analysis of the international research in the field, the chapter begins with a short account of this background and names the assumptions about transition evident in the literature, in terms of three broad categories: as induction, development and becoming. These frame the sections that follow and the discussion about what they mean for resourcing students' capacities to navigate change. In their references to how students experience transition, each also draws attention to legitimated forms of 'knowledge', particularly 'academic capital' (Bourdieu, 1988). In this they support Bernstein's observation, that 'educational knowledge is a major regulator of the structure of experience' (2003: 85). Hence, underlying questions implicit in the discussion that follows include: 'How are forms of experience, identity and relation evoked, maintained and changed by the formal transmission of educational knowledge and sensitivities?' (Ibid.)

Background

Contemporary student transition studies are part of a broader research endeavour focused on life transitions, although this broader field remains dominated by an interest in student transition (Ingram, Field and Gallacher, 2009). Indeed, this interest in students has increased with the growing importance of lifelong learning in late modernity (Field, 2010; Giddens, 1990; Bauman, 2001). A complementary observation is that most of the life transition research is concentrated on children and youth. Hence, when it comes to adult life, research on transitions is still relatively underdeveloped. There is a comparatively mature literature on transitions among young people, and particularly on the transition from youth to adulthood and from school to work ... [Of the limited research focused on adult transitions] by far the largest body of work has concerned movement into higher education. (Ingram, Field and Gallacher, 2009: 3-4)

One reason for this emphasis on HE in adult transition research is the most recent wave of HE expansion in OECD nations, aimed at shifting HE systems from mass (16 per cent to 50 per cent) to universal (50+ per cent) participation (Trow, 1974, 2006). The Bradley *Review of Australian Higher Education* (Bradley et al., 2008), and the then Australian Government's targeted response (*Transforming Australia's Higher Education System*, 2009), is just the most recent example of this aspirational expansion, seeking to deliver more and different kinds of students into university. Others include but are not restricted to HE expansion agendas in the UK (target: 50 per cent of 30-year-olds with a degree by 2010; DfES 2003), in Ireland (target: 72 per cent of 17 to 19-year-olds participating in HE by 2020; Bradley et al., 2008: 20) and in the USA (target: 60 per cent of 25 to 34-year-olds to hold college degrees by 2020; Kelly, 2010: 2).

This policy imperative to enrol increased numbers of HE students from diverse backgrounds and have them graduate and contribute to a global knowledge economy has also drawn attention to the need to improve student engagement and retention. That is, student transition into HE has expanded beyond its traditional focus on access (see Belyakov et al., 2009) — which 'until recently generally meant the study of recruitment, with a particular focus on constraints — often described as barriers — to recruitment' (Ingram, Field and Gallacher, 2009: 4) — to include the outcomes of students' studies (Osborne and Gallacher, 2007: 11). Among HE institutions, practitioners and researchers, this expansion has increased the centrality and importance of student transition in HE (Heirdsfield et al., 2008; Hultberg et al., 2009; Kift, Nelson and Clark, 2010), an importance often expressed in the context of the first year in higher education (FYHE) and the first-year experience (FYE), and, increasingly, undergraduate study more generally.

Yet, despite the increased attention, and perhaps because of recent additions to its purview, 'there is no agreed-upon definition of what constitutes a transition' (Ecclestone, Biesta and Hughes, 2010: 5). Indeed, in many studies transition is rarely explicitly considered, despite the fact that 'different conceptualizations and theories ... lead to different ideas about how to manage or support transitions' (ibid.). This is not to say that researchers are unaware of different forms of transition:

> Many researchers have discussed how transitions have changed — how they no longer follow a traditional linear path — but much of this research on youth transitions does not really provide an alternative to the linear model that is fundamentally different. Instead research often provides supporting case studies that suggest how transitions are now radically different, without taking the opportunity to add to transition theory. (Worth, 2009: 1051)

In contributing to this theorisation, we define transition as *the capacity to navigate change*. This imagines more for transition than just 'a process of change over time' (Colley, 2007: 428). The capacity to navigate change includes the resources to engage with change, without having full control over, and/or knowledge about, what the change involves. In this sense it resembles Bourdieu's account of the logic of practice, which is a logic of the moment. It is 'caught up in "the matter in hand", totally present in the present and in potentialities' (Bourdieu, 1990: 92). Transition understood as the capacity to navigate change also alludes to the mutuality of agency and structure in transitions (Ecclestone, 2009; Ecclestone, Biesta and Hughes, 2010); navigation evokes agency in relation to structure. Conceptually, transition is also related to the social capacities of mobility, aspiration and voice (Sellar and Gale, 2011; Smith, 2009) and shares their intended outcomes: to enable people to access, benefit from and transform economic goods and social institutions. In this respect, transition is a central plank in the current social inclusion in HE agenda, particularly given the 'risk society' (Beck, 1992) and 'liquid modernity' (Bauman, 2000) that now characterise advanced economies. Like mobility (Bauman, 1998), transition has become a marker of social distinction.

While not always explicitly named in the research literature, it is possible nonetheless to discern three distinct ways (summarised in Table 1.1) in which student transition is conceived in higher education:

1. as *induction*: sequentially defined periods of adjustment involving pathways of inculcation, from one institutional and/or disciplinary context to another (T_1);

2. as *development*: qualitatively distinct stages of maturation involving trajectories of transformation, from one student and/or career identity to another (T_2); or

Conceptions of student transition	Transition metaphors	Types of transitional change: from one to another	Transition dynamics	Illustrative transition activities / emphases / systems
Transition as Induction (T_1)	Pathway; Journey; Milestones	Inculcation: sequentially defined *periods* of adjustment From one institutional and/or disciplinary *context* to another	• Navigating institutional norms and procedures • Linear, chronological, progressive movement • Relatively fixed structures and systems • Crisis as culture shock (contextual familiarity)	• Orientation/familiarisation with campus (facilities etc.) and significant staff • 'Just-in-time' information re procedures, curriculum content, assessment requirements • First year seminars • 'Transition pedagogy'
Transition as Development (T_2)	Trajectory; Life stage;	Transformation: qualitatively distinct *stages* of maturation From one student and/or career *identity* to another	• Navigating socio-cultural norms and expectations • Linear, cumulative, non-reversible movement • Discrete, singular, consecutive identities • Crisis as critical incident (identity forming)	• Mentoring programs • Service learning and field placements • Career and research culture development activities/emphasis • Championing narratives of student and career trajectories by successful students and staff
Transition as Becoming (T_3)	Whole of life; Rhizomatic	Fluctuation: perpetual *series* of fragmented movements Lived reality or *subjective* experience, from birth to death	• Navigating multiple narratives and subjectivities • Rhizomatic, zigzag, spiral movement • Flexible systems/fluid (ephemeral) identities • Crisis as neither period-/stage-specific or necessarily problematic	• Flexible student study modes, including removal of distinction between full- and part-time study and min./max. course loads • Flexible student study pathways, including multiple opportunities to change course and enter, withdraw and return to study throughout life • Pedagogy that integrates learning support *within* the curriculum • Curriculum that reflects and affirms marginalised student histories and subjectivities

Table 1.1: A typology of student transition into higher education

3. as *becoming*: a perpetual series of fragmented movements involving whole-of-life fluctuations in lived reality or subjective experience, from birth to death (T_3).

Given their potential to 'lead to different ideas about how to manage or support transitions' (Ecclestone, Biesta and Hughes, 2010: 5), these three conceptualisations frame the discussion of student transition in HE research that follows. A common element in each is reference to a life period or stage (bounded by time and/or circumstance, variously defined), which is characterised by change (also variously defined).

Transition as induction (T_1)

The traditional definition of transition is of 'a fixed turning point which takes place at a preordained time and in a certain place' (Quinn, 2010: 122). For students transitioning into HE, this means 'the move from upper secondary school to higher education' (Hultberg et al., 2009: 48). That said,

> [c]learly, all students new to Australian universities, whether from local or international high schools, colleges or other post-secondary institutions, or whether returning to study as mature-aged learners, face a period of transition. (Beasley and Pearson, 1999: 303)

As well as recognising that school is not the only source of university students, T_1 researchers distance themselves from conceptions of transition as access (Belyakov et al., 2009), rejecting a 'point' of transition for commencing students in favour of the 'smooth transition' (Gill et al., 2011: 63) evoked by metaphors (often replicated in policy documents) such as 'journey' and 'pathway' (Furlong, 2009; Wyn and Dwyer, 2000; Pallas, 2003). This transition pathway or 'period' is conceived as a linear progression through a number of 'phases', including

> Pre-transition (or Beginning to Think About University), Transition (or Preparing for University), Orientation Week, First Year Student Induction Programs, The Middle Years, and The Capstone or Final Year Experience. (Burnett, 2007: 24)

The shift in emphasis from a 'pivotal moment of change' to a transitional period has focussed T_1 researchers' attention on how students encounter HE when they initially enter, rather than on student experiences prior to entry. Rather than a point that separates these experiences, student transition into HE is understood as the domain of the FYE. Indeed, T_1 student transition research suggests that the first year is 'arguably the most critical time' (Krause, 2005: 9): it can 'inform a student's success or failure in tertiary settings' (Burnett, 2007: 23).

Hence, 'understanding the first-year experience plays a critical role in managing transitions to tertiary study' (Krause and Coates, 2008: 495). The first year is frequently portrayed by T_1 researchers as 'a complex and often difficult period of a young student's life' (ibid: 499), particularly for students from 'diverse' backgrounds (Kift, 2009; Kift and Nelson, 2005; McInnis, James and McNaught, 1995). The solution to these difficulties lies in students' *induction* (Hultberg et al., 2009), requiring 'varying degrees of adjustment to Australian university culture in general and the conventions and expectations of students' individual disciplines in particular' (Beasley and Pearson, 1999: 303). Transition, then, is best managed by institutions (Kift and Nelson, 2005; Krause and Coates, 2008), although this also places significant onus on students regarding their commitment and motivation to study, engagement with learning, interaction with staff and participation in out-of-class activities (Kift, Nelson and Clarke, 2010; Nelson, Kift and Harper, 2005; Krause and Coates, 2008; Burnett, 2007).

T_1 researchers justify an institutional response to or regard for student transition by pointing out that 'access [to the HE curriculum] without support is not opportunity' (Tinto, 2008). Of course, there are other justifications:

> High levels of student attrition may be viewed as a waste of institutional resources, particularly in a climate of limited financial, and other, resources in many institutions. Unhappy initial experiences for students and high levels of attrition can damage the reputations of individual institutions.
> (Hillman, 2005: 2)

Institutional activity and research directed at supporting the adjustments required of students, represent what Wilson (2009) has characterised as first and second generation FYE approaches: (1) university student support services (including 'course advice and student decision-making' support; Krause and Coates, 2008: 499) and other co-curricular activities (including orientation activities; see Gill et al., 2011 for a categorisation of these); and (2) curricula activities, including the 'core practices of education' (that is, curriculum, pedagogy, assessment; Wilson, 2009: 10) as well as the broad 'curriculum' of institutions (Nelson et al., 2006; Kift, 2009; Kift, Nelson and Clarke, 2010).

While many T_1 or induction transitionists would see these as distinctive, albeit complementary, approaches (e.g. Wilson, 2009), others — those who hold to a 'broad' curriculum perspective — take a cumulative or 'holistic approach', arguing that transition from a second generation FYE orientation combines 'intentionally blended curricular *and* co-curricular' activities (Kift, Nelson and Clarke, 2010: 10; emphasis added). There are good reasons for institutions to take a whole-of-university-life approach to student transition. For instance, many claim that 'social integration and academic performance have both been identified as strong predictors of attrition from study'; both are required for 'the successful integration of first year students' (Hillman, 2005: 1). Indeed, for Kift, addressing student transition with this one-two combination[1] of transition activity provides the optimum institutional approach

> when first generation co-curricular and second generation curricular approaches are brought together in a comprehensive, integrated, and coordinated strategy that delivers a seamless FYE across an entire institution and all of its disciplines, programs, and services. (2009: 1)

This 'joined-up' institutional approach to the FYE is embodied in what Kift and her colleagues (e.g. Kift, 2009; Kift and Nelson, 2005; Kift, Nelson and Clarke, 2010; see also Nelson et al., 2006) refer to as 'transition pedagogy', a rational and comprehensive approach to designing higher education that is, as summarised below,

- *coherent* (institution-wide policy, practice and governance structures)
- *integrated* (embedded across an entire institution and all of its disciplines, programs, and services)
- *co-ordinated* (a seamless FYE that is institution-wide, rather than separate, 'siloed' initiatives)
- *intentional* (an awareness that curriculum is what students have in common and using curriculum to influence the experience of all students)

---

[1] Kift (2009) and Kift, Nelson and Clarke (2010) have also referred to the 'combination' of co-curricular and curricular activities as a third generation approach to the FYE, given the addition of a 'whole-of-institution' emphasis. While this 'joined-up' institutional approach represents a distinctive strategic move in T_1 approaches, reminiscent of social inclusion policy in the UK (Colley, 2007: 429), it does not provide a significant conceptual difference to Kift, Nelson and Clarke's (2010) previous conceptualisation (of how to approach the FYE) and is probably better described as Wilson's (2009) second-generation account writ large.

- *cumulative* (a long-term approach to learning; gradual withdrawal of scaffolding)
- *interconnected* (curriculum principles that stand out in the research as supportive of first-year learning engagement, success, and retention)
- *explicit* (with links between what is taught, why, and its assessment).

Explicit, rigorous and coherent curricula, pedagogies and assessment have long been advocated as a primary and central strategy for supporting students from diverse backgrounds (e.g. Delpit, 1995; Lingard et al., 2001). However, in a context of increasing diversity of students transitioning to university, what appears missing from T_1 research and policy is a 'third generation' approach to the FYE (Gale, 2009: 14; Kift, 2009: 16): specifically, a 'southern theory of higher education' (Gale, 2009; see also Sellar and Gale, 2011; Gale, 2011b), which advocates spaces in HE institutions for diverse knowledges and ways of knowing (Said, 1979; Connell, 2007; Sefa Dei, 2008), not simply institutional spaces for different kinds of students.

This regard for what students embody raises the more general point (alluded to by Bernstein, 2003 above), which is not well understood or considered by T_1 researchers: that is, 'the terms of the transition are set by others' (Quinn, 2010: 119). Student transition from an induction perspective is a matter of fit 'between the individual's and the institution's characteristics' (Thomas, 2002: 427), but in a context where the transition is 'institutionally-managed' (Nelson et al., 2006: 2). From this point of view, successful transition requires of students 'navigation of institutionalised pathways or systems' (Ecclestone, Biesta and Hughes, 2010: 6), albeit with support provided to assist their navigation. There is little acknowledgment that

> educational institutions are able to determine what values, language and knowledge are regarded as legitimate, and therefore ascribe success and award qualifications on this basis. Consequently, pedagogy is not an instrument of teaching, so much as of socialization and reinforcing status ... [I]ndividuals who are *inculcated* in the dominant culture are the most likely to succeed, while other students are penalized. (Thomas, 2002: 431; emphasis added)

T_1 researchers generally fail to recognise this 'hidden curriculum' (Lynch, 1989) and hence fail to respond with transition strategies that move beyond students' socialisation and induction into dominant norms.

Transition as development (T_2)

An alternative definition of student transition evident in the research literature is focused on identity (Terenzini et al., 1996); specifically, 'a shift from one identity to another' (Ecclestone, Biesta and Hughes, 2010: 6). The traditional example of identity change portrays youth or adolescence as a 'stage' in which individuals make 'the transition from childhood to adulthood' (Baron, Riddell and Wilson, 1999: 484). In the context of HE, 'transition is a time during which students develop their identity as a university student' (Krause and Coates, 2008: 500), although being a university student itself is also a transitional stage; it is preparation for 'becoming somebody' (Ecclestone, 2009: 12; Ecclestone, Biesta and Hughes, 2010: 7): a scientist, musician, nurse, teacher and so on (e.g. Rice, Thomas and O'Toole, 2009; Webb, 2005). In this sense, transition is about students' transformation or development from one life stage to another.

Evident in this account are a number of similarities with, and differences from, conceptions of transition as induction. For example, like inductionists, developmentalists imagine transition as a linear, albeit developmental, process:

> The processes by which young people come to identify with, and become members of, a study community have been likened to the processes by which individuals ascend from youth to full adult status in traditional societies, or by which migrant peoples are accepted into a new community: the stages of separation (from the previous group), transition (interaction with the new group), and finally incorporation or integration into the new group. It is during these first two stages — separation and transition — that the first year tertiary student may be at greatest risk in terms of withdrawing from study altogether or from a particular institution. (Hillman, 2005: 1)

Clearly, for T_2 researchers the idea that transition is developmental is closely related to the notion that development happens not so much in 'periods' but in 'stages'. That is, rather than a 'smooth transition' (Gill et al., 2011: 63) along pathways (à la T_1), the developmental process is stilted or, in developmental psychology terms, 'discontinuous' (e.g. see Werner, 1957). The differences between stage and period can appear subtle, given that both are bounded by time (for example, the first year). However, at issue is the role ascribed to time. In conceiving of transition as a stage — the first year in higher education (FYHE), for example — T_2 researchers regard time as contributing to an individual's development (for example, time in the 'right' company, good use of time and so on), but time itself only loosely determines when that development begins or is completed. Hence, the time available might be exhausted but this does not guarantee transition to the next stage. Indeed, critics of transition stages point out that often 'the rhythms of the young people's learning lives do not synchronise with the set time frames offered to them' (Quinn, 2010: 122). Whereas, in conceptions of transition-as-period, time makes no significant contribution to the FYE, except to record when it begins and ends. It is time *in situ* that distinguishes transitional periods.[2]

Differences between the approaches of induction and development transitionists are also evident in the respective metaphors they use to describe transition. While T_1 researchers employ images of 'pathways', T_2 researchers prefer a 'trajectory' as a way of signalling 'a series of stages, linear, *cumulative* and non-reversible' (Baron, Riddell and Wilson, 1999: 484; emphasis added). According to Pallas,

> pathways are well-travelled sequences of transitions that are shaped by cultural and structural forces ... A trajectory is an attribute of an individual, whereas a pathway is an attribute of a social system. (2003: 168)

These different conceptions of transition have different implications for when, how long and what kind of strategies to employ in supporting student transition into HE. For example, programs that 'encourage students to consider carefully ... the suitability and desirability of the career pathways associated with their [course] choices' (George, Lucas and Tranter, 2005: 145), by providing first-year students with information, introductions to campus and staff, and 'icebreaker' activities with fellow students (Gill et al., 2011), are informed by a view of transition as induction. In contrast, transition programs that have first-year students shadowing student mentors (Heirdsfield et al., 2008; Keup and Barefoot, 2005) and courses featuring a field placement or 'service learning' component (Jamelske, 2009) derive largely from a regard for transition as a developmental stage. Moreover, critics of mentoring as a form of development suggest that it is 'about the maintenance and reproduction of the existing hierarchy and the status quo, [with] the primary beneficiary [being] the institution' (Margolis and Romero, 2001: 80).

---

[2] See Colley (2007, 2010) on how time is differently conceived in, and formative of, transition types.

Whether period or stage, T_1 and T_2 researchers agree that the first year can be difficult for students. Inductionists in particular draw attention to the situational difficulties: '[i]t is not only a change of the type of study situation, with higher demands on students' use of time, but also a new social situation: moving away from home, financial stress, new friends, etc' (Hultberg et al., 2009: 48). However, for developmentalists, the difficulties tend to be internal to individuals rather than external:

> One of the reasons students find transition to university so tumultuous is that it often challenges existing views of self and one's place in the world. Many students from disadvantaged backgrounds, for example, experience significant culture shock on entering an institution whose practices and traditions are alien to them. Transition is a time of identity re-shaping and coming to terms with whether expectations about university life have been met, or need to be revised, or, in fact, if the mismatch between expectation and reality is too great to warrant persistence. (Krause and Coates, 2008: 500)

In short, the fundamental difference between induction and developmental approaches to student transition into HE lies in their differing psychological orientations: whether the transition 'problem' is best addressed at the level of institutions (an *organisational* psychology of student transition) or at the level of individuals and groups (a *developmental* and *social* psychology of student transition). Researchers inspired by the first hold to a 'vision of a pathway along which learners can be led to goals that are predefined, neat and orderly' (Quinn, 2010: 127). In contrast, researchers with a developmental perspective regard the FYHE as 'a valuable time for promoting changes in thinking, particularly in relation to beliefs about learning and knowing' (Brownlee et al., 2009: 600), and such changes are required to 'awaken intellectual curiosity' (Jamelske, 2009: 377).

Missing from this developmental account is recognition that beliefs about learning and knowing, which currently dominate HE, are socially exclusive and require students to adopt identities that do not always follow their life trajectories (Quinn, 2010; Sellar and Gale, 2011; Gale, 2011b). A more socially inclusive regard for university student identities in T_2 research and practice would acknowledge that 'the curriculum itself should reflect and affirm working-class students by ensuring that working-class histories and perspectives are presented with respect rather than marginalised and ignored' (Quinn, 2010: 125-6). More typically, for students from under-represented backgrounds, the HE curriculum constitutes 'a challenge to one's identity and a threat to familiar ways of knowing and doing' (Krause, 2006: 1). There are obvious implications for student transition: '[i]f a student feels that they do not fit in, that their social and cultural practices are inappropriate and that their tacit knowledge is undervalued, they may be more inclined to withdraw early' (Thomas, 2002: 431).

Transition as becoming (T_3)

A third view of student transition into HE is, in many ways, a rejection of transition as a useful concept, at least in how the term is often understood within HE (see T_1 and T_2 above). T_3 researchers (given this nomenclature for the purposes of the categorisation here) argue that 'we need to change the terms of the discussion and recognise that the concept of transition itself does not fully capture the fluidity of our learning or our lives' (Quinn, 2010: 127).

Much of the impetus for this reconceptualisation of student transition into HE has come from the life transition literature more generally. While it has found traction among some HE researchers in the UK, for the most part others have ignored it. Indeed,

> [t]he study of transitions has been largely conducted in isolation from wider analyses of occupational and social mobility ... The separation of transitions and mobility has left a disconnect between transitions theorists and some of the wider sociological concerns seen in the analysis of mobility, class structure and processes of class formation. (Smith, 2009: 371)

Informed by a critical sociology of education and critical cultural studies, T_3 researchers emphasise the complexities of life and the interdependence of 'public issues' and 'private troubles' (Mills, 1959; see also Field, 2010: xxi). They take issue with T_1 and T_2 accounts that represent student transition into HE as

1. a *particular* time of crisis
2. part of a *linear* progression' and
3. *universally* experienced and normalised.

While they recognise that 'it is not enough to say that transitions are no longer neat and linear, or to briefly mention their complexity' (Worth, 2009: 1051), these provide points from which to develop a more dynamic account of student transition.

On the issue of crisis, for example, T_3 researchers accept the 'anxiety and risk' (Field, 2010: xix) experienced by some students in 'the challenges faced by transition (and particularly first year students) trying to navigate the unchartered waters of their new university experience' (Nelson, Kift and Harper, 2005: 2). However, they do not necessarily accept the implied problematic of transition, nor do they accept that transition into HE is a time of crisis for all students. On the contrary,

> transitions can lead to profound change and be an impetus for new learning, or they can be unsettling, difficult and unproductive. Yet, while certain transitions are unsettling and difficult for some people, risk, challenge and even difficulty might also be important factors in successful transitions for others. (Ecclestone, Biesta and Hughes, 2010: 2)

In short, T_3 scholars reject the view that transitions are always times in which people experience crisis and that these are bracketed by relatively stable life experiences (Baron, Riddell and Wilson, 1999: 484). For instance, the to-ing and fro-ing between home and university — between different identities (Kimura et al., 2006: 70) — has to be negotiated on a daily basis, not merely in moments of crisis (Hughes et al., 2010): 'So, transition rather than being a rare event is actually an everyday feature' (Quinn, 2010: 124). Similarly, the idea that life is experienced in a linear way (for example, from high school to university to the world of work; or from childhood to youth to adulthood) is not sensitive to the ongoing changes, transformations, and the back and forward movements experienced by many people. We are not situated within fixed identities or roles either before or after significant events such as the move to HE. For example, university students

> do not view work and study in the linear sequential way implied by the conventional career paradigm and by the policy formulations based upon it. Images about 'pathways' and linear transitions from school via further study and then into the world of work and an independent adult way of life *do not reflect the actual experience.* (Cohen and Ainley, 2000: 83-4; emphasis added)

The absence of students' experiences and understandings from HE policy and practice is informed by normative accounts of student transition (Elder, Kirkpatrick Johnson and Crosnoe, 2003), which represent variations from the norm as 'deviant', 'deficient' (Colley, 2007: 430), 'unruly' and 'inadequate' (Quinn, 2009: 126). Such norms and their variations frustrate student transition. They focus attention on different students, on their difference, rather than on the changes to be made by institutions and systems in order to accommodate difference. They mobilise narratives and histories that render students voiceless, unable to speak 'in one's own name' (Couldry, 2009: 580; see also Sellar and Gale, 2011). For example, knowledge — the central narrative of HE — and ways of knowing associated with under-represented groups, are often unspeakable in HE (Said, 1979; Connell, 2007; Sefa Dei, 2008). This 'yoking together of the speakable with transition, inevitably leaves those with lives that are marginal [to institutional narratives] and [with] incoherent [genealogies] unable to make the transition to fully "educated person"' (Quinn, 2010: 123).

In short, T_3 scholars argue that the normative and the universal do not capture the diversity of student lives, their experiences of university or of universities themselves. It is impossible, then, to speak of student transition into HE in the singular, in the same way that 'there is no such thing as *an* identity, or *a* discrete moment of transition' (Quinn, 2010: 127; emphasis added). Subjectivity and flux better describe the contemporary experience of navigating extended periods of formal education (Smith, 2009), multiple career paradigms and life patterns (Cohen and Ainley, 2000), and 'the fluid experience of time' (Worth, 2009: 1051). Student transition into HE is less about isolated and stilted movements from one context or identity to another:

> [i]nstead it must be understood as a series of flows, energies, movements and capacities, a series of fragments or segments capable of being linked together in ways other than those that congeal it into an identity. (Grosz, 1993: 197-8)

T_3 researchers describe this rendition of transition as 'a condition of our subjectivity' (Quinn, 2010: 123) and liken it to 'becoming', a concept with a rich tradition in social theory and philosophy (see for example Deleuze and Guattari, 1987; Grosz, 1999, 2005; Semetsky, 2006). 'Becoming', as it is conceived here, rejects notions of the linearity and normativity of life stages implicit in much student transition research. It diverts attention away from

> transformation from one identity to another and attends instead to what Deleuze and Guattari call 'multiplicities' composed of heterogeneous singularities in dynamic compositions … To put this another way, Deleuze and Guattari have described the [transition] movement as 'rhizomatic',

a term that refers to underground root growth, the rampant, dense propagation of roots that characterizes such plants as mint or crabgrass. Each rhizomatic root may take off in its own singular direction and make its own connections with other roots, with worms, insects, rocks or whatever. (Sotirin, 2005: 99-100)

This has significant implications for notions of the self, identity, life stages and transitions generally: 'Becoming explodes the ideas about what we are and what we can be beyond the categories that seem to contain us ... [It] offers a radical conception of what a life does' (2005: 99). If education systems, structures, institutions and procedures do not take account of the multiplicities of student lives that enter HE, then transition practices will be less effective. Indeed, T_3 researchers argue that the 'failure to prioritize the actual views, experiences, interests and perspectives of young people as they see them' (Miles, 2000: 10), particularly 'the lived reality for disadvantaged young people' (Barry, 2005: 108) but also university students generally, has been counter-productive. It has led to an overly 'structural perspective on transitions' (Miles, 2000: 10). Certainly, HE 'must have structures and processes ... but ultimately it needs greater openness and flexibility. It should mirror the flux of our being, rather than trying to subjugate it with rigidity' (Quinn, 2010: 127).

For Quinn, being more open and flexible means that

[i]nstitutions should not hide the fact that withdrawal is a possibility, but rather be open about its implications. They should offer better opportunities to change course and provide more meaningful information about individual subjects to enable students to make well-informed choices. Personal planning of 'non-traditional pathways' into and through HE should be facilitated, which remove the distinction between full- and part-time mode and permit less than full-time study on all courses. Opportunities and support for students to change modes of study from full- to part-time and vice versa should be easily available. (2010: 125-6)

In the same way, T_3 researchers argue (see also above) that HE also needs to be more accommodating of diverse knowledges and ways of knowing (Gale, 2009; Gale, 2011b). This may include taking account of what Foucault (1970) terms 'subjugated knowledges' or unsettling 'the centre-periphery relations in the realm of knowledge' (Connell, 2007: viii). From a social inclusion and widening participation perspective, it is about the need for a curriculum that provides room for different ways of thinking about, and different ways of engaging with knowledge, and indeed inserting different kinds of understandings that perhaps have not been part of Australian higher education before. It is about how we structure the student learning experience in ways that open it up and make it possible for students to contribute from who they are and what they know. (Gale, 2009: 12)

Appreciating who students are and 'how they identify themselves' (2009: 11) — specifically, appreciating the dynamic compositions of their heterogeneous singularities (Sotirin, 2005: 99) — is at the heart of understanding student transition as becoming. For T_3 scholars, the appropriate response is to adjust HE systems and practices, including their knowledge systems and practices, to make them more open and flexible.

Conclusions

At least four conclusions about student transition into HE can be drawn from this analysis of the research literature. First, transition tends to be conceived of in three ways — as induction, transformation and becoming — each of which lead to different transition policies, programs and research endeavours. Often these conceptual preferences are not well-articulated or recognised, so that policies, research and practice in the field tend to be predicated on taken-for-granted concepts and normative assumptions regarding preferred and ideal student experiences and trajectories. In our view, many of the problems associated with these silences could be addressed in future research that explicitly names how it defines transition. This should result in improved focus and greater clarity about what informs the research, providing policymakers, researchers and practitioners with the wherewithal to subject it to critique. Research that names how it defines transition will also require locating it in relation to other definitions within the field and/or enable it to contribute to redefining the field.

Second, much policy, research and practice (particularly T_1 and T_2) in relation to student transition into HE is disconnected from the extensive research literature on youth and life transitions and from education and social theory. This limits how student transition is conceived and hence limits the policies, research and practices which flow from these conceptions. Some researchers are drawing on these broader literatures to reconceptualise transition in a way that reflects students' lived realities and has the potential for new approaches to transition. However, they tend to be in the minority. As a way forward, future research needs to draw on the extensive research literature from related fields. This has the potential for transition research to make connections with how (student) transitions are elsewhere experienced and theorised and to reinvigorate the field with new and innovative ideas. In particular, it will enable the research to draw on and contribute to the considerable bodies of knowledge in arenas such as education (with regards to curriculum, pedagogy and assessment), cultural studies (of knowledge production and legitimation) and social theory (for example, exploration of the implications for student transition of conditions such as 'liquid modernity', the 'risk society', 'becoming' and so on).

Third, the current dominant conception of student transition into HE tends to lead to policy, research and practice that are largely system-driven and system-serving. University students are expected to make the transition into HE while conforming to existing institutional requirements. The possibility of broader systemic or structural change to meet the needs of a diverse student population tends to be marginal. Inasmuch as institutional practices change, these are limited to devising ways to enable students to more successfully navigate pre-existing and dominant structures and practices, including knowledge structures and practices embodied in formal and informal curricula, pedagogy and assessment. Future research in the field needs to be cognisant of students' lived reality, not just institutional and/or systemic interests. This includes research, policy and practice aimed at making HE (at the level of classrooms and courses through to institutions and systems) more flexible and responsive to students. It also includes efforts aimed at redressing the marginalisation of certain forms of knowledge and ways of knowing.

Finally, to date, interest in student transition into HE has focused narrowly on undergraduate students, particularly those in their first year, who are undertaking courses in a select cluster of disciplines. This concentration on 'vertical' (Lam and Pollard, 2006) or 'diachronic' (Bransford et al., 2006) transitions — transitions across time and similar contexts (for example, from school to university) — is partial, given the limited interest in transition issues prior to students' first year in HE *and* in their later years of undergraduate and postgraduate study. In contrast, analyses of 'horizontal' (Lam and Pollard, 2006) or 'synchronic' (Bransford et al., 2006) transitions — transitions within the same time frame and between different contexts (for example, from one course or university to another; from home to university to home) — are almost non-existent. Clearly, future research should add to the corpus of investigations on the full range of 'vertical' and 'horizontal' transitions. This includes research with vertical foci beyond the 'first year' (for example, prior to HE entry, the latter years of undergraduate and postgraduate study, the first year of work and so on) as well as horizontal interests (for example, from home to university, from one course or university to another and so on). It also includes research focused on discipline areas (for example, the social sciences, humanities, cultural studies, some areas of science and so on) not yet represented in student transition studies, for their potential to bring new insights into how student transition is experienced, conceived and addressed.

These are the directions that policy, research and practice in the field now need to take if we are to develop more sophisticated conceptions of transition issues and more robust ways of resourcing students' capacities to navigate change.

Acknowledgments

An earlier version of this chapter appeared as part of an Australian Learning and Teaching Council Good Practice Report. Financial support to undertake the study was provided by an ALTC grant.

References

Australian Government. 2009. *Transforming Australia's higher education system*. Canberra: Commonwealth of Australia.

Baron, S., S. Riddell and A. Wilson. 1999. 'The secret of eternal youth: identity, risk and learning difficulties'. *British Journal of Sociology of Education*, 20(4): 483-99.

Barry, M. 2005. *Youth policy and social inclusion*. London: Routledge.

Bauman, Z. 1998. 'Time and class'. *Arena Journal*, 10: 69-83.

Bauman, Z. 2000. *Liquid modernity*. Cambridge: Polity Press.

Bauman, Z. 2001. *The individualized society*. Cambridge: Polity Press.

Beasley, C.J. and C.A.L. Pearson. 1999. 'Facilitating the learning of transitional students: strategies for success for all students'. *Higher Education Research & Development*, 18(3): 303-21.

Beck, U. 1992. *Risk society: towards a new modernity*. London: Sage.

Belyakov, A., L. Cremonini, M.X. Mfusi and J. Rippner. 2009. *The effect of transitions on access to higher education*. Washington, DC: Institute for Higher Education Policy.

Bernstein, B. 2003. *Class, codes and control: volume III — towards a theory of educational transmission*. Milton Park, Oxon: Routledge.

Bourdieu, P. 1988. *Homo Academicus*. Cambridge: Polity Press.

Bourdieu, P. 1990. *The Logic of practice* (R. Nice, trans.). Cambridge: Polity Press.

Bradley, D., P. Noonan, H. Nugent and B. Scales. 2008. *Review of Australian higher education: final report*. Canberra: Commonwealth of Australia.

Bransford, J., R. Stevens, D. Schwartz, A. Meltzoff, R. Pea, J. Roschelle, N. Vye, P. Kuhl, P. Bell, B. Barron, B. Reeves and N. Sabelli. 2006. 'Learning theories and education: toward a decade of synergy', in P. Alexander and P. Winne (eds), *Handbook of educational psychology*. New Jersey: Erlbaum (209-44).

Brownlee, J., S. Walker, S. Lennox, B. Exley and S. Pearce. 2009. 'The first year university experience: using personal epistemology to understand effective learning and teaching in higher education'. *Higher Education*, 58(5): 599-618.

Burnett, L. 2007. 'Juggling first year student experiences and institutional changes: an Australian experience'. Conference paper. *20th International Conference on First Year Experience*, July, Hawaii. http://www98.griffith.edu.au/dspace/bitstream/10072/32622/1/51648_1.pdf [accessed 7 June 2011].

Cohen, P. and P. Ainley. 2000. 'In the country of the blind? Youth Studies and Cultural Studies in Britain'. *Journal of Youth Studies*, 3(1): 79-95.

Colley, H. 2007. 'Understanding time in learning transitions through the lifecourse'. *International Studies in Sociology of Education*, 17(4): 427-43.

Colley, H. 2010. 'Time in learning transitions through the lifecourse: a feminist perspective', in K. Ecclestone, G. Biesta and M. Hughes (eds), *Transitions and learning through the lifecourse*. London: Routledge (130-46).

Connell, R.W. 2007. *Southern Theory: the global dynamics of knowledge in social science*. Crows Nest, NSW: Allen & Unwin.

Couldry, N. 2009. 'Rethinking the politics of voice'. *Continuum: Journal of Media and Cultural Studies*, 23(4): 579-82.

Deleuze, G. and F. Guattari. 1987. *A thousand plateaus: capitalism and schizophrenia* (B. Massumi, trans.). Minneapolis and London: University of Minnesota Press.

Delpit, L. 1995. *Other people's children: cultural conflict in the classroom*. New York: The New Press.

Department of Employment Education and Training [DEEWR]. 2009. *An indicator framework for higher education performance funding — discussion paper*. December. Australian Government: Canberra. http://www.deewr.gov.au/HigherEducation/Documents/HIEDPerformanceFunding.pdf [accessed 17 June 2011].

Department for Education and Skills [DfES]. 2003. *The future of higher education (White Paper)*. Norwich: The Stationery Office Limited.

Ecclestone, K. 2006. *The rise of transitions as a political concern: the effects of assessment on identity and agency in vocational education*. Working paper for the teaching and learning research programme thematic seminar series on 'Transitions through the lifecourse'.

Ecclestone, K. 2009. 'Lost and found in transition', in J. Field, J. Gallacher and R. Ingram (eds), *Researching transitions in lifelong learning*. London and New York: Routledge (9-27).

Ecclestone, K., G. Biesta and M. Hughes. 2010. 'Transitions in the lifecourse: the role of identity, agency and structure', in K. Ecclestone, G. Biesta and M. Hughes (eds), *Transitions and learning through the lifecourse*. London: Routledge (1-15).

Elder, G.H., M. Kirkpatrick Johnson and R. Crosnoe. 2003. 'The Emergence and Development of Life Course Theory', in J.T. Mortimer and M.J. Shanahan (eds), *Handbook of the life course*. New York: Plenum (4-19).

Field, J. 2010. 'Preface', in K. Ecclestone, G. Biesta and M. Hughes (eds), *Transitions and learning through the lifecourse*. London: Routledge (xvii-xxiv).

Foucault, M. 1970. *The order of things: an archaeology of the human sciences*. London: Tavistock Publications.

Furlong, A. 2009. 'Revisiting transitional metaphors: reproducing social inequalities under the conditions of late modernity'. *Journal of Education and Work*, 22(5): 343-53.

Gale, T. 2009. 'Towards a southern theory of higher education'. Keynote address. *12th Pacific Rim First Year in Higher Education Conference: Preparing for Tomorrow Today: The First Year Experience as Foundation*. 30 June, Townsville. http://www.fyhe.com.au/past_papers/papers09/ppts/Trevor_Gale_paper.pdf [accessed 2 June 2011].

Gale, T. 2011a. 'Student equity's starring role in Australian higher education: not yet centre field'. *Australian Educational Researcher*, 38(1): 5-23.

Gale, T. 2011b. 'Expansion and equity in Australian higher education: three propositions for new relations'. *Discourse: Studies in the Cultural Politics of Education*, 32(5): 669-85.

George, R., J. Lucas and D. Tranter. 2005. 'Portfolio entry: alternative university access for year 12 students', in A. Brew and C. Asmar (eds), *Higher education in a changing world: research and development in higher education*, 28. Proceedings of the 2005 HERDSA Annual Conference. Sydney Australia 3-6 July (142-9).

Giddens, A. 1990. *The consequences of modernity*. Stanford: Stanford University Press.

Gill, B., L. Ramjan, J. Koch, E. Dlugon, S. Andrew and Y. Salamonson. 2011. 'A standardised orientation program for first year undergraduate students in the College of Health and Science at UWS: a practice report'. *The International Journal of the First Year in Higher Education*, 2(1): 63-9.

Grosz, E. 1993. *Volatile bodies: towards a corporeal feminism*. Bloomington: Indiana University Press.

Grosz, E. 1999. 'Thinking of the new: of futures yet unthought', in E. Grosz (ed.), *Becomings: explorations in time, memory, and futures*. Ithaca: Cornell University Press (15-28).

Grosz, E. 2005. 'Bergson, Deleuze and the becoming of unbecoming'. *Parallax*, 11(2): 4-13.

Heirdsfield, A.M., S. Walker, K. Walsh and L. Wilss. 2008. 'Peer mentoring for first-year teacher education students: the mentors' experience'. *Mentoring and tutoring: partnership in learning*, 16(2): 109-24.

Hillman, K. 2005. *The first year experience: the transition from secondary school to university and TAFE in Australia*. Camberwell, Vic.: Australian Council for Education Research.

Hughes, M., P. Greenhough, W.C. Yee and J. Andrews. 2010. 'The daily transition between home and school', in K. Ecclestone, G. Biesta and M. Hughes (eds), *Transitions and learning through the lifecourse*. London and New York: Routledge (16-31).

Hultberg, J., K. Plos, G.D. Hendry and K.I. Kjellgren. 2009. 'Scaffolding students' transition to higher education: parallel introductory courses for students and teachers'. *Journal of Further and Higher Education*, 32(1): 47-57.

Ingram, R., J. Field and J. Gallacher. 2009. 'Learning transitions: research, policy, practice', in J. Field, J. Gallacher and R. Ingram (eds), *Researching transitions in lifelong learning*. London and New York: Routledge (1-6).

Jamelske, E. 2009. 'Measuring the impact of a university first-year experience program on student GPA and retention'. *Higher Education*, 57(3): 373-91.

Kelly, P.J. 2010. *Closing the college attainment gap between the US and most educated countries, and the contributions to be made by the States*. National Center for Higher Education Management Systems. http://www.nchems.org/pubs/docs/Closing%20the%20U%20S%20%20Degree%20Gap%20NCHEMS%20Final.pdf [accessed 14 February 2011].

Keup, J.R. and B.O. Barefoot. 2005. 'Learning how to be a successful student: exploring the impact of first-year seminars on student outcomes'. *Journal of the First-Year Experience and Students in Transition*, 17(1): 11-47.

Kift, S. 2009. *Articulating a transition pedagogy to scaffold and to enhance the first year student learning experience in Australian higher education: final report for ALTC Senior Fellowship Program*. Strawberry Hills, NSW: Australian Learning and Teaching Council.

Kift, S. and R. Field, 2009. 'Intentional first year curriculum design as a means of facilitating student engagement: some exemplars'. Conference paper. *12th Pacific Rim First Year in Higher Education Conference: Preparing for Tomorrow Today: The First Year Experience as Foundation*. 30 June, Townsville. http://www.fyhe.com.au/past_papers/papers09/content/pdf/16D.pdf [accessed 2 June 2011].

Kift, S. and K. Nelson. 2005. 'Beyond curriculum reform: embedding the transition experience'. Conference paper. *HERDSA Conference 2005: Higher Education in a Changing World*, 3-6 July, Sydney (225-35). http://conference.herdsa.org.au/2005/pdf/refereed/paper_294.pdf [accessed 1 June 2011].

Kift, S., K. Nelson and J. Clarke 2010. 'Transition pedagogy: a third generation approach to FYE — a case study of policy and practice for the higher education sector'. *The International Journal of the First Year in Higher Education*, 1(1): 1-20.

Kimura, M., K. Brian, D. Ganga, T. Hudson, L. Murray, L. Prodgers, K. Smith, K. Straker and J. Willott. 2006. *Ethnicity, education and employment*. London: University of East London, Continuum — The Centre for Widening Participation Policy Studies.

Krause, K. 2005. 'The changing face of the first year: challenges for policy and practice in research-led universities'. Keynote paper. The University of Queensland First Year Experience Workshop, October, Brisbane.

Krause, K. 2006. 'On being strategic about the first year'. Keynote paper. First Year Forum, Queensland University of Technology, Brisbane.

Krause, K.-L. and H. Coates. 2008. 'Students' engagement in first-year university'. *Assessment & Evaluation in Higher Education*, 33(5): 493-505.

Lam, M.S. and A. Pollard. 2006. 'A conceptual framework for understanding children as agents in the transition from home to kindergarten'. *Early years: an international journal of research and development*, 26(2): 123-41.

Lingard, B., J. Ladwig, M. Mills, M. Bahr, D. Chant, M. Warry, J. Ailwood, R. Capeness, P. Christie, J. Gore, D. Hayes and A. Luke. 2001. *Queensland School Reform Longitudinal Study (QSRLS)*. Brisbane: Education Queensland.

Lynch, K. 1989. *The hidden curriculum: reproduction in education, a reappraisal*. Lewes and Philadelphia: Falmer Press.

Margolis, E. and M. Romero. 2001. '"In the image and likeness ...": how mentoring functions in the hidden curriculum', in E. Margolis (ed.), *The hidden curriculum in higher education*. New York: Routledge (79-96).

McInnis, C., R. James and C. McNaught. 1995. *First year on campus: diversity in the initial experience of Australian undergraduates*. Canberra: AGPS.

Miles, S. 2000. *Youth lifestyles in a changing world*. Buckingham: Open University Press.

Mills, C.W. 1959. *The sociological imagination*. Oxford: Oxford University Press.

Nelson, K.J., S.M. Kift and W. Harper. 2005. '"First portal in a storm": a virtual space for transition students'. *Australian Society for Computers in Learning in Tertiary Education Conference*. 7 December, Brisbane. http://eprints.qut.edu.au/3943/1/3943_1.pdf [accessed 10 June 2011].

Nelson, K., S. Kift, J. Humphreys and W. Harper. 2006. 'A Blueprint for enhanced transition: taking an holistic approach to managing student transition into a large university'. Conference paper. *9th First Year in Higher Education Conference: Engaging Students*. 14 July, Gold Coast. http://www.fyhe.com.au/past_papers/2006/Papers/Kift.pdf [accessed 2 June 2011].

Osborne, M. and J. Gallacher. 2007. 'An international perspective on researching widening access', in M. Osborne, J. Gallacher and B. Crossan (eds), *Researching widening access to lifelong learning: issues and approaches in international research*. London: Routledge (3-16).

Pallas, A.M. 2003. 'Educational transitions, trajectories, and pathways', in J.T. Mortimer and M.J. Shanahan (eds), *Handbook of the life course*, New York: Plenum (165-84).

Quinn, J. 2010. 'Rethinking "failed transitions" to higher education', in K. Ecclestone, G. Biesta and M. Hughes (eds), *Transitions and learning through the lifecourse*. London: Routledge (118-29).

Rice, J.W., S.M. Thomas and P. O'Toole. 2009. *Tertiary science education in the 21st century — final report*. Strawberry Hill, NSW: ALTC. http://www.altc.edu.au/project-reconceptualising-tertiary-science-uc-2006 [accessed 7 June 2010].

Said, E.W. 1979. *Orientalism*. New York: Vintage Books.

Sefa Dei, G.J. 2008. 'Indigenous knowledge studies and the next generation: pedagogical possibilities for anti-colonial education'. *Australian Journal of Indigenous Education*, 37 (Supplementary): 5-13.

Sellar, S. and T. Gale. 2011. 'Mobility, aspiration, voice: a new structure of feeling for student equity in higher education'. *Critical Studies in Education*, 52(2): 115-34.

Semetsky, I. 2006. *Deleuze, education and becoming*. Rotterdam and Taipei: Sense.

Smith, D.I. 2009. 'Changes in transitions: the role of mobility, class and gender'.

Journal of Education and Work, 22(5): 369-90.

Sotirin, P. 2005. 'Becoming Woman', in C.J. Stivale (ed.), *Gilles Deleuze: key concepts*. Quebec: McGill-Queen's University Press (98-109).

Thomas, L. 2002. 'Student retention in higher education: the role of institutional habitus'. *Journal of Education Policy*, 17(4): 423-42.

Tinto, V. 2008. 'Access without support is not opportunity'. 36th Annual Institute for Chief Academic Officers, The Council of Independent Colleges. November, Seattle.

Terenzini, P.T., L.I. Rendon, S.B. Millar, M. Lee Upcraft, P.L. Greg, R. Jalomo Jr and K.W. Allison. 1996. 'Making the transition to college', in R.J. Menges and M. Weimer (eds), *Teaching on solid ground: using scholarship to improve practice*, San Francisco: Jossey-Bass (43-74).

Trow, M. 1974. 'Problems in the transition from elite to mass higher education', in *Policies for higher education*. Paris: OECD (51-101).

Trow, M. 2006. 'Reflections on the transition from elite to mass to universal access: forms and phases of higher education in modern societies since WWII', in J.F. Forrest and P.G. Altbach (eds), *International handbook of higher education. Part one: global themes and contemporary challenges*. Dordrecht: Springer (243-80).

Webb, M. 2005. 'Becoming a secondary-school teacher: the challenges of making teacher identity formation a conscious, informed process'. *Issues in Educational Research*, 15(2): 206-24.

Werner, H. 1957. 'The concept of development from a comparative and organismic point of view', in D.B. Harris (ed.), *The concept of development: an issue in the study of human behaviour*, Minneapolis: University of Minnesota Press (125-48).

Wilson, K. 2009. 'The impact of institutional, programmatic and personal interventions on an effective and sustainable first-year student experience'. Keynote address. *12th Pacific Rim First Year in Higher Education Conference: Preparing for Tomorrow Today: The First Year Experience as Foundation*. 29 June, Townsville. http://www.fyhe.com.au/past_papers/papers09/ppts/Keithia_Wilson_paper.pdf [accessed 2 June 2011].

Worth, N. 2009. 'Understanding youth transition as "becoming": identity, time and futurity'. *Geoforum*, 40(6): 1050-60.

Wyn, J. and P. Dwyer. 2000. 'New patterns of youth transition in education'. *International Social Science Journal*, 52(164): 147-59.

2 University transitions in practice: research-learning, fields and their communities of practice

Deane Fergie

Abstract

This chapter is about university transitions in practice. It seeks to extend the scope of enquiry from a narrow concern with undergraduate student transition (see Parker and Gale, Chapter 1, this book) to a university- and field-wide approach by developing a practice perspective on universities and the university field. Practice is our point of departure. Universities are the focus. The concept of research-learning is introduced as the generic but richly variegated practice at the heart of any university. Analysis moves to consider how fields of research-learning practice are constituted in and through communities of practice and how learning and transition are at the heart of communities of practice. This brings consideration to tensions at the intersection of potentially global and diasporic research-learning fields and their position in local universities and communities, broader social forms and the global university field. The chapter then turns to explore how these insights can inform the design and delivery of courses of research-learning practice in a university. I introduce a practicum approach to research-learning.

Introduction[1]

In this chapter I seek, with Parker and Gale (Chapter 1, this book), to broaden the scope of inquiry into university transition. Student transitions, Parker and Gale argue — and especially the transitions of undergraduate students — have dominated inquiry. Such student-centred inquiries sit behind 'transition programs' orienting, inducting, informing and enhancing the first-year experience of neophyte students coming to university. Meanwhile, what a university is or does remains largely taken for granted. But what is it that students — indeed undergraduate students in particular — navigate their way around when they enrol to study at university? Can we understand student transition if we do not understand what they are transitioning through? What of those who remain or return to make a career in a university? How do universities themselves, as corporate bodies, navigate change and undergo transition? I suggest that these are all important, but largely unaddressed, questions of university transition.

I begin a process of addressing such lacunae and broadening the base of inquiry by exploring the core question: what is a university? In doing this I draw on practice theory. My objective is to understand universities and university transition in, and through, practice. The horizon of this practice perspective extends from any particular research university[2], to the (ordinarily national and sometimes

---

[1] I thank and acknowledge my co-editors, and particularly my close colleague Michael Maeorg, together with Agapi Amanatidis, Chilla Bulbeck, Berenice Carrington, Georgina Drew, Celia Frank, Gerry Groot, Lucy Hackworth, Christine Ingleton, Rod Lucas, Cassandra McCreadie, Naomi Offler, Lucy Potter, Mandy Paul and Megan Warin, for critically engaging with the ideas on which this paper is based. I also thank and acknowledge the University of Adelaide for two learning and teaching development grants, which enabled some of these ideas to be developed in the ReOrientation Project, 'a research-learning approach to university', which was delivered by Christine Ingleton, Mandy Paul, and Naomi Offler in 2008 and 2009. I thank the Commonwealth Attorney-General's Department for Native Title Anthropologist grants in 2011-12 and 2013-14, which enabled the development of the practicum approach to higher education introduced in this paper.

[2] I use the term 'university' relatively narrowly here to connote a research university rather than a 2nd or 3rd tier teaching-only institution of higher education (see, for example, Shavit, Arum and Gamoran, 2007: 5). Coaldrake and Stedman (2013) have noted that in the year 2000 Australia settled on a formal definition of a university which is instructive for its generalisability and its (Australian) specificity. Australian universities, they noted, award qualifications 'across a range of fields and set standards for those qualifications which are equivalent to Australian and international standards'. In addition they noted that teaching and learning should 'engage with advanced knowledge and

regional) university systems[3] in which they are enmeshed and regulated, to the now well-recognised global university field.

With what might a practice perspective on the university field begin? My point of departure is 'social practice' — patterned and socially situated human action which has been dynamically reproduced over time.[4] Social practice in my view is inherently dynamic and its dynamism, as Shove, Pantzar and Watson (2012) show, needs to be front and centre in analysis.

Inquiring about social practice in universities I ask firstly: is there a generic, yet dynamic, practice at the heart of any (research) university? Practices of coming to know appear as central practice in any university. I will argue that, indeed, a key thing that universities share is practices of coming to know. I introduce the conceptualisation of these practices as 'research-learning' and inquire into the communities of research-learning practice, which constitute fields of knowledge and connect practitioners in uneasy arrangements locally and internationally, through space and time.

My focus on social practice entails attention to communities of practice and, in the context of universities, the relationship between fields of research-learning practice and communities of research-learning practice. Such an orientation better situates us to recognise and explore all manner of trajectories that members of various and overlapping communities of research-learning practice can take into,

---

enquiry' with 'a culture of sustained scholarship extending from that which informs inquiry and basic teaching and learning, to the creation of new knowledge through research, and original creative endeavour' (2013: 74). I note that contemporary universities are likely to be multi-campus and might include campuses in more than one country.

[3] Coaldrake and Stedman (2013) provide a recent analysis of change in the Australian university system. Shavit, Arum and Gamoran (2007) in their comparative study of stratification in higher education provide an indicative introduction to a large number of national university systems. I note also that, after Bologna, the national university systems of Europe are now framed and provided with interlocking pathways in an overarching European arrangement and they are now beginning to act like regional university systems.

[4] For a useful introduction to practice in contemporary theory see Schatzki, Cetina and Savigny (2001). In this chapter I develop a practice approach informed by Bourdieu's reflexive sociology of science and the French university field, Lave and Wenger's analysis on situated learning and communities of practice, and Brew and Shove, Pantzar and Watson on the dynamics of social practice.

out of, and within such communities, from 'legitimate peripheral participation' (Lave and Wenger, 2007 [1991]) to varying levels of 'adept', and even 'exemplary', practice.

I signal that trajectories of university transition may seem to have an apparent clear 'upward' trajectory of progress, but they are, in practice, uncertain. Few of us have, as Bourdieu might put it, 'consecrated careers' (1996 [1989]). Students, and indeed employed academics, drop in and out without graduating. Careers do not go to plan. For many, university life is pregnant with possibilities of detour, stall, unexpected acceleration, exit and sometimes re-entry. A miniscule minority make uninterrupted progress in their university life from neophyte undergraduate through graduate study to academic employment, ending their academic career celebrated as meritorious professor.

I seek to demonstrate that a practice perspective can be as productive in pedagogy as in analysis. In the final section of this chapter I introduce a case study of a practicum approach to show how practice perspectives can provide a fecund framework for intentionally designing and facilitating courses of research-learning practice.

Research and teaching: core university practice?

Let us return to the basic question of what universities do. I am looking for a core practice or set of social practices which underpin and structure what happens in a university.

It is uncontroversial to note that contemporary universities articulate two main purposes or core activities: the transmission of knowledge (education or higher education) and the production of knowledge (or research).[5]

---

[5] Most Australian universities are organised and, in important respects, have been funded by government. In an analysis of governmentality in higher education (after Foucault) Marginson outlines how, by means of the mechanism of agreeing in a standard format an 'educational profile' between government and university as a basis of government funding in the 1990s (after the so-called 'Dawkins reform' and development of a 'unified national system'), 'the Government homogenised not only government funding and accountability but also institutional planning' (1997: 71. See also Croucher et al. (eds) for a detailed discussion of the Dawkins reforms). By developing educational profiles separately with each university Marginson argued that '[t]he government shaped both the work of institutions and the system as a whole without undergoing a multi-lateral process' (ibid.). In subsequent work with Considine (2000) commonality of change across the higher education system

Intriguingly, integrating research and teaching in universities has been a long-held aspiration in Australia.[6] Brew reported a survey of the institutional strategic and teaching and learning plans in publicly funded Australian universities, which showed that 33 of 39 aspired to integrate teaching and research in some way (2010: 139). Indeed the University of Adelaide[7] has placed a (re)union of teaching and research at the heart of its most recent strategic plan (University of Adelaide, 2012). The narrative of planned change was that teaching will be reunited with research in an Adelaide education experience. This, it said,

> does not mean merely inviting students to study an individual topic in depth, with initiative and creativity. In a true research university, the study of existing knowledge is secondary to the making of new knowledge. Moving away from knowledge delivery, now increasingly eroded by the universal availability of free online content, a university should focus on the essence of what research offers: the rigour of the scientific method, the search for empirical evidence, the beauty of logic and of patterns, the value of innovation, the creativity of problem-solving and the intrinsic worth of knowledge. (2012: 8)

It remains to be seen whether the University of Adelaide can transform its practice whilst also navigating funding cuts. Brew has noted that 'the aspiration to integrate research and teaching is not well translated into practical strategies for implementation' (2010: 139). Mayson and Schapper (2012) have shown

---

was further demonstrated (see 2000: 11). Brew (2010: 142) and also Access Economics (2010) discuss the challenge of assessing the relative funding of university teaching and research. In 2010, on the eve of the introduction of the demand-driven system of university funding in Australia, Schapper and Mayson noted that 'publication quality and output (as determined by whatever research assessment exercise prevails) has become the dominant and uncritically accepted indicia of research productivity and quality. Adopting these as system-wide research measures together with student evaluations of teaching performance serves as the basis of resource allocation from Australia's Federal government' (2010: 644). More recently Coaldrake and Stedman (2013) argue that the stakes of the university game have been raised again.

[6] This stands in contrast to the first century of tertiary education in Australia in which, while some academics managed to do research, the expressed purpose of a university was teaching (Davis, 2010: 60).

[7] The University of Adelaide website can be found at www.adelaide.edu.au. Institutional narratives of a variety of kinds are available on the website. Duncan and Leonard (1973) and Linn (2011) have each written detailed histories of the University. Finnis (1975) has undertaken a study of the Adelaide University [student] Union.

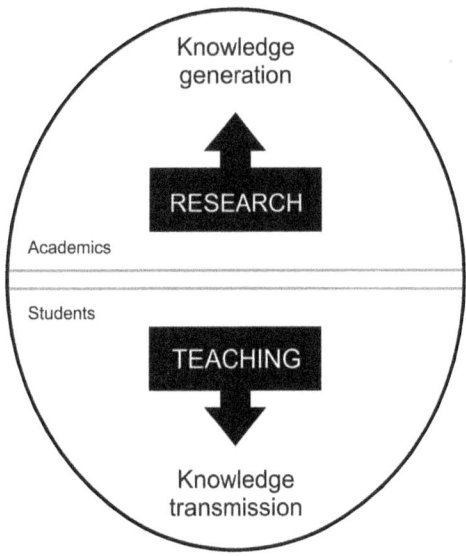

Figure 2.1: A 'teacher focussed / information transmission' (with knowledge conceived of as objective and separate from knowers) model of the relationship between teaching and research (after Brew, 2003, 2006 and 2012: 108)

that change is easy to obfuscate by simply shifting rhetoric. In their analysis of the talk and texts discourse[8], a major Victorian university at one point named research and teaching 'the twin peaks' of academic practice. Later the talk and texts changed. The erstwhile twin peaks were rescaled as 'research-led teaching' in the wake of changes in funding metrics which made research outcomes count more.[9]

More positively, Angela Brew has sought to rethink the relationship between teaching and research in universities (see Brew and Boud, 1995; Brew, 1999, 2001; and especially Brew, 2006, 2010 and 2012). Brew's recent analysis builds

---

[8] See Roxå and Mårtensson (2009) for an insightful distinction between the 'discourse of talk and texts' and its contrast with capital 'D' 'Discourse' in Foucauld's sense.

[9] Our broader work, which sees social practice as patterned and dynamic action which is socially situated and constituted, critically extends the elemental work of Shove, Pantzar and Watson in *The Dynamics of Social Practice: Everyday Life and How it changes* (2012). We understand practices as constituted when elements of 'material', 'meaning', 'capacity' and 'social relations' (which is an element we have introduced to this approach) are all linked. This framework enables changes in practices to be tracked over time. In this example a change in the element of 'meaning', from research and teaching as 'twin peaks' to 'research-led teaching', got momentum from a change in the element of 'material'; that is, changes in funding following the introduction of Excellence in Research Australia (ERA) funding metrics. These two elements of practice triggered a change in 'social relations' as researchers successful in ERA metrics gained reputation and power over those who were less successful in those terms, and in particular teachers. In some universities this caused initiatives designed to get more people working more successfully on ERA tracks; that is, in terms of this elemental approach to tracking the dynamics of social practice, it triggered change in the element of 'competency'.

Figure 2.2: Mandy Paul lecturing to the students in ANTH 2055 Native Title Anthropology: Society, Law and Practice, in Napier Building LG29

on the fundamental work of the Boyer commission in the US, which interrogated the scholarly work of academics. In her work on the relationship between teaching and research, Brew (2012) noted that the status-quo (which she optimistically referred to as the 'old') teacher-focused model, concentrated upon 'information transmission'. She presented these ideas figuratively (see Figure 2.1; see also Figure 2.2 as an illustration of teacher-focused learning).[10]

Brew used this diagram (Figure 2.1) to bring home the view that for contemporary academics in Australia, and I think likely globally, it seems as if 'teaching and research constantly pull away from each other, vying for resources and an academic's time' (2012: 108; see also University of Adelaide, 2012: 8; see also Figure 2.3).

In 2010 Brew reflected that:

[h]igher education can be considered a split community: academics who teach and do research; students who learn; and general/support staff who provide service. Separate arrangements, even separate social spaces in some institutions, exist for each of these groups. (2010: 142)

Why is this so?

---

[10] Brew's new conception sees both research and teaching 'as activities where individuals and groups negotiate meanings, building knowledge within a social context' (Brew, 2003: 12).

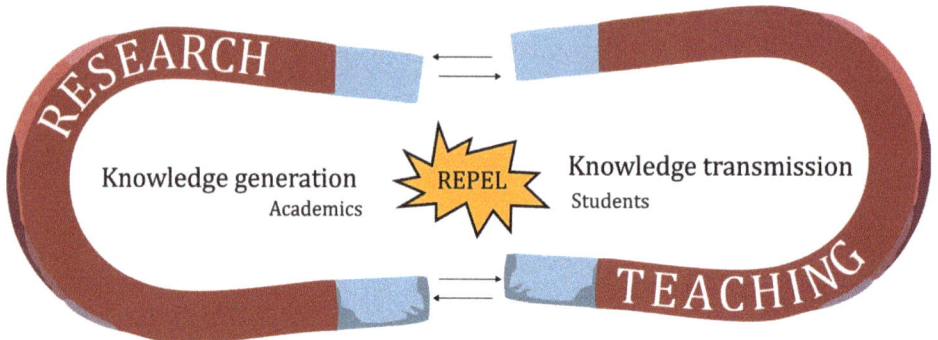

Figure 2.3: In contemporary universities research and teaching seem 'poles apart' (Figure by Lucy Hackworth)

Might the apparent antagonism of research and teaching practice offer insight into universities, their core practices and transitions? If we eschew perspectives whose point of departure is social roles (which in this context result either in academic-centric or student-centric analysis) and start instead with social practices might we see things differently? Do students and academics share a university practice?

Research-learning: paradigmatic and richly variegated practice

In a fascinating discussion of identity and mimetic conflict in Melanesia and the West, Simon Harrison builds an insightful analysis on a tradition of social theory which recognises that 'the deepest and most destructive antagonisms often occur in the closest relationships and between those who have the most in common' (2006: 1). As with electrical polarity: like repulses like to create a space of difference. In this chapter, I take this basic idea — that commonality can drive antagonism — in a somewhat different direction to explore social practice. As Brew has noted:

> [i]ntegrating research and teaching requires academics to think about what they mean by teaching and about how learning occurs for them as academics and for their students; to reconsider what they think research is and ideas about who generates it. They need to reassess what kind of knowledge is being generated and by whom. (2010: 148)

Here I shift the question from two views that have dominated discussion about universities: 'governance' and 'role-centred' perspectives[11] (such as that represented in Figures 2.1 and 2.2) to practice perspectives. I ask: what is it that the practices of teaching and research have in common which makes them seem antagonistic and antithetical to each other? Is there more between them than surface repellence? Can we think about the unity of teaching and research differently if we adopt a practice perspective as our analytic frame?

More specifically I ask: is there a practice, a fundamentally shared practice, which underpins the work done in a university and whose different sameness creates a centrifugal or polarising force in the way academics presently work, driving different dimensions away from each other?

I think there is.

In my view, practices of 'coming to know' are at the heart of what people in any university do. Practices of coming to know unite all members of its community as well as the academic labours of teaching and research and the work of those who support this practice. Learning in a university is disciplined by the critical rigour of a research-founded orientation to coming to know. I call this research-founded approach to coming to know 'research-learning'. The Boyer Commission put it this way:

> The ecology of the university depends on a deep and abiding understanding that inquiry, investigation, and discovery are at the heart of the enterprise, whether in funded research projects or in undergraduate classrooms or graduate apprenticeships. Everyone at a university should be a discoverer, a learner. That shared mission binds together all that happens on a campus. (1998: 9)

Brew amplifies this:

> Both learning and research are about making meanings. Research and learning both involve the pursuit of intellectually challenging ideas … [B]oth learning and research are concerned with discerning the critical features of phenomena. Both teaching and research involve exploring existing knowledge and trying to go beyond it. Both involve the human act of making sense of the world. (2012: 112; citations omitted)

---

[11] See Clark (1986) and more recently in Australia, Marginson and Considine (2000). I include the 'talk and texts' analysis — or what Alvesson and Kärreman (2011) would call discourse (with a small 'd') analysis — like that of Schapper and Mayson (2010) and Mayson and Schapper (2012).

The point is that the *learning practices* at the heart of a university are *coming to know through research practice and products* just as *research* itself is *a kind of practice of coming to know and learn*. This kind of learning is founded on an approach to coming to know which, as a matter of routine, questions the taken-for-granted assumptions of 'common sense'. Initially at least its outcomes tend to go beyond 'common knowledge', although they may over time become incorporated into such generally held knowledge. I refer to learning which is research-founded and call it 'research-learning' to indicate the constitutive fecundity of this 'two-in-one' practice.

I introduce the concept 'research-learning' to clarify the broad ensemble of social practices which entail practitioners in a search for new and significant knowledge, inspiration, insight, lucidity, meaning and understanding by: skilling up and applying in practice disciplined and critical questioning; finding new (if only fleeting) frameworks for focusing, observing, experimenting, creating, evoking, gathering 'evidence', considering and analysing; and then, when new understanding and insight is found through these processes, communicating this in ways that enable others to see, to understand and then, again, to test. Searching and informed, disciplined *re*-searching is at the heart of research-learning practice.

Echoing Boyer's admonition on research in a research university, I say *everyone at a university should be a research-learner* engaged in practices of knowledge discovery and transmission. Research-learning has some shared and generic practices: critical appraisal and flexibility of mind, consideration, recognition, inspiration and case-making. Research-learning is *uncommon sense-making* applicable across the range of fields, from the inspirational arts to fields of 'hard' scientific practice.

If research-learning is the paradigmatic or generic social practice which unites all in a university, it is also a richly variegated and dynamic practice. Practitioners in the discipline of geology or its sub-field, geomorphology, have a fundamentally different approach to enquiry from those in the inter-disciplinary field of gender studies or genetics or the discipline of German. Each might be studied in a contemporary university.

But the nomenclature of disciplined difference is changing. The label 'discipline' now appears anachronistic and too narrow a referent for the dynamically forming, transforming, deforming and reforming 'fields of research-learning practice' which contemporary universities (in the east as in the west) host. So I use the term 'field' to refer to the specialised subjects of research-learning practice. As a rule of thumb, different and emerging and disappearing fields of research-learning practice can be identified by their accepted (yet always contestable)

- name(s)
- ambits of interest
- focal subjects or sub-fields of enquiry
- practices or 'methods' of doing things, including questioning, enquiring, investigating and composing
- substantive material or data which practitioners focus on and work with
- theoretical paradigms, analytic frames and key concepts through which patterns are recognised or insight achieved in practice
- principles of rigour/rules of the game for making and critically evaluating narrations, soundings, calculations, cases and 'findings' as acceptable within their community of practice
- conventions for presenting 'findings' and 'creations' as significant and compelling, and accomplished practice — including accomplished use of distinctive notational forms, citation conventions and linguistic expressions (see Hyland and Bondi, 2006; Hyland, 2008)
- histories of practice
- social relations and communities of practice (including local, system-wide and global social forms, internal distinctions, recognitions and progressions, as well as 'external' alliances and oppositions)
- habitus, personal styles and demeanours of practice, transition and struggle in the field (after Bourdieu).

My usage of the term 'field' is consonant with Bourdieu's concept of a 'field' in *Homo Academicus* (1990 [1984]) but also in *The Field of Cultural Production* (1993) and his final lecture series *Science of Science and Reflexivity* (2004). Bourdieu discussed the concept of 'field' in both its generic and specific manifestations, with the field of science as his example. A field, he wrote,

> is a structured field of forces, and also a field of struggles to conserve or transform this field of forces ... The agents, [in this case] isolated scientists, teams of laboratories, create, through their relationships, the very space that

determines them, although it only exists through the agents placed in it, who, to use the language of physics, 'distort the space in their neighbourhood', conferring a certain structure upon it. It is in the relationship between the various agents (conceived as 'field sources') that the field and the relations of force that characterize it are generated. (2004: 33)

Bourdieu's analytic use of the term 'field' enables us to recognise both fields of research-learning practice (as might be labelled 'disciplines' or 'fields' in everyday speech) and a university field, which in the international context of academic interactions and publications, for example, and the 'internationalisation' of university study and global rankings of universities which have bitten hard for just over a decade or so, is now unquestionably a global field of forces and struggles.

As with struggle, change also must be recognised at the heart of any analysis of research-learning fields. As we confront 'super-complexity' (after Barnett, 2000), with changes in global power and the emergence of 'wicked problems', our once apparently even intellectual keels are destablised. Inter-disciplinary, cross-disciplinary and a variety of innovative problem-oriented fields have surfaced in the ever-more choppy confluence of cross-currents in which universities seek to provide individuals and societies with light by which to understand and navigate (see Strathern, 2004; Holland et al., 2010).

To consolidate the point: research-learning is the generic and core practice of any university, any university system and of the global university field. But research-learning is also richly variegated practice — differentiated into a range of dynamic but generally distinguishable fields of practice as diverse in their research-learning practices as anatomy, Arab studies, or astrophysics (just to start an indicative list starting with 'A').

The next section of this chapter focuses on the social context of learning and transition in practice: communities of practice. I argue that research-learning practice constitutes, and is constituted by, the practices of people in communities of practice.

Communities of research-learning practice

How is a field of research-learning practice constituted? In practice a research-learning field is constituted in and through communities of practice. I will argue that communities of practice can be localised or more broadly based. They can be constituted in the face-to-face interactions of everyday life or over the horizon through occasional visitation, web connection and the like. In respect of communities of research-learning practice, they can be constituted in particular units of particular universities, in the occasional get-togethers and virtual communications of 'diasporic' learned societies. Conferences, seminars and electronic bulletin boards no less than lectures, degrees and academic posts constitute the communities of research-learning practice, which in their turn are constitutive of their fields of research-learning practice and struggle.

Once dominated by more or less established disciplines, research-learning is constituted in particularities of practice, as Chandler sought to make clear:

> Although disciplines, in the academic sense, can be taken to mean something less like submission to rules and more like a field of study — one's academic speciality — there remains an important distinction to be made between a discipline and a subject matter ... The kinds of practices associated with the academic disciplines might be said to involve styles of thought, that is, procedures for identifying and gathering evidence, ways of posing and sequencing questions, conventions for distinguishing productive from unproductive questions and practices for establishing sound demonstrations, building arguments, citing authorities, or making cases. (2009: 732)

I put the case here that a more fecund approach to enquiry is one which focuses on social practice and explores the dynamics of social practice in the actions, relations, learning, 'feel', styles, demeanours, productions, struggles, competitions, and transitions which are constitutive of the field and its communities of its practice.

Lave and Wenger's 'situated' practice perspectives offer us insight into how we come to know in context, in action and in social interaction. In short these research-learners are interested in how we learn in communities of practice and how communities of practice are constituted by learning. Lave and Wenger argue that the 'defining characteristic' of learning is a process they call 'legitimate peripheral participation'. Such participation has the potential to move newcomers toward full participation in a community of practice.

> A person's intentions to learn are engaged and the meaning of learning is configured through the process of becoming a full participant in a sociocultural practice. This social process includes, indeed it subsumes, the learning of knowledgeable skills. (2007 [1991]: 29)

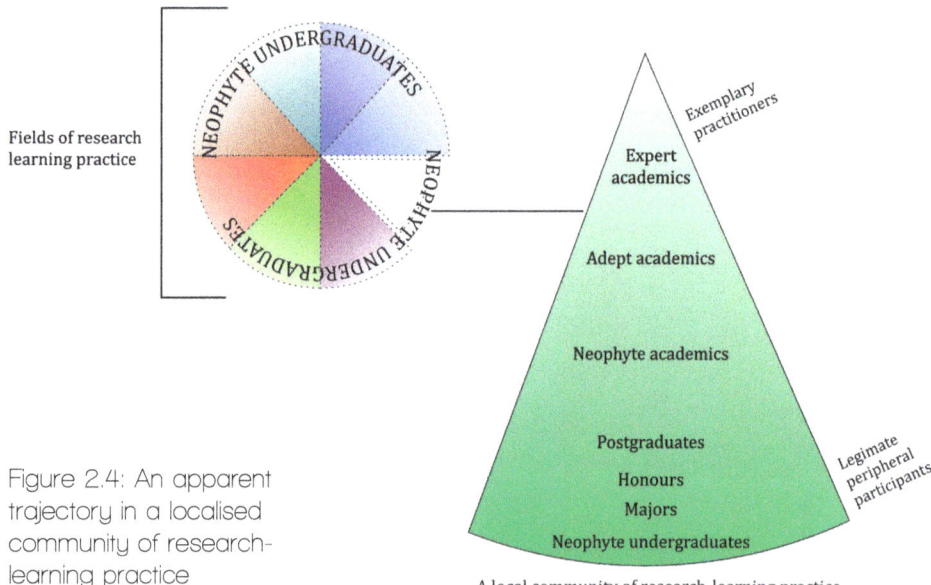

Figure 2.4: An apparent trajectory in a localised community of research-learning practice

Legitimate peripheral participants do not simply learn skills as members of a community of practice. They see and in time undertake themselves exemplary practices producing typical and, perhaps eventually, exemplary products. But more than this: they see how exemplary practitioners act — their typical personal styles, demeanours, interactions and being in the world.

Legitimate peripheral participation is pregnant with the possibility of transition. Transition takes place not just by moving into a position of legitimate peripheral participation but also by learning and becoming increasingly adept within a community of practice. At a university a neophyte first-year student arguably becomes a legitimate peripheral participant in fields of research-learning practice when they enrol in learning units (courses, subjects) which introduce and develop those fields of research-learning practice in their undergraduate practice (see Figure 2.4).

But a senior academic moving into a new university, a new locus of practice, is also, for a time at least, a legitimate peripheral participant in its local communities of practice. Despite their professional status, new professors need to know how to get a book out of their new research library, need to learn the taken-for-granted purchasing or IT or meeting practices of that local community of institutional practice.

Despite its clumsy expression, the concept of 'legitimate peripheral participation' elucidates characteristic ways of belonging so that such participation is more than a condition of learning; it is a 'constitutive element of its content' (Lave and Wenger, 2007 [1991]: 35). First-year courses (such as say 'Anthropology 101') introduce students to a field of research-learning practice as it admits them as its most peripheral of legitimate peripheral participants. Some students do not complete their introductory courses. Others complete but do not proceed to further units in the field. Over the course of their studies, students may consolidate their participation by concentrating their studies in one field of research-learning practice (for example in a major sequence, or in a major sequence leading to a year of Honours focus in the present system of Australia).

An analytic focus on communities of practice, the learning practices through which they are constituted and the trajectories of transition necessary for their reproduction is clearly a potentially productive approach to the understanding of transitions in the university field. As Lave and Wenger note:

> [i]n any given concrete community of practice the process of community reproduction — a historically constructed, ongoing, conflicting, synergistic structuring of activity and relations among practitioners — must be deciphered in order to understand specific forms of legitimate peripheral participation through time. This requires a broader conception of individual and collective biographies than the single segment encompassed in studies of 'learners'. Thus we have begun to analyse the changing forms of participation and identity of persons who engage in sustained participation in a community of practice: from entrance as a newcomer, through becoming an old-timer with respect to new-comers, to a point when those newcomers themselves become old-timers. (2007 [1991]: 56)

Loci in the university field

Studies of situated learning have focused particularly on the development of adept practice through apprenticeship. Studies of institutions of intentional instruction, such as schools and universities, have not been at the centre of situated inquiry. Indeed when developing their ideas Lave and Wenger deliberately steered away from considering what this meant for traditional educational forms like 'schooling' (2007 [1991]: 39-42) or indeed universities, which have also been sites of 'intentional instruction'. Their comments on the study of schooling are clearly germane to considering contemporary universities as places of learning. Lave and Wenger wrote:

> Even though we decided to set aside issues of schooling in this initial stage of our work, we are persuaded that rethinking schooling from the perspective afforded by legitimate peripheral participation will turn out to be a fruitful exercise. Such an analysis would raise questions about the place of schooling in the community at large in terms of possibilities of developing identities of mastery. These include questions of the relation of school practices to those of the communities in which the knowledge that schools are meant to 'impart' are located, as well as issues concerning relations between the world of schooling and the worlds of adults more generally. Such a study would also raise questions about the social organisation of schools themselves into communities of practice, both official and interstitial, with varied forms of membership. (Ibid.: 41)

They suggest that what is needed is a detailed understanding of the social world (ibid.: 55). This sounds to me, as an anthropologist, like a detailed practice-oriented ethnography.

> To furnish a more adequate account of the social world of learning in practice, we need to specify the analytic units and questions that would guide such a project. Legitimate peripheral participation refers both to the development of knowledgeably skilled identities in practice and to the reproduction and transformations of communities of practice. It concerns the latter insofar as communities of practice consist of and depend on a membership, including its characteristic biographies, trajectories, relationships, and practices. (Ibid.: 55)

The agenda they set is clear but, in respect of the university field, particularly complex. From one vantage, universities house and sponsor a discrete subset of possible fields of research-learning practice. Brew for example highlights 'academic communities of practice' for analysis:

> We can treat academic departments, disciplines, sub-specialisms, a university as a whole, or networks of professionals as communities of practice. In an academic community of practice, students, academics, professionals and indeed anyone else who shares this site of practice, are responsible for the maintenance of the community of practice, for inducting newcomers into it,

for carrying on the tradition of the past and carrying the community forward into the future. (2012: 109)

Similarly Becher and Trowler (2001 [1989]) wrote of connections between cultures of 'academic tribes' and their epistemological 'territories'. Their work took 'disciplines' whose cultures they inquired into, and 'departments' in which they were located, for granted, even if they recognised a gap between them (2001: 41). Bourdieu, too, adopts the same general approach to describing the basic units of academic organisation:

> A discipline is a relatively stable and delimited field, and is therefore relatively easy to identity: it has an academically and socially recognised name (meaning one that is found, in particular, in library classifications, such as sociology as opposed to 'mediology', for example); it is inscribed in institutions, laboratories, university departments, journals, national and international fora (conferences), procedures for the certification of competence, reward systems and prizes.
>
> A discipline is defined by its possession of a collective capital of specialised methods and concepts, mastery of which is the tacit or implicit price of entry to the field. It produces a 'historical transcendental', the disciplinary habitus, a system of schemes of perception and appreciation (where the incorporated discipline acts as a censorship). It is characterized by a set of socio-transcendental conditions, constitutive of a style. (2001: 64-5)

It is easy to conflate the organisational forms (units, departments, centres) which host representatives of research-learning fields and their localised university-based communities of practice with their broader, territorially transcendent, communities of practice. Indeed Becher and Trowler conflate academic 'tribes' with their territory (for examples see 2001 [1989]: 23).

But are we missing something here?

I think so.

In my view analysis is impoverished if we conflate different, even if overlapping and connected, communities of practice in inquiry and analysis. There is often an important dynamic tension, for any member, in the overlap between communities of research learning practice. In important ways this is a polarising tension, important for better understanding transition, that needs to be elucidated.

Where to start? Why not the organisational units and degree structures through which neophyte students are introduced to fields of research-learning practice when they enrol in university? Becher and Trowler have drawn attention to 'well-established areas of pure, monodisciplinary knowledge' naming anthropology, history and philosophy as examples (2001 [1989]: 20). Depending on the university, academics in these disciplines might be found within an overarching unit such as a Faculty of Arts or Faculty of Humanities and Social Sciences. Study units in these disciplines might be offered as part of Bachelor degrees, typically indeed a Bachelor of Arts degree. Courses in these research-learning areas might form a concentration, named perhaps as a major sequence in an undergraduate degree.

We might then imagine some long-term correlation between such named disciplinary fields and the administrative units that house them in most universities — with the research-learning field of anthropology housed, say, in a Department of Anthropology. Yet this does not follow in practice. In my own experience of studying anthropology at undergraduate level I was a student in a 'Department of Anthropology and Sociology' (Faculty of Arts, The University of Papua New Guinea, in the early 1970s), which offered courses as diverse as 'Introduction to Social Anthropology', 'Race Relations' and 'Community Development'. Later I continued my BA studies in the 'Department of Prehistory and Anthropology' (in the School of General Studies at the Australian National University). There I took courses with names like 'The Anthropology of Art', 'Economic Anthropology' and 'Kinship and Marriage'. Only as a postgraduate and then post-doctoral scholar did I work in a singular 'Department of Anthropology' (Faculty of Arts, University of Adelaide, in the late 1970s and early 1980s; and Research School of Pacific Studies, Australian National University, in the late 1980s).

Here at the University of Adelaide in recent years the erstwhile Department of Anthropology was renamed 'The Discipline of Anthropology' in a Faculty of Humanities and Social Sciences. 'The Discipline' changed its focus and was renamed 'The Discipline of Anthropology and Development Studies'. We will soon become 'The Department of Anthropology and Development Studies', again with our Faculty called the Faculty of Arts. My colleagues and I teach courses that can contribute generally to, and as part of, a named major in the Bachelor's degrees in Arts (BA), Social Sciences (B. Soc. Sci.) and Development Studies (B. Dev. Stud.) and as options in a wide range of other degrees (from Medicine to Law to Science).

As you read you may be reflecting on the changing nomenclature and structure of your own research-learning practice in universities.

Academic units such as mine might house between 8 and 18 academic staff members. They might host 18 to 50 postgraduate research students. They would offer study units to as many as 800 to 2000 students each year. We do not often think of those students as part of 'us'. But we might well ask whether their learning and our academic lives might be improved if we did.

At the same time we need to recognise that in practice students experience their research-learning practice somewhat differently from 'us'. The 'first-year experience' is often predicated on a requirement to enrol in courses from several different fields of research-learning, even if in subsequent years many will be able to concentrate their subject choices in major (or similar) sequences. Their struggle is to make sense of difference across fields in research-learning practice. And, if they are lucky, they will join a variety of non-academic communities of practice — student societies, interest and political groups — during their time as students. Most, but far from all, first-year students proceed to complete an undergraduate degree even as they are members of a number of other university-based communities of practice.

The often unseen transition in practice is the exit experience: what practice, and membership of communities of practice, students continue beyond the locus of the university. This is of course a different kind of inquiry from the usual foci in student-centred studies of university transition. The majority of students make a transition out of university during, or at the end of, their first-degree studies. What practices of coming to know do they take with them? Are they still in some sense members of communities of research-learning practice? Certainly that would seem to be the case for graduates of professional degrees (Architecture, Dentistry, Engineering, Law, Medicine) whose transition to professional work is successful. Indeed the transition to work in such areas of research-learned professional practice is often effected by work-experience and internship placements which are designed to bridge 'academic' learning in theory to learning through practice where the student is a legitimate peripheral participant in a community of research-learned professional practice.

And although there seems to be a clear trajectory from neophyte student to expert academic and exemplary practitioner (see Figure 2.4) this is misleading.

Road-blocks emerge not just in the crises and attrition associated with the 'first-year experience' but at every point of engagement in a community of practice.

In the same way that neophyte undergraduates are invited to become legitimate peripheral participants in a number of fields of research-learning practice by being required to enrol in different courses in the first years of their undergraduate studies, some successful academics participate in a number of different fields of practice. I am thinking of a successful colleague of mine: a feminist anthropologist who is an adept member of a university's community of anthropological practice as well as its community of gender studies practice and, indeed, its community of public health practitioners.

Adept practice in local communities of research-learning practice ramify outward in 'space' to include membership of supra-local, national, regional and international communities of research-learning practice. Adept practitioners at least are entailed in a range of linked and sometimes nested communities of research-learning practice: minimally perhaps a class, or a group of co-practitioners (at various levels), medially at state, or national or regional level (see Figure 2.5), maximally at global level (see Figure 2.6). Through relations established in the preparation and reading of publications, processes of peer review, supervisions, exchange, correspondence, examination, conferences, meetings, certification and the like, communities of practice are constituted by legitimate peripheral participants and more and less adept practitioners as well as exemplary and meritorious practitioners. These typifications are in no way meant to indicate stability or clear trajectory. Delays and detours abound. In any case most academics move over their careers. A unit's new professorial leader, no less than a neophyte student, will for a time join a local community of research-learning practice as a legitimate peripheral participant.

The university field, as Bourdieu showed in his pioneering but now somewhat dated study of the French system of higher education, is a field of struggle amongst a plurality of hierarchies and co-existing but incommensurate forces of academic prestige, university power and external renown (1996 [1989]: 20). I remember being struck by the mismatch Bourdieu wrote of in a young American scholar's expectation of national and international recognition in the early 1970s. Bourdieu explained to his young visitor

Universities in Transition

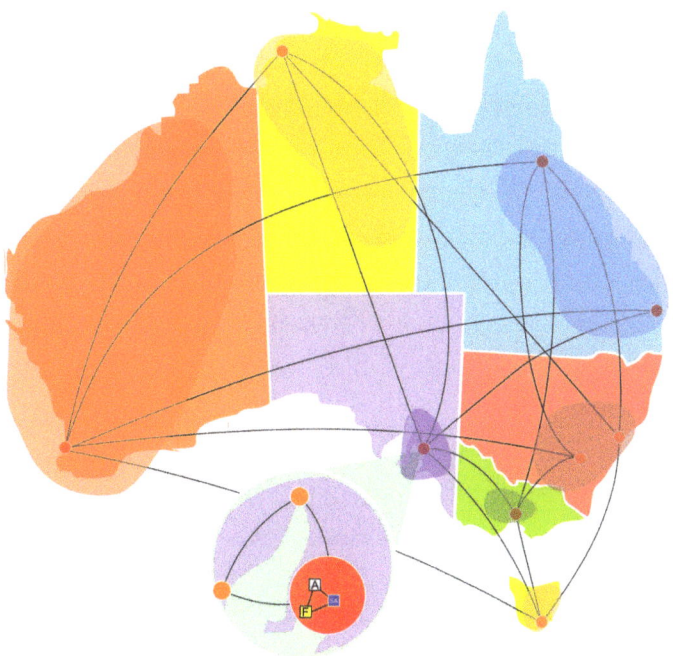

Figure 2.5: People and the places in which they practice link to create nested communities of research-learning practice at say, university, city, state and national levels

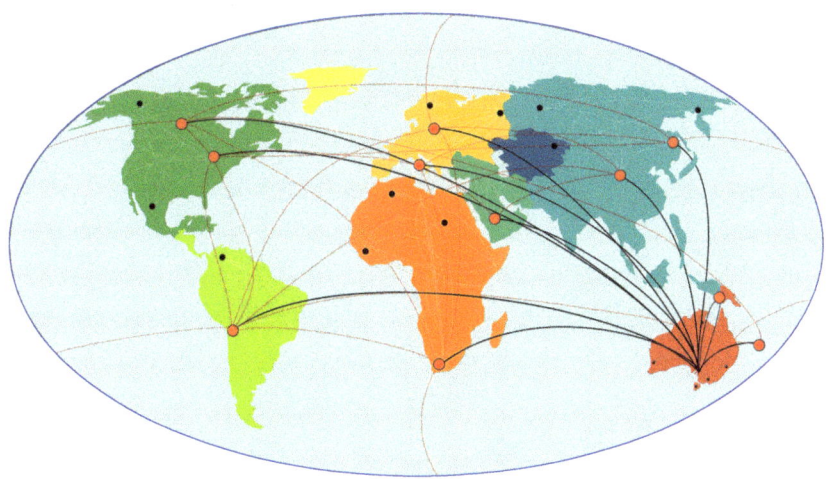

Figure 2.6: 'Maximal' communities of research-learning practice are founded in practitioners' global connections

> that all his intellectual heroes, like Althusser, Barthes, Deleuze, Derrida and Foucault ... held marginal positions in the university system which often disqualifie[d] them from officially directing research (in several cases, they had not themselves written a thesis, at least not in canonical form, and were therefore not allowed to direct one). (1990 [1984]: xviii)

These scholars of outstanding international repute did not have 'consecrated careers' in the French national university system (Bourdieu, 1996 [1989]). This points up a sometimes uneasy tension between the local organisational formations which host research-learning practitioners (in laboratories, departments, centres, faculties), who may form local communities of practice of their field of research-learning practice, and the broader potentially global communities of research-learning practice in which they are enmeshed and struggle for status, and indeed which, in their practice, they constitute. This resonates strangely with my experience of listening to scholars of growing or well-established global repute who, when they fail in the 'promotion rounds' of their local university, complain that they have been told that they need to take on administrative roles — Head of Department, member of the university's occupational health and safety committee or education committee — to be promoted. If there is a tension between research and teaching for academics in Australia there is also a tension between local university communities of practice and an academic's (global) field of research-learning practice and struggle.

Transition, whether into, within, or 'beyond' a class, a field or a locus of practice, is a fundamental feature of the membership of communities of research-learning practice. Few staff or students stay in the same local community of practice over the course of their career. Those who do stay in place are unlikely to reach recognition as exemplary practitioners, since research-learning practice is global and its membership diasporic. The movement of members from one university to another, and from country to country, entails that even exemplary global practitioners will be legitimate peripheral practitioners when they move.

Putting theory into practice

Brew has made the point that

> [i]f we are really serious about linking research and teaching, we need to consider the scholarly communities as mutual engagement and as joint

enterprise, that is to say, with all who participate including students ....
(2010: 142)

But how can we frame our educational practice like this without bankrupting academic lives and organisational budgets? Brew, I think, signals the way forward: situate students and their learning at university in practice and through communities of research-learning practice.

A practicum approach to research-learning

In my opinion, the challenge of practice theory to pedagogy is how to frame curriculum in practice. Professional areas of practice like law and medicine have over time developed a series of strategies to bring practice (often figured as 'problem-based learning') into their curricula through placements and internships.

But disciplines like mine in the social sciences are still in the experimental stages of finding more effective ways to engage our students in learning practices. Here I present a case study: an undergraduate unit that intentionally seeks to build a community of research-learning practice in a senior undergraduate course, 'Native Title Anthropology: Society, Law & Practice'.

A small group of colleagues working in the Locus of Social Analysis and Research (LocuSAR) at the University of Adelaide — Michael Maeorg, Lucy Hackworth and I — have been working to develop a 'practicum approach' to higher education to frame the Australian Native Title Studies (ANTS) program[12] we are developing in Native Title anthropology, a specialised field of research-learning practice.[13]

---

[12] At the time of writing, we are working to develop a national curriculum in Native Title anthropology. Scoping and foundational pedagogical work on this project has been supported by grants in 2011-12 and 2012-13 from the Attorney-General's Native Title Anthropologist grant program.

[13] Native Title anthropology has developed as an area of practice since the Mabo Decision of the High Court of Australia in 1992 and the bringing in of the Native Title Act in 1993, to give effect to that landmark judgement in Australian law (*Mabo v Queensland* (No 2) (1992) 175 CLR; *Native Title Act 1993* (Cth)). Native Title is a 'recognition space' in which Australian law recognises the law of Australia's First People's (see Mantziaris and Martin, 2000: 9-12). This recognition space is also a space for specialist anthropological practice. Native Title anthropology is also a hotly contested practice in Australian anthropology more generally. Some anthropologists declare it is not anthropology at all. Others assert that Native Title anthropologists fail to realise that they are

So what might a practicum approach look like? First and foremost a practicum approach *pivots on practice*. Our practicums aim progressively to open up and engage students with, and in, a field of research-learning practice. Secondly, our practicum approach works from the premise that learning and practice is socially situated and constituted in communities of practice, as it is constitutive of them. For this reason we aim *to bring participants into communities of practice* firstly by intentionally establishing the class itself as a community of practice (see Figure 2.9) and then by facilitating participants to engage with members of this community of practice more broadly over the duration of the course and beyond it. We do this by bringing adept, expert and exemplary practitioners into our classrooms to engage with the class about their practice, but also by enabling students to join them in their places of practice (see Figures 2.8 and 2.10). Thirdly our practicum approach seeks to provide a framework for course practice through which participants can 'do', and in their practice progressively link, master and ultimately innovate from, typically patterned (albeit dynamic) actions and outcomes in these communities of practice. But this framework is not intended to provide a clockwise trajectory. Rather participants have some control, particularly in the online portion, of what they do when. We anticipate trajectories that navigate back and forth around these planned pivots of research-learning practice (see Figure 2.7).

We open our own Native Title practice for inspection through 'Blue print briefs'. These 'interactive' briefing papers are so called because the links they provide to online material appear in blue print. By hitting a blue print link students are taken from the narrative of the brief to other relevant material that can extend perspectives. Typically these well-illustrated introductions to the field of practice provide links to official (court) accounts of the cases we introduce, films (including controversial films to debate), scholarly writing, radio, television and newspaper reports and documentaries and even publicly available primary evidence.

---

part of the governmentality of dispossession. Meanwhile there is a high demand for expert Native Title anthropologists and a recognition of the fact that there are not enough capable people coming through the ranks to take on these roles and indeed to replace aging experts who are leaving practice. The 'blockage' in the Native Title system that this contributes to has meant that funds have been available to try and bring students into training and practice, increase the capabilities of practitioners in the system and retain practitioners in the system. Support for a number of projects under the Attorney-General's Native Title Anthropologist grant program has enabled us to develop research-learning courses, and for Adelaide to become a locus for a national community of Native Title anthropological practice.

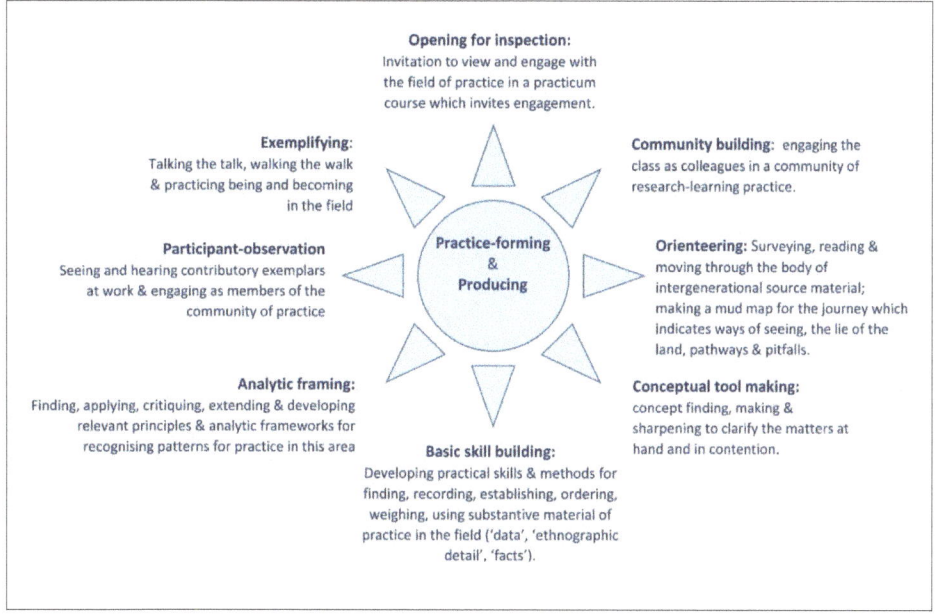

Figure 2.7: Pivots in a practicum-based research-learning approach

In the delivery of our undergraduate course in Native Title anthropology we seek community-forming from the start: by making a student's first task the posting on the class website of an introduction of themselves and their reasons for doing the course to everyone else. We encourage interaction by assessing the extent and quality of contributions to the discussion board in the first two weeks of the course. In an intensive on-campus week (in an otherwise online offering), we purposefully develop the class community through a number of class exercises. Over the on-campus week we bring Native Title practitioners into this locus of learning to discuss their work and be available as exemplars of practice. Over the week we encourage students, course staff and visiting practitioners to lunch together in the 'University Hub' (see Chapter 7, this book).

Assessment strategies are central to these endeavours. Community engagement through online introductions and interactions is rewarded. Regular quizzes provide formative experience and incentives to engage with the scholarly literature. Practicum assignments require students to undertake a typical practical process in the terms of typical practitioners. Students already working in the field of Native Title anthropology are encouraged to negotiate a project with their employer and the course co-ordinator so that their research-learning practice might also be integral to their workplace practice. ANTS also 'commissions' Native Title work through a 'Call for Contributions' brochure. Students may also negotiate a project with teaching staff who, in this course, take on the position of commissioning client. The staged assignment progression involves students in

- negotiating a project assignment (in this case 60 hours)
- finalising their project brief with their client
- developing a project plan with costings and milestone progress and payment points

Figure 2.8: Steve Goldsmith welcomed students to his country and gave his own perspective on Native Title, 20 January 2014

- delivering (for assessment) and invoicing a specified progress milestone outcome
- delivering and invoicing for payment the final outcome against the brief.

At the time of writing, we are seeking virtual ways to bring exemplary practitioners and exemplary practice to students as an online community of practice. Our online virtual space, 'the ANTS nest', is being further developed to support engagement in the broader community of practice in Native Title anthropology. We are developing 'untethered' curricula organised around topical, skill-developing, re-

Figure 2.9: Maddison and Clara conferring as part of a workshop exercise, 20 January 2014

Figure 2.10: Guest panellists discussing the De Rose Hill Native Title case, (from left, top); Karina Lester (chair of the Native Title holding group), Susan Woenne-Green (senior anthropologist for the claimants), Jon Willis (witness for the claimants), Kim McCaul (anthropologist for the 'State Crown'), Andrew Collett (lawyer for the claimants), and (bottom, far right) Peter Tonkin (lawyer for the State Crown), Native Title Summer School, University of Adelaide, January 2014

search-learning practice packages. One example revolves around a 30-minute research-learning film, 'Exploring Society', made by film-maker Caro McDonald for the ANTS program. The film introduces the 'genealogical method' developed by Rivers in the early twentieth century as practised by exemplary practitioner Professor Peter Sutton, eliciting responses from Karina Lester, a Yunkunytjatjara woman. In this package the key skills of eliciting a genealogy, and through it kin terminology, are introduced. The relevance of such material to the practice of Native Title anthropology is outlined. A core reading by the skill's inventor (Rivers, 1910) is attached and students are required to take 'research reading notes' on it. Students will watch the high-quality and engaging video of the practice in action and will 'write up' the case study. We have designed an interactive context for students to practise the skill amongst themselves. Then they will be asked to critically assess the usefulness of the method in Native Title analysis.

Figure 2.11: Giving concurrent expert evidence, *The Barngarla Native Title Trial* by Bronya McGovern

At the time of writing, other skill development learning packages are in planning with our film-maker. Planned for inclusion in these learning packages is a unit on Native Title litigation. Here we will use footage shot while our team has been doing the in-court fieldwork for our ethnography of Native Title litigation. This unit will not only include ethnographic film but will also draw on sketches made by an experienced courtroom artist, Bronya McGovern, whom we commissioned to make this visual record of court proceedings (see Figure 2.11). The outcome will be research-learning exemplars — a richly illustrated and multi-faceted ethnographic monograph on Native Title litigation, and an enticing video documentary that will bring research-learners into the courtroom and the court into our research-learning practice. None of these products will be bound by 'traditional' teaching or research forms. All will make fundamental contributions to our community of practising Native Title anthropologists.

Conclusion

This chapter has sought to reach over a horizon of enquiry and understanding dominated by student transition, and undergraduate transition in particular, to conceptualise the university field and university transitions more broadly. In this chapter I have sought to demonstrate the analytic and pedagogical fecundity of practice perspectives. I have sought to show how, by making practice rather than governance or social roles (teachers versus students, researchers versus teachers) our point of departure, we can better understand the social life of universities, fields and the research-learning practices which constitute them. I have also sought to indicate how pedagogical design organised around research-learning and its communities of practice can bring the strengths of situated learning into universities. Indeed a practice orientation opens up what, for me, is the biggest lacuna in our understanding of university transitions: what do our students take away with them into the practices of their everyday lives when, whenever they do it, they leave university?

References

Access Economics. 2010. 'Study of relative funding levels for university teaching and research activities'. Report for Universities Australia available at: http://www.universitiesaustralia.edu.au/page/submissions---reports/commissioned-studies/relative-funding/ [accessed 29 June 2013].

Alvesson, M. and D. Kärreman. 2000. 'Varieties of discourse: on the study of organizations through Discourse Analysis'. *Human Relations*, 53 (9): 1125-49.

Alvesson, M. and D. Kärreman. 2011. 'Decolonizing discourse: critical reflections on organizational discourse analysis'. *Human Relations*, 64(9): 1121-46.

Barnett, R. 1990. *The idea of higher education*. Buckingham: The Society for Research into Higher Education and Open University Press.

Barnett, R. 2000. *Realizing the university in an age of supercomplexity*. Buckingham: The Society for Research into Higher Education and Open University Press.

Becher, T. and P. Trowler. 2001 [1989]. *Academic tribes and territories: intellectual enquiry and the culture of the disciplines*. 2nd edn. Buckingham: Open University Press.

Bourdieu, P. 1990 [1984]. *Homo Academicus*. Cambridge: Polity Press.

Bourdieu, P. 1993. *The field of cultural production: essays on art and literature.* Cambridge: Polity Press.

Bourdieu, P. 1996 [1989]. *The state nobility.* Stanford: Stanford University Press.

Bourdieu, P. 2004. *Science of science and reflexivity.* Cambridge: Polity Press.

Boyer Commission on Educating Undergraduates in the Research University. 1998. *ReInventing undergraduate education: a blueprint for America's research universities.* http://www.niu.edu/engagedlearning/research/pdfs/BoyerReport.pdf [accessed 24 July 2014].

Brew, A. 1999. 'Research and teaching: changing relationships in a changing context'. *Studies in Higher Education,* 24(3): 291-301.

Brew, A. 2001. *The nature of research: inquiry in academic contexts.* London: Routledge Falmer.

Brew, A. 2006. *Research and teaching: beyond the divide.* London: Palgrave Macmillan.

Brew, A. 2010. 'Imperatives and challenges in integrating teaching and research'. *Higher Education Research & Development,* 29(2): 139-50.

Brew, A. 2012. 'Teaching and research: new relationships and their implications for inquiry-based teaching and learning in higher education'. *Higher Education Research & Development,* 31(1): 101-14.

Brew, A. and D. Boud, 1995. 'Teaching and research: establishing the vital link with learning'. *Higher Education,* 29: 261-73.

Brew, A. and J. Weir, n.d. 'Teaching-Research Nexus Benchmarking Project: The University of Sydney and Monash University'. Unpublished report available. http://www.dm.monash.edu.au/cheq/academic/ [accessed 24 July 2004].

Chandler, J. 2009. 'Doctrines, disciplines, discourses, departments'. *Critical Inquiry,* 35(4): 729-46.

Clark, B. 1986. *The higher education system: academic organization in cross-national perspective.* Berkeley: University of California Press.

Coaldrake, P. and L. Stedman. 2013. *Raising the stakes: gambling with the future of universities,* St Lucia: University of Queensland Press.

Croucher, G., S. Marginson, A. Norton and J. Wells (eds). 2013. *The Dawkins Revolution 25 years on.* Carlton: University of Melbourne Press.

Davis, G. 2010. *The Republic of Learning: higher education transforms Australia, Boyer Lectures 2010.* Melbourne: HarperCollins Publishers.

Donald, J. 2009. 'The commons: disciplinary and interdisciplinary encounters', in C. Kreber (ed.), *The university and its disciplines: teaching and learning within and beyond disciplinary boundaries*. New York: Routledge.

Dourish, P. and G. Bell. 2011. *Divining a digital future: mess and mythology in ubiquitous computing*. Cambridge, Mass: MIT Press.

Duncan, W.G.K. and R.A. Leonard. 1973. *The University of Adelaide, 1874-1974*. Adelaide: Rigby.

Ecclestone, K. 2009. 'Lost and found in transition', in J. Field, J. Gallacher and R. Ingram (eds), *Researching transitions in lifelong learning*. London and New York: Routledge.

Finnis, M. 1975. *The lower level: a discursive history of the Adelaide University Union*. Adelaide: Adelaide University Union.

Harrison, S. 1995. 'Anthropological perspectives: on the management of knowledge'. *Anthropology Today*, 11(5): 10-14.

Harrison, S. 2006. *Fracturing resemblances: identity and mimetic conflict in Melanesia and the West*. New York: Berghahn Books.

Hattie, J. and H. Marsh. 1996. 'The relationship between research and teaching: a meta-analaysis'. *Review of Educational Research*, 66(4): 507-42.

Holland, D., D. Powell, E. Eng and G. Drew. 2010. 'Models of engaged scholarship: an interdisciplinary discussion'. *Collaborative Anthropologies*, 3: 1-36.

Hyland, K. 2008. 'Genre and academic writing in the disciplines'. *Language Teaching*, 41(4): 543-62.

Hyland, K. and M. Bondi (eds). 2006. *Academic discourses across disciplines. Linguistic insights: studies in language and communication* (42). Bern: Peter Lang.

James, R., K.-L. Krause and C. Jennings, 2010. 'The first year experience in Australian universities: findings from 1994 to 2009'. Melbourne: Centre for the Study of Higher Education, The University of Melbourne. http://www.cshe.unimelb.edu.au/research/experience/docs/FYE_Report_1994_to_2009.pdf [accessed 24 July 2014].

Jenkins, A., T. Blackman, R. Lindsay and R. Paton-Saltzberg. 1998. 'Teaching and research: student perspectives and policy implications'. *Studies in Higher Education*, 23(2): 127-41.

Kreber, C. 2009. 'The modern research university and its disciplines', in C.

Kreber (ed.), *The university and its disciplines: teaching and learning within and beyond disciplinary boundaries*. New York: Routledge.

Lave, J. and E. Wenger. 2007 [1991]. *Situated learning: legitimate peripheral participation*. Cambridge: Cambridge University Press.

Linn, R. 2011. *The spirit of knowledge: a social history of the University of Adelaide North Terrace Campus*. Adelaide: Barr Smith Press.

McInnis, C. and R. James. 1995. *First year on campus: diversity in the initial experiences of Australian undergraduates*. Melbourne: Centre for the Study of Higher Education, The University of Melbourne. http://www.cshe.unimelb.edu.au/people/james_docs/FYE.pdf [accessed 24 July 2014].

Mantziaris, C. and D. Martin. 2000. *Native Title corporations: a legal and anthropological analysis*. Annandale, NSW: Federation Press.

Marginson, S. 1997. 'Steering from a distance: power relations in Australian higher education'. *Higher Education*, 34: 63-80.

Marginson, S. 2007. 'Rethinking academic work in the global era'. *Journal of Higher Education Policy and Management*, 22(1): 23-35.

Marginson, S. and M. Considine. 2000. *The enterprise university: power, governance and reinvention in Australia*. Cambridge: Cambridge University Press.

Matusov, E., N. Bell and B. Rogoff. 2009. 'Review'. *American Ethnologist*, 21(4): 918.

Mayson, S. and J. Schapper. 2012. 'Constructing teaching and research relations from the top: an analysis of senior manager discourses on research-led teaching'. *Higher Education*, 64: 473-87.

Michaels, E. 1985. 'Constraints on knowledge in an economy of oral information'. *Current Anthropology*, 26(4): 505-10.

Nielsen, M. 2012. *Reinventing discovery: the new era of networked science*. Princeton: Princeton University Press.

Northedge, A. and J. McArthur. 2009. 'Guiding students into a discipline: the significance of the teacher,' in C. Kreber (ed.), *The university and its disciplines: teaching and learning within and beyond disciplinary boundaries*. New York: Routledge.

Nursey-Bray, M., D. Fergie, V. Arbon, L.-I. Rigney, R. Palmer, J. Tibby, N. Harvey and L. Hackworth. 2013. *Community based adaptation to climate change: the Arabana, South Australia*. Gold Coast: National Climate Change Adaptation Research Facility.

Rivers, W.H.R. 1910. 'The genealogical method of anthropological enquiry'. *The Sociological Review*, 3(1): 1-2.

Rowland, S. 2006. *The enquiring university: compliance and contestation in higher education*. Maidenhead, Berkshire: The Society for Research into Higher Education and Open University Press.

Roxå, T. and K. Mårtensson. 2009. 'Teaching and learning regimes from within: significant networks as a locus for the social construction of teaching and learning', in C. Kreber (ed.), *The university and its disciplines: teaching and learning within and beyond disciplinary boundaries*. New York: Routledge.

Sahlins, M. 2013. *What kinship is — and is not*. Chicago: University of Chicago Press.

Schapper, J. and S. Mayson. 2010. 'Research-led teaching: moving from a fractured engagement to a marriage of convenience'. *Higher Education Research & Development*, 29(6): 641-51.

Schatzki, T., K. Cetina and E. Savigny. 2001. *The practice turn in contemporary theory*. London: Routledge.

Shavit, Y., R. Arum and A. Gamoran (eds). 2007. *Stratification in higher education: a comparative study*. Stanford: Stanford University Press.

Seaman, M. 2008. 'Birds of a feather? Communities of practice and knowledge communities'. *Curriculum and Teaching Dialogue*, 10(1-2): 269-79.

Shove, E., M. Pantzar and M. Watson. 2012. *The dynamics of social practice: everyday life and how it changes*. London: Sage.

Smith, K. 2008. '"Who do you think you're talking to?" — the discourse of learning and teaching strategies'. *Higher Education*, 56: 295-406.

Strathern, M. 2004. *Commons and borderlands: working papers on interdisciplinarity, accountability and the flow of knowledge*. Oxford: Sean Kingston Publishing.

Trowler, P. 2009. 'Beyond epistemological essentialism: academic tribes in the twenty-first century', in C. Kreber (ed.), *The University and its disciplines: teaching and learning within and beyond disciplinary boundaries*. New York: Routledge.

Universities Australia. 2013. 'A smarter Australia: an agenda for Australian higher education 2013-2016'. http://www.universitiesaustralia.edu.au [accessed 24 July 2014].

The University of Adelaide. 2012. *Beacon of enlightenment: strategic plan 2013-*

2023. Adelaide: The University of Adelaide. http://www.adelaide.edu.au/VCO/beacon/ [accessed 24 July 2014].

The University of Adelaide. 2013. *2012 Annual report*. Adelaide: The University of Adelaide. http://www.adelaide.edu.au/publications/pdfs/a-report-12.pdf [accessed 24 July 2014].

Part 2

Revaluing: 'non-traditional' student groups in higher education

3 Classism on campus? Exploring and extending understandings of social class in the contemporary higher education debate

Angelique Bletsas and Dee Michell

Abstract

In this chapter we introduce the term 'classism' into the higher education debate in Australia. By 'classism' we mean the tendency to construct people from low socio-economic status (SES) backgrounds as inherently deficient according to prevailing normative values. Using an analysis of the Bradley Review, we show that low SES students are constructed as inherently lacking in aspirations in current policy discourse and are regarded as 'needier' higher education students in comparison with their higher SES peers. This construction, we argue, is an example of classism, and therefore we suggest that adding 'classism' to existing understandings of disadvantage will help to raise awareness of discrimination as well as formulate best practice in higher education.

Introduction

On gaining office in 2007 the Labor government (2007-13) commissioned a comprehensive review of the higher education sector. Released in 2008 and known after its lead author, Professor Denise Bradley, 'the Bradley Review' (Bradley et al., 2008) identifies diversity and equity as key areas of concern in the sector. Consequently, the issue of equity in the Australian university system has re-emerged as a point of lively policy and public debate. Taking the Bradley Review as our starting point, in this chapter we examine the ways in which equity goals, as they relate to social class and socio-economic status (SES), are articulated in contemporary government policy. Informed by the work of policy analyst Carol Bacchi (2009), we ask: what kind of a problem is social class represented to be in this policy discourse? The chapter demonstrates that social class is represented to be a problem of individual (student) deficit. We posit that this conceptualisation of social class, as a problem of individual deficit, is a product of 'classism'. We understand this term broadly, as referring to pervasive cultural and institutional norms which construct individuals who are of a low SES as inherently deficient in a variety of ways.

Classism: towards a definition

Our argument in this chapter is that contemporary debates on higher education continue to be predicated on a 'deficit' understanding of low SES students. That is, in addressing participation rates of low SES students, low SES students themselves are frequently represented as 'the problem'. It is our contention that this representation of low SES students, in terms of a deficit model, persists even when policy and literature otherwise promote an egalitarian agenda of equal access and equal opportunity, as is the case of the Bradley Review, which we analyse below. In order to account for how it is that the deficit model persists even in egalitarian accounts of higher education, we posit the notion of 'classism'. We therefore foreground our discussion of the Bradley Review with an elaboration of this term.

'Classism' is not a term widely used in Australia. In particular, the term is largely absent from critical higher education literature. For instance, a database search of the term in Equity101, the national online repository of research and other material on social inclusion in education, does not return any material. This absence may arise from the fact that in education literature there has been a methodological preference for talking in the language of SES rather than social class. Nor is the term 'classism' much in use in the United Kingdom either, where class-based discrimination, and the low social esteem in which low SES groups are held, is increasingly described through the language of 'social racism'. It seems this is the preferred language for some in the UK who argue that classist derogations there demarcate and create distance from particular 'white' ethnic groups (Nayak, 2006; Tyler, 2008; Webster, 2008).

By contrast, in the United States the term 'classism' is broadly used. Here it is a term which arises in a range of literatures to name the way in which the low social esteem in which low SES people are held impacts perceptions of low SES people and, more precisely, impacts service delivery to low SES communities. Given the current focus on increasing participation of low SES students into higher education, our purpose in this chapter is to suggest that the concept of classism and its potential impact on service delivery may well be instructive. In this context we argue that 'classism' could usefully be added to existing understandings of disadvantage and attempts to raise awareness of discrimination as well as to formulate best practice in higher education and elsewhere.

Emphasis on low *social* esteem and low *cultural* valuation, which presupposes a deficit model of low SES people, makes up the key aspects of our preferred definition of classism. At least, it forms the core of a definition on which we could both agree. We also both preferred the term 'classism' to that of 'social racism' because we consider it highly problematic to suggest that only 'white' ethnic groups are included in the category of low SES, or that social class can be made discrete from, and separate to, other politicised identity categories. However, as indicated below, existing definitions from the literature often diverge from our own as well, with different ones emphasising particular aspects of the concept. Some definitions emphasise individual prejudice, treating classism as primarily an attitudinal problem (e.g. Lott, 2002, see below). Others emphasise the way in which classism becomes internalised and the implications of this (e.g. Barone, 1998, see below). The different emphases indicate a variety of theoretical underpinnings, and in reviewing this literature we found that we did not share an underlying theoretical position. Therefore, we are not endorsing these definitions intrinsically. Rather, we merely review them as evidence of the ways in which the concept of classism has been developed in existing literature.

In the US, use of 'classism' extends back to at least the late 1960s (Bazelon, 1969). However, according to economist Chuck Barone (1998) it was never clearly defined and while many scholars were keen to analyse class as it intersected with other categories of difference, particularly race and gender, focus was primarily on structural or institutional class oppression. For Barone, though, what is needed is an understanding of classism operating at multiple levels in society. At the individual or 'micro' level, according to Barone, 'classist beliefs, attitudes, and behaviour' are internalised through a socialisation process (1998: 4). At the 'meso' or intra-group level, he goes on to argue, prejudices 'based on negative attitudes toward and classist stereotypes' of low SES people as well as discrimination, result in distancing and exclusion (ibid.: 5-6). Macro-level classism then results in the reproduction of the class system through social institutions, particularly education, where the epistemologies of low SES groups are 'depreciated and invalidated in schools' and 'middle and owning class' epistemologies are highly esteemed and normative (ibid.: 18). But what is termed Barone's 'ecological' understanding of classism appears not to have been taken up by other than a few academics, although US psychologist Bernice Lott has generated more interest with her definition of the term.

In 2002 Lott called on clinical psychologists to examine their professional practice for ways in which they may reproduce class-based discrimination at both interpersonal and institutional levels. Lott's aim is to show that people who are poor are usually regarded as 'Other', and as morally and personally deficient. For Lott, classism leads to exclusion from 'full participation in social institutions':

> I propose that a dominant response [to people from low SES backgrounds] is that of distancing, that is, separation, exclusion, devaluation, discounting, and designation as 'other', and that this response can be identified in both institutional and interpersonal contexts. In social psychological terms, distancing and denigrating responses operationally define discrimination. These, together with stereotypes (i.e., a set of beliefs about a group that are learned early, widely shared, and socially validated) and prejudice (i.e., negative attitudes) constitute classism. (2002: 108)

Lott's account of classism, and her claim that clinical psychologists reproduce classism, provoked a spirited discussion. For example, in 2008 Laura Smith argued for the inclusion of classism in clinical psychology's social justice agenda, echoing her earlier attempts (Smith, 2005, 2006). According to Smith, classism needs to be added to the racism, sexism and heterosexism that clinical psychologists have already tackled. She also calls for colleagues to confront, where appropriate, their privilege and any internalised discrimination with regard to social class, including recognising social location, becoming informed about the lived experience of low SES people, challenging assumptions and prejudices, and analysing everyday classed experiences (Smith, 2008).

Other key contributors to the move to include classism on the social justice agenda include William Liu and Saba Rasheed Ali (2005). Also clinical psychologists, their focus is on vocational counselling and they argue that without attention to classism it is easy to assume upward mobility is unproblematic and always preferable. Outside of psychology, US social worker Kathryn Newton (2010) has also called for facilitators of therapeutic and support groups to become aware of their internalised classism in order to reduce conflicts and silencing that may otherwise occur because of social class barriers (Newton, 2010).

In a rare Australian example, Smith's position is echoed by a team of Queensland psychologists. Peter McIlveen et al. (2010) argue that autoethnography — using oneself as the subject of research — is one way for psychologists undertaking diversity training to become better informed about their own class identity and related values and beliefs. Another notable contribution from Australian research is the work of Elizabeth Hatton. As early as the 1990s Hatton sought to bring attention to the way in which existing diversity training had limited impact in teacher training because potential school teachers 'come from a narrow range of relatively privileged backgrounds' (1998: 217). She claimed further that the consequent narrow range of experiences of this group limited their understanding of diversity. In Hatton's analysis, without effective intervention and training teachers from middle class backgrounds will carry with them 'classist' attitudes that potentially serve to disadvantage the low SES children and young people they work with (ibid.: 222).

From this brief review of key literature it is clear that there are multiple accounts of the concept of 'classism'. What they have in common, and what specifically interests us in this chapter, is that they identify a tendency to represent or understand low SES people in terms of a deficit model. While psychological approaches to classism identify this tendency at the attitudinal level, as a product of un-interrogated prejudice, we suggest that this is, at best, an incomplete analysis. It is certainly likely that there exist individuals who hold prejudiced views, but the deficit model of low SES people also exists at a discursive level where it is not fairly or adequately explained as the product of individual bias but rather indicates a cultural logic. It is the discursive construction of low SES people that we now turn to explore in the Bradley Review.

Understanding problem representations: equality as a contested problem

This chapter discusses the 2008 Bradley Review because of the way it has reinvigorated debates on equality in education, specifically in relation to low SES groups. However, the 'problem' of equality and equitable participation in higher education is by no means a new issue. With the possible exception of reforms undertaken during the Howard Coalition government — where increased productivity and efficiency were central aims — it could be argued that almost all major reforms to the university sector since the 1970s have been made in the name of advancing equity goals. The Whitlam Government's move to abolish university fees was famously made in the pursuit of an egalitarian agenda (Whitlam, 1972: 1-3). Likewise, when the Hawke Government reintroduced fees through the (then named) HECS deferred payment system, equity was also invoked (Dawkins, 1987: 2-3, 21-4). At this time fees were forwarded as a possible means by which to fund the increased costs brought about by mass participation in university education (ibid.: 87; Gale and Tranter, 2011: 36). The Bradley Review (2008: 27, 38), which nowhere recommends repealing the fee-paying system, nonetheless claims that measures undertaken in the period of the Dawkins reforms have failed to solve the equity problem and that the university sector is failing to achieve proportional access by 'non-traditional' students. Thus, while equity is generally held as a common goal, what is required to achieve it remains contested. In the words of Bacchi (2009), policy proposals advanced to achieve equity represent the problem differently.

Bacchi's approach to policy analysis, the 'What's the Problem Represented to be?' approach (WPR), which we employ in our analysis of the Bradley Review below, involves studying policy texts for the way they represent the social phenomena they address. Importantly, in this analysis policy 'problems' are understood in a very specific sense. Bacchi (2009: ix-24) suggests that in analysing policy proposals we ask: what is it, precisely, that the policy seeks to change? From the entry point of the policy proposal and what it specifically aims to change, it is possible to work backwards to understand what the policy represents the problem to be:

> To study problematisations it is useful to open them up to analysis by 'reading off' (or identifying) the implied 'problem' — what is seen as in need of 'fixing' — from the plan of action that is proposed (the policy or policy

> proposal). It is possible to do this because what we propose to do about something indicates what we think needs to change ('the problem'). This characterisation of the 'problem' is the place to start in order to understand how an issue is being understood. I call this implied 'problem' — described by Dean as the 'problem space of rule' — a problem representation. (2009: xi)

For Bacchi, studying problem representations is crucial, for it allows the researcher to query how a particular phenomenon comes to have the status of a 'policy problem' (or problematisation). Investigating problem representations also usefully highlights that, frequently, there is contestation over what the problem is represented to be.

To treat problem representations as socially constituted is not to infer that it is never appropriate to claim that some social phenomena are problematic. Rather, this approach merely asserts that the process by which some social phenomena come to be considered policy 'problems' is an appropriate field of inquiry. Thus it is not our claim that the lack of proportional representation of so-called 'non-traditional' students *should not* be constituted a problem. Instead, in keeping with Bacchi, we argue that it is of fundamental importance that policy proposals towards this goal are closely interrogated for the specific way they represent the problem. If equity in education is a normative goal, then policy proposals to achieve it ought also to be examined for their logical and normative presuppositions. While it is the case that in our analysis of the Bradley Review we are specifically concerned with what kind of a problem low SES participation is represented to be, it would be possible to examine the Review for the way it understands equality more generally. Indeed, there is already literature which does this (e.g. Gale, 2011; Gale and Tranter, 2011). We have narrowed our focus in this chapter, however, in order to provide a close reading of the underlying presuppositions which are implicit to the way social class is constituted as a particular kind of problem.

Equity, class and the Bradley Review

As stated above, the Bradley Review is a comprehensive survey of the Australian higher education sector. It evaluates the functional effectiveness of the sector and recommends a number of measures government ought to take in order to improve performance. A key finding of the Review is that participation among low SES groups is not representative of the demographic make-up of the population.

Towards this end the Review sets a target of increased participation by low SES students from 15 per cent of university enrolments in 2008 to 20 per cent by 2020 (Bradley et al., 2008: xiv).[1] Because of this recommendation and the frank discussion in which it is advanced, with the authors asserting that existing policy approaches were failing to achieve equity targets, the Bradley Review has been widely received as promoting an equity agenda in education (e.g. James, 2009; Putnam and Gill, 2011; Ferguson, 2011; Klinger and Murray, 2011), with debate arising over the specific recommendations advocated and whether they will ensure that equity targets are more adequately addressed in future. With some notable exceptions (e.g. Gale, 2011; Gale and Tranter, 2011; Bok, 2010; Brook, 2011), the existing debate takes for granted the way in which the problem of social class and equity is understood in the Bradley Review. In the analysis that follows, we sidestep debates about whether the recommendations made in the Review are the 'right' ones in order to interrogate just what it is that they represent the problem to be.

In examining the way participation of low SES students is represented as a problem in the Bradley Review, we note first that increased participation in university is a target established across the board in the Review. Thus, the target of 20 per cent participation for low SES groups is not set out of a simple concern for equity. Rather, it is posited following a long discussion of findings from an Access Economics report, which claims that in the near future labour market demand for university graduates will far outpace current enrolment levels (Bradley et al., 2008: 9-10, 15-21).[2] The aim to increase the participation rates of low SES groups to a representative level is a subset of this wider goal. This is significant because it suggests an instrumental market-focused understanding of social class and equality. This instrumental market-focused rationale becomes quite apparent when applying Bacchi's 'What's the Problem Represented to be?' approach in a methodical way: by starting with the recommendations and working backwards.

The Bradley Review contains a total of 46 recommendations. Of these, two directly concern the issue of equitable participation for low SES groups as detailed in the chapter dedicated to this issue: 'Providing Opportunities for all Capable Students to Participate' (ibid.: 27-45). They are as follows:

---

[1] In 2009 the then Labor Government pledged to adopt this recommended target (Gillard, 2009).

[2] Interestingly, a similar line of argument is also advanced in the 1987 Dawkins policy paper.

- Recommendation 3: That the Australian Government commission work on the measurement of the socio-economic status of students in higher education with a view to moving the current postcode methodology to one based on the individual circumstances of each student.
- Recommendation 4: That the Australian Government set a national target that, by 2020, 20 per cent of higher education enrolments at undergraduate level are people from low socio-economic status backgrounds. (ibid.: xviii)

Recommendation 3 is made out of a concern with the methodology by which low socio-economic students are identified. It problematises the analytic process by which equity targets are reported and evaluated. It is, in other words, a technical recommendation. Recommendation 4 is more substantive and has attracted significant controversy. Before moving on to analyse it in detail, we note that two additional recommendations (Recommendation 5 and Recommendation 6) in the Review explicitly address the issue of Commonwealth allowances for eligible students and, consequently, impact participation rates of low SES students. In the case of Commonwealth allowances and the Review's recommendation that these be brought in line with rising costs of living, it could be said that the problem is represented to be 'structural' — brought about by inadequate support for students who are unable to rely solely on family for financial support throughout their studies. Certainly the Review's recommendations on this matter acknowledge such pressures (ibid.: 49-56).[3]

The issue of Commonwealth allowances has been the source of inquiry and reform in the period since the Bradley Review. Considering such reforms in further detail is beyond the scope of this chapter. It is, however, important to acknowledge that there is more than one problem representation in the Review and that this in itself is not unusual in policy discourse.

In debate following the Review the key point of contention has been Recommendation 4, and its relationship to an additional recommendation, Recommendation 31, which proposes that participation levels of low SES students should become a performance indicator in evaluating universities and,

---

[3] However, even in so doing they are careful to delimit the role of government in assisting students. On two occasions budget constraints are explicitly stated in the rationale of the Review's authors' recommendations for income support structures for students (Bradley et al., 2008: 62, 65).

more specifically, that a quantum of Commonwealth funding be predicated on performance in this area (ibid.: xxiii). This recommendation is consistent with the general emphasis on performance measurement and evaluation which occurs throughout the Review. Given that the Review acknowledges that the current funding structure of the university sector is inadequate to meet present demand and that this situation has led to strained budgets and to eroding student satisfaction levels (ibid: 148-50), it is not difficult to sympathise with the feeling of frustration that additional performance criteria and expectations placed upon universities provoked among some stakeholders (e.g. Gallagher, 2009; McWha as cited in Holderhead, 2011). However, to engage the debate at this level is to leave the presuppositions embedded in the Review and its representation of the problem of equitable participation un-interrogated. In keeping with the WPR approach it is necessary to 'dig deeper' into the Review. Doing so highlights that, while the Review makes specific university institutions *responsible* for addressing the problem by tying funding to performance, it is ultimately not the university system it represents as needing to change but low SES students themselves.

A thoroughgoing analysis of the Review and its discussion of equitable participation reveals 'aspiration' to be a repeated theme of its discourse: specifically the aspirations of low SES communities. The Review (Bradley et al., 2008: 27) claims that people from low SES groups need to be made aware of the university sector and of the benefits of university. Recommending 'aspiration building' as the solution to the problem of inequitable participation represents low socio-economic communities as the problem: *their* aspirations are what need to change (see also Bok, 2010). This representation of the problem was clear in a speech replying to the Review by then Education Minister Julia Gillard:

> The aspiration to attend university ... comes from many sources, but one of the most crucial is parental attitudes towards tertiary study ...
>
> Positive cultural attitudes towards higher education can be extended to even the poorest of families ... The building blocks of education start in the home.
>
> In suburbs, in country towns, in remote Australia and in the poorest households across the nation, Australian parents need to encourage a positive attitude towards education, to nurture a love of learning and to rejoice in learning success as children grow and mature. (Gillard, 2009)

This interest in aspiration building has since been implemented into policy with the Australian Government offering funding for projects designed to provide 'outreach', awareness and aspiration building programs with 'non-traditional' students and communities (Australian Commonwealth Government, 2009a: 13-14, 2009b; see also DEEWR, 2011).

It is useful at this juncture to draw out some of the logical and normative presuppositions upon which this representation of the problem of equitable participation is necessarily premised. Of relevance is that the aspiration building proposed in the Review aims to engage low SES students in terms of their *private* aspirations. That is, the Bradley Review, and subsequent government discourse, does not recommend building the aspirations of low SES communities in terms of inculcating a right or *entitlement* to access education as a public institution. This is apparent, and consistent with, the wider terms of the Review and its understanding of the role of education. As noted above, the Review's concern to increase participation rates is phrased in terms of projected labour market demand for graduates. Clearly, this is an understanding of education that is focused on the relation between education and the labour market. It is, as such, a 'private' understanding of education concerned with labour market opportunities afforded to individuals as individuals and not a view of education as a public entitlement: the right to learn and to be an educated citizen.

What is more, though advocating a 'demand driven' education system and recommending that caps on Commonwealth supported places be abandoned, the Review nonetheless supports a (deferred) fee-paying system. Indeed, at times in its discussion it appears to endorse moves to set fees in accord with the 'private benefits' that different degrees are likely to bestow upon graduates (Bradley et al., 2008: 156). This demonstrates that the wider logic upon which the representation of participatory equity rests takes for granted a global 'free market' system wherein individuals are understood as being in competition for limited opportunities (see also Gale, 2011; Gale and Tranter, 2011). Education is not so much a citizen entitlement, then, as it is necessary to the human capital building that 'fair competition' requires. Aspiration building in this context means inculcating an appropriate set of norms into low SES communities who, it is inferred, have to date failed to be competitive in the global labour market.

It is worth pausing to consider the full implications of this representation of the problem. This problem representation constructs individuals of low SES as not participating in the university sector because they have failed to recognise the benefits, personal and financial, which arise from a university qualification. When identified in this way and stated as such, this presupposition seems highly unlikely. In what possible context could large groups of the community have failed to recognise a relationship between private benefits — including higher incomes — and university qualifications? We contend that this is not a reasonable assumption and that it arises as a consequence of classism. We do *not* suggest by this that the authors of the Review consciously hold 'classist' views or are deliberately prejudiced towards low SES people. Nor do we mean to single out the Bradley Review as uniquely informed by the cultural attitudes we identify. Instead, we acknowledge that the Bradley Review is in many ways a progressive statement and that it is clearly committed to improving outcomes for low SES students. For instance, the Review readily endorses research which demonstrates that at the level of performance, low SES students are at much the same level of achievement as their peers (Bradley et al., 2008: 30). Our more circumscribed claim in analysing the Review is that understandings of low SES students as they appear in the document are still tacitly informed by pervasive cultural attitudes which presuppose that individuals on low incomes are inherently different from, and in some ways deficient in relation to, the social 'mainstream'. It is this pervasive classism, we argue, which underlies the 'deficit' understanding of low SES students and their allegedly limited or misplaced 'aspirations'. As Jessica Bok (2010: 176) puts it, 'the policy rhetoric of "raising aspirations" … is offensive in its suggestion that students attending schools categorised as low SES "lack" adequate desires for their futures'.[4]

A deficit understanding of low SES students can be further identified in the Bradley Review. For example, it is implicit in the claims that it is more expensive for universities to educate/service students from low SES backgrounds than their peers (Bradley et al., 2008: 27-8). The reason given for this assertion is that students from low SES backgrounds rely more regularly on student support services than their peers do (e.g. Bradley et al., 2008: 27-8). It may in fact be the

---

[4] For a critical discussion of 'aspiration' in the higher education debate see also Brook, 2011; Bland, 2011.

case that low SES students access university support services more readily than their peers (counselling and so on) but there may be a range of reasons for this. For example, students with greater financial means may be able to access similar services privately, off campus. Thus, it may not be that low SES students access the services more frequently; it might simply be a difference in *where* such services are accessed. Perhaps this is less a fact about low SES students and more a reflection on a lack of support services being publicly offered at the level of the community sector and local councils.

Nonetheless, even if it is the case that low SES students do in fact access support services more frequently than their peers this does not tell us anything about *why* such variation occurs. The absence of analysis on this point effectively 'naturalises' the issue. Without any detailed analysis of why there might be higher rates of support services accessed, low SES students appear in the discussion as innately 'needier' than their peers. Given that the Bradley Review acknowledges that means-tested Commonwealth incomes for eligible students have not merely failed to rise but have in fact depreciated in purchasing power in recent years (Bradley et al., 2008: 49, 54-6, 59), this seems a significant oversight. The Review acknowledges that students who rely on Commonwealth support are increasingly facing income stress, but does not consider this policy failure as a potential contributing factor as to why students from low SES backgrounds require additional support services.

To clarify, our intention is not to suggest that this is a deliberate oversight, or that the authors of the Review personally or consciously hold a view of low SES students as 'needy'. The example does, however, amplify the way a 'deficit' model of low SES students is implicit in policy discourse and the Bradley Review in particular. Furthermore, the purpose of drawing attention to this discursive construction of low SES students as 'the problem' is to demonstrate that the problem could be thought about differently. Instead of seeing students from low SES groups as 'needy' and expensive to educate, the problem could be thought of in terms of a wider context of policy failure — that is, failure to provide at federal and community levels the basic personal and social infrastructure necessary for *all* students to excel. No such analysis is advanced in the Review and, consequently, social class itself comes to be tacitly positioned as the reason for the high needs of low SES students.

As a conceptualisation of social class and equity, this representation, in our view, is unacceptably truncated. Along with Trevor Gale and critical researchers like him (e.g. Thomas, 2011), we argue that such approaches take too much for granted. The willingness to accept education as primarily a source of private benefit and of students from low SES backgrounds as invariably 'deficient' delimits the extent to which the transformative potential of an equity agenda is imagined:

> under-explored in policy and practice debates around equity is what under-represented groups potentially bring to and do for higher education ... The question of equity needs to shift from access, to a consideration of what is being accessed.
>
> ...
>
> Indeed, the rethinking required is actually about the value of these resources and about what valuable resources are missing ... What if we recognized that if the higher education system deals unjustly with some of its students, they are not the only ones to suffer, that the quality of education for all the others is degraded? (Gale, 2011: 17)

A practical example in the context of our discussion easily illuminates Gale's point. The discussion advanced in the Review about low SES students accessing services, with its inference that these students are 'needier' than their peers for doing so, implicitly suggests that students should not over-rely on university services. This runs counter to an understanding of students as necessarily needing support and direction because of their status as learners. If our default view of students is that they should be self-reliant and not overly seek support and assistance, then this most certainly has the capacity to disadvantage *all* students, regardless of their SES, by imposing upon them a burdensome, and we would venture, unrealistic expectation of 'independence'. It is apparent in this example that, as Gale contends, the way we treat students from low SES backgrounds has implications for the way we treat all students.

In Gale's view (2011: 17), what is needed in the equity debate is recognition that increased participation of under-represented students has the potential to do more than transform their personal, private trajectories and their ability to attract high salaries. The 'inclusion' of all members of the community into our education system has the potential to transform that system and the lives of all citizens who are touched by it. This is an egalitarian aspiration that we believe to be far more worthy of the higher education sector. If we are to achieve it, however, it is necessary to think beyond the presumed deficits of individual students to question more widely what it is that students from low SES backgrounds encounter when they do aspire to a university experience. It is in this context that we suggest that 'classism' might usefully be added to existing understandings of the discrimination and disadvantage which students face in higher education.

Classism on campus?

There is already a substantial literature within critical education studies which argues that class, as a cultural phenomenon, is relevant to students' embodied experience. In this literature, sociologist Pierre Bourdieu's concept of 'habitus' is relied upon as an explanation of why and how low SES students face additional difficulties at university (e.g. Devlin, 2011; Bok, 2010). Frequently in this literature, class is talked about in terms of cultural capital and a 'misfit' between the cultural capital of low SES students and the cultural capital of the university as a socio-cultural field. While there are many important insights in this literature, our interest in this chapter is not with the university as a discrete cultural field but with wider socio-cultural trends in the valuation of social class. In this regard, and at the most practical level, we are concerned with students' experience on campus. Taking insight once more from research in the US, we suggest that classist attitudes may well be present on campus and that research which explores this aspect of low SES students' experience may usefully contribute to the existing debate on equity and participation.

In 2009, psychologists Regina Day Langhout, Peter Drake and Francine Roselli set out to test their hypothesis that classism was a factor affecting the sense of belonging felt by students from low SES backgrounds. On the small campus of what they describe as a progressive college where most students saw themselves as left-leaning and liberal, they found that many students *and* staff members made derogatory remarks about people who are poor. The impact of this behaviour on students from similar backgrounds was such that they 'were more likely to seriously consider leaving school before finishing their degree' (Langhout, Drake and Rosselli, 2009: 176). Opening the doors of universities, therefore, is not sufficient, they argue. Instead, it is incumbent upon universities to specifically address classism and ensure that the institutions are welcoming places for those from low SES backgrounds.

Another example comes from Canadian scholar Brenda Beagan's study (2005) of the implications arising from the fact that Canadian medical students are predominantly drawn from high SES backgrounds. Her project explored the experiences of those 40 per cent of medical students in one medical school who self-identified as coming from poor, working class and lower middle class backgrounds, and it confirmed the normativity of middle and upper class values in that school. These values prompted some students to 'pass' as middle class in order to fit in, and others to feel disadvantaged because of not having the 'right' social networks, while others experienced a growing distance from their families and friends. Importantly for our argument, students also felt marginalised on hearing disparaging comments about patients and other workers in the hospital who were from similar backgrounds to their families and friends, as well as comments that they did not belong in the medical profession because of their low SES backgrounds (Beagan, 2005).

Drawing from this research, we want to suggest that if universities are to transition into spaces that are more welcoming of low SES students, 'classism' as a feature of society must be addressed. By this we are not suggesting that classism only exists in universities. Rather, our argument is that classism is a feature of contemporary society, and that as universities are social institutions, it is likely to be a factor of their institutional life. Indeed, in our view, to single out universities as somehow more 'classist' than other social institutions is problematic for two reasons. First, taking this narrow view reproduces the rather classist idea that low SES people do not excel at research and that they cannot flourish in universities. While low SES students are under-represented at universities, research cited in the Bradley Review, noted above, finds that those who do attend perform just as well as their peers (Bradley et al., 2008: 30). The second reason why we consider taking a narrow view of universities as 'elitist' to be problematic is that it risks reproducing precisely the rationale that the Howard coalition government repeatedly deployed in justifying public funding cuts to the sector (e.g. Nelson, 2003). The Bradley Review (Bradley et al., 2008: xii) acknowledges that the pressures on universities brought about by inadequate funding have negatively impacted the student experience — and this would include the experience of low SES students. Thus, in advocating the addition of 'classism' to the existing framework, we are very determinedly not suggesting that classism is restricted to, or uniquely a product of, university culture. Very precisely, we are claiming that classism is a feature of contemporary society, and as social institutions universities are not immune from it.

Additionally, in proposing further research into the experience of students on campus, we suggest that it is important that any such research investigates not only the negative experiences low SES students might have, but also the positive. Indeed, in order to fully examine the experience of students from low SES backgrounds, it is necessary to survey not only those students but the wider university community. This is required in order to move beyond the deficit model and to document not only instances of 'misfit' that the cultural capital researchers are concerned with, but to also be open to moments of connection: connection between students, between students and academics, and across social classes. Those moments of connection do happen, and when they do they are likely to be transformative. They are not transformative in a narrow sense of providing private benefits to individuals, but transformative in the sense that Gale describes. Moments of connection have the potential to transform the educational exchange from one that delivers individual benefits at a private cost to an exchange that pushes at the limits of the cultural logics which structure our lives. We believe that those moments are, therefore, worth exploring alongside instances where the *cultural devaluation* of low SES people makes them feel unwelcome on campus.

Conclusion

In this chapter we have demonstrated where and how social class is represented to be a problem of individual (student) deficit in the Bradley Review. We have also suggested that this conceptualisation of social class, as a problem of individual deficit, is a product of 'classism', where classism is defined as referring to pervasive cultural and institutional norms which construct individuals who are of a low SES as inherently deficient in a variety of ways. In line with Gale's analysis, we have argued that the increased representation of low SES students in higher education has the potential to transform this education for the benefit of all students, but that an important first step is to raise awareness of classism in the sector.

References

Australian Government. 2009a. 'Transforming Australia's higher education system'. http://www.deewr.gov.au [accessed 17 February 2012].

Australian Government. 2009b. 'Funding to support low SES participation targets'. http://www.deewr.gov.au [accessed 17 February 2012].

Bacchi, C. 2009. *Analysing policy: what's the problem represented to be?* Frenchs Forest, NSW: Pearson Longman.

Barone, C. 1998. 'Political economy of classism: towards a more integrated multilevel view'. *Review of Radical Political Economics*, 30(1): 1-30.

Bazelon, D.L. 1969. 'Racism, classism, and the juvenile process'. *Judicature*, 53: 373.

Beagan, B.L. 2005. 'Everyday classism in medical school: experiencing marginality and resistance'. *Medical Education*, 39: 777-84.

Bland, D. 2011. 'From classroom resistance to school reform'. *Institutional transformation to engage a diverse student body*, Special Edition edited by L. Thomas and M. Tight, *International Perspectives on Higher Education Research*, 6: 57-65.

Bok, J. 2010. 'The capacity to aspire to higher education: "It's like making them do a play without a script"'. *Critical Studies in Education*, 51(2): 163-78.

Bradley, D., P. Noonan, H. Nugent and B. Scales. 2008. *Review of Australian higher education: final report*. Canberra: Commonwealth of Australia.

Brook, H. 2011. 'Preparation and aspiration: access to higher education for working-class students'. *Australian Universities Review*, 53(1): 84-8.

Dawkins, J.S. 1987. 'Higher education: a policy discussion paper'. Australian Government Publishing Service: Canberra. http://www.voced.edu.au/content/ngv1033 [accessed 27 January 2012].

Department of Education, Employment and Workplace Relations (DEEWR). 2011. 'Higher Education Participation and Partnerships Program' Website. http://www.deewr.gov.au/highereducation/programs/equity/pages/heppprogram.aspx [accessed 3 February 2012].

Devlin, M. 2011. 'Bridging socio-cultural incongruity: conceptualizing the success of students from low socio-economic status backgrounds in Australian higher education'. *Studies in Higher Education*, DOI:10.1080/03075079.2011.613991.

Ferguson, K. 2011. 'Achieving a "fair go" at La Trobe University', *Institutional transformation to engage a diverse student body*, Special Edition edited by L. Thomas and M. Tight, *International Perspectives on Higher Education Research*, 6: 107-18.

Gale, T. 2011. 'Student equity's starring role in Australian higher education: not yet centre field'. *Australian Education Research*, 38: 5-23.

Gale, T. and D. Tranter. 2011. 'Social justice in Australian higher education policy: an historical and conceptual account of student participation'. *Critical Studies in Education*, 52(1): 29-46.

Gallagher, M. 2009. 'Bradley's flawed vision', *The Australian*. 18 February. http://www.theaustralian.com.au/higher-education/opinion/bradleys-flawed-vision/story-e6frgcko-1111118881130 [accessed 17 February 2012].

Gillard, J. 2009. *Speech to Australian Financial Review —Higher Education Conference*. Ministerial keynote address. 9 March, Sydney.
Transcript available at http://ministers.deewr.gov.au/gillard/australian-financial-review-higher-education-conference-9-march-2009 [accessed 2 February 2011].

Hatton, E. 1998. 'Writing and teaching about the oppressive "isms" in teacher education: taking a new direction through alternate forms of data representation'. *Asia-Pacific Journal of Teacher Education*, 26(3): 217-34.

Holderhead, S. 2012. 'Vice-chancellor critical: policies hurting our unis abroad'. *The Advertiser*, 14 February: 23.

James, R. 2009. 'Implications of the Bradley Review's recommendations for student equity groups'. Conference paper. *ANU Equity Panel*, National Centre for Student Equity in Higher Education. 25 February. http://www.equity101.info/files/ANU_Equity_Panel_Richard%20James.pdf [accessed 2 February 2011].

Klinger, C.M. and N.L. Murray. 2011. 'Access, aspiration and attainment: foundation studies at the University of South Australia'. *Institutional transformation to engage a diverse student body*, Special Edition edited by L. Thomas and M. Tight, *International Perspectives on Higher Education Research*, 6: 137-46.

Langhout, R.D., P. Drake and F. Rosselli. 2009. 'Classism in the university setting: examining student antecdents and outcomes'. *Journal of Diversity in Higher Education*, 2(3): 166-81.

Liu, W.M. and S.R. Ali. 2005. 'Addressing social class and classism in vocational theory and practice: extending the emancipatory communitarian approach', *The Counseling Psychologist*, 33: 189-96.

Lott, B. 2002. 'Cognitive and behavioral distancing from the poor'. *American Psychologist*, 57(2): 100-10.

McIlveen, P., G. Beccaria, J. du Preez and W. Patton. 2010. 'Autoethnography in vocational psychology: wearing your class on your sleeve'. *Journal of Career Development*, 37(3): 599-615.

Nayak, A. 2006. 'Displaced masculinities: chavs, youth and class in the post-industrial city'. *Sociology*, 40(5): 813-30.

Nelson, B. 2003. 'Students national day of action: transcript'. Edited transcript of media conference, 27 August. Dr Brendan Nelson Media Centre Archive. http://www.dest.gov.au/ministers/nelson/aug_03/transcript_270803.htm [accessed 17 February 2012].

Newton, K. 2010. 'A two-fold unveiling: unmasking classism in group work'. *The Journal for Specialists in Group Work*, 35(3): 212-19.

Putnam, T. and J. Gill. 2011. 'The Bradley challenge: a sea change for Australian universities?' *Issues in Educational Research*, 21(2): 176-91.

Smith, L. 2005. 'Psychotherapy, classism, and the poor'. *American Psychologist*, 60(7): 687-96.

Smith, L. 2006. 'Addressing classism, extending multicultural competence, and serving the poor'. *American Psychologist*, 61(4): 338-9.

Smith, L. 2008. 'Positioning classism within counseling psychology's social justice agenda'. *The Counseling Psychologist*, 39: 895-924.

Thomas, L. 2011. 'Institutional transformation to engage a diverse student body'. *Institutional transformation to engage a diverse student body*, Special Edition edited by L. Thomas and M. Tight, *International Perspectives on Higher Education Research*, 6: 1-15.

Tyler, I. 2008. 'Chav Mum Chav Scum'. *Feminist Media Studies*, 8(1): 17-34.

Webster, C. 2008. 'Marginalized white ethnicity, race and crime'. *Theoretical Criminology*, 12(3): 293-312.

Whitlam, G. 1972. 'Australian Labor Party Policy Speech 1972'. Speech. 13 November, Blacktown Civic Centre, NSW. http://static.oph.gov.au/timeline/media/docs/pms-speeches/1972%20Whitlam%20policy%20speech.pdf [accessed 27 January 2012].

4 Reframing 'the problem': students from low socio-economic status backgrounds transitioning to university

Marcia Devlin and Jade McKay

Abstract

As higher education populations further diversify, new thinking and approaches are needed to ensure the successful transition to university of all students who are given access to higher education. This chapter challenges the notion of the student as 'the problem' when considering the transition to university of students from low socio-economic status (SES) backgrounds. Based on an examination of key literature from Australia, New Zealand, the United Kingdom and North America, this chapter argues that a deficit conception of students from low SES backgrounds is limited. It further argues that a deficit conception of the institutions into which these students transition is equally limited. Drawing on a recent national study (Devlin et al., 2012), this chapter examines a recently developed new conception, which positions successful transition to university for students from low SES backgrounds as a joint venture toward bridging socio-cultural incongruity (Devlin, 2011). This new conception privileges the agency, experience and contributions that these students bring to higher education, as well as institutional efforts to help students make the transition. The chapter proposes teaching and learning the discourse as a critical way to contribute to bridging socio-cultural incongruity and thereby assist students from low SES backgrounds to transition successfully to university.

Introduction

In an increasingly massified higher education system with greater numbers of students from low socio-economic status (SES) backgrounds studying alongside more traditional cohorts of students, it is not only appropriate, but also essential, that institutions work towards successful experiences for all students (Devlin, 2010).[1] This is particularly pertinent considering the federal policy changes in Australia following the 2008 *Bradley Review of Australian Higher Education*, which increased the diversity of higher education student cohorts as the sector worked to meet targets related to increased participation of students from low SES backgrounds (Bradley et al., 2008). Pointing to the International Association of Universities (2008: 1), who have adopted the principle that 'access without a reasonable chance of success is an empty phrase', Devlin (2011) argues that the increasing number of diverse students in the Australian context necessitates a focus not only on access to university but also on success and achievement for all students once they have gained access.

One critical component of both achievement and success in higher education is a successful transition into university. In their extensive research on the first-year experience, Yorke and Longden (2008) identify the proactive management of student transition as an institutional activity that radically improves the chances of student success overall. Pittman and Richmond (2008) explain that students experience multiple transitions upon entering higher education, including changes in their living situations, negotiating academic environments, developing new friendships and, for younger students at least, adapting to greater independence and responsibility in their academic lives. Many students struggle with the transition to university, experiencing loneliness, distress, academic disengagement and even depression (see Wintre and Bowers, 2007; Adlaf et al., 2001; Gall, Evans and Bellerose, 2000; Wintre and Yaffe, 2000). However, Rose-Krasnor et al. (2010) claim that while the transition to university entails the adjustment to new roles and responsibilities, the transition can also present a positive opportunity for forging a new identity, forming new friendships and developing new interests (see also Lefkowitz, 2005). Christie et al. (2008) likewise refer to the excitement and exhilaration students can experience while making the transition to university.

---

[1] Note that Marcia Devlin is a co-author of this chapter.

Based on a study of factors affecting the academic performance of Latino students in the United States (US), Cole and Espinoza (2008) raise the notion of cultural congruity and incongruity. This notion has resonance in relation to SES status and in particular to the level of socio-cultural congruence between students from low SES backgrounds and the higher education institutions in which they transition and study (Devlin, 2011). This chapter adopts a framework for conceptualising the transition of students from low SES backgrounds into higher education based on socio-cultural incongruence. It examines the notions of students from low SES backgrounds as 'the problem' and the institutions into which they move as 'the problem'. The chapter explores some of the characteristics associated with students from low SES backgrounds, providing a context for discussion about supporting their transition to university. Finally, it proposes teaching and learning the discourse as a critical way to contribute to bridging socio-cultural incongruity and thereby assist students from low SES backgrounds to transition successfully to university.

Reframing 'the problem'

Literature and thinking related to students from low SES backgrounds often adopt a deficit conception. While some theorists problematise students, others view institutions as the 'problem'. Both discourses are premised on a deficit conception that this chapter argues is limited. Drawing on Devlin (2011), this chapter articulates the notion of socio-cultural incongruence as a way of conceptualising the differences in cultural and social capital between students from low SES backgrounds and the high SES of the institutions into which they move to study. In an attempt to reframe the problem of the deficit discourse, the chapter proposes a more nuanced approach to framing the complexities of the transition experience of students from low SES backgrounds — one that prioritises both the agency of students as well the role of the institution.

Cultural capital is a notion that is important to understanding the experiences of students from low SES in higher education. Cultural capital has been defined as 'proficiency in and familiarity with dominant cultural codes and practices' (Aschaffenburg and Mass, 1997: 573). Bourdieu (1977, 1984) suggests that the primary vehicle for the transmission of the 'ruling class' culture is the education system. He suggests further that teachers and other staff, arguably those representing the ruling class, have the authority and the means to assess students and do so based on a set of assumptions, values and expectations that are not always made explicit. University students from higher socio-economic strata and more traditional backgrounds build familiarity with these assumptions, values and expectations over a lifetime (Devlin, 2010). They have what Margolis et al. (2001) refer to as a 'reservoir' of cultural and social resources and familiarity with 'particular types of knowledge, ways of speaking, styles, meanings, dispositions and worldviews' (ibid.: 8) when they come to university, which helps them to transition easily into, and feel comfortable at, university. Devlin (2009) has pointed out that some university students do not have such a 'reservoir' and that many students from low SES backgrounds fall into this second group (Devlin, 2011). Contrary to feeling comfortable at university, many such students can feel very uncomfortable and out of place. A comment from a student from a low SES background in the United Kingdom (UK) illustrates this discomfort:

> I find it really hard to integrate with ... middle class people ... I feel quite intimidated by this university and I feel as if I'm working class and I shouldn't be here ... I just feel I'm no' good enough. (As cited in Christie et al., 2008: 576)

According to Lawrence (2005), achievement at university relies on socio-cultural capabilities relevant to the high SES context of university study. One element of such university socio-cultural competency includes appropriately seeking help and information. Seeking assistance would be particularly relevant to many students transitioning into university. Lawrence points out that the specific verbal and nonverbal means of asking for help can differ from subculture to subculture, and that seeking help may not be 'culturally "valued"', for example in 'individualist self-reliant sub-cultures' (ibid.: 250). However, at university, students are expected to be independent learners and this often means asking for help when necessary. In a recent (2011-12) national research project funded by the Office for Learning and Teaching (OLT) in which both authors were research team members (see Devlin et al., 2012) student interviews were undertaken examining the effective teaching and support of students from low SES backgrounds. 40 out of 89 students from low SES backgrounds interviewed (45 per cent) commented on the importance of asking for help in terms of succeeding at university. In proffering advice to other students, 34 out of 89 students (38 per cent) identified asking for help as critical to student success at university.

If a student does choose to ask for help, they also need to consider the words to use, whether to ask directly or indirectly and whether to include explanations or reasons, or not (Lawrence, 2005). As Lawrence explains, students may feel that they do not have the right to ask, or may equate seeking help as remedial. One student in Lawrence's study reported:

> I don't feel confident enough to speak to my tutor about the essay question because they might think I am stupid or something. (Psychology student, as cited in ibid.: 250)

Another student in Lawrence's study who had some experience of challenging feedback and who subsequently understood some of the tacit expectations explains:

> It's not a good idea to just walk in and say 'look this is crap'. You can't bulldoze your way through you have to be tactful about it … 'Look, I agree with this, but I think I've been hard done by with this bit for this reason'. (Nursing student, as cited in ibid.: 250)

According to Read, Archer and Leathwood (2003), there is a culture of academia that encompasses ways of thinking and acting that are dominant. Without guidance in the ways of this culture, students from low SES backgrounds may only learn that the sort of approach outlined above is 'not a good idea' through trial and error as they are transitioning into university (Devlin, 2011). This is not an ideal method of learning, especially given the significant risks involved for students entering and attempting to navigate a new culture.

When students unfamiliar with the norms and expectations of higher education transition in, they have to learn to become a university student (Christie et al., 2008) and master the university student 'role' (Collier and Morgan, 2008). Collier and Morgan refer to the 'implicit expectations' and 'tacit understandings' (ibid.: 426) which permeate the university study experience. Based on their North American research, they note that mastering the student role requires students to both understand the expectations of them and to meet those expectations successfully. This distinction between understanding and meeting expectations is important in relation to conceptualising the transition of students from low SES backgrounds. Collier and Morgan (ibid.) distinguish between a student's academic skills and actual capacity on one hand and their cultural capital and demonstrated capacity on the other. They argue that whatever a student's actual capacity, their background and cultural capital affect their ability to understand tacit requirements and appropriately perform a university student's role and thereby demonstrate their capacity. They also point out that demonstrated capacity is what is examined and assessed at university. These researchers argue that if a comparison was made between two students who had equivalent understanding of course material, the student who better understood the need to respond to the tacit expectations of university staff members would perform better (ibid.). Success transitioning into, and participating at, university depends on understanding these unspoken requirements and being able to perform in ways that meet them (Devlin, 2011). But as Devlin (2010) points out, many students from low SES backgrounds do not know that these unspoken requirements exist, never mind that they must understand and then respond appropriately to them.

Collier and Morgan (2008) claim that how closely students can understand and relate to the tacit expectations of staff will have an impact on their performance, success and achievement at university. The following comments are examples of students from the study by Collier and Morgan (ibid.). These students were the first in their family to go to university and they found themselves 'getting it wrong' because they did not understand tacit expectations:

> The assignment we had said, 'write about some field experience' and I literally wrote the two-page thing out. It said 'write' and I took it literally and wrote it out, and then I got a note back that said 'see me'. It was in red and everything, and I went and she was like 'you were supposed to type this up'. But the instructions were to 'write'. I wasn't sure what she wanted. (As cited in ibid.: 440)

> I am taking biology ... I do not have experience in writing, and the main thing is that they require writing for research papers, and I'm expecting doing a lot of work trying to figure out how to do that. I did two papers already and ... He said, 'You have to go back and do it again, this is not scientific writing' ... I thought it was scientific because it was from a biology textbook, and I did study at [community college], and he said 'No, this is not scientific writing'. So it is really hard to see what they want because they already see it, they already know it; they see what I don't. (As cited in ibid.: 440)

The first deficit conception: students are 'the problem'

Much research has been conducted on elements of success at university within the individual student's sphere of influence (Devlin, 2011). This includes research on resilience (see Morales, 2000), self-efficacy (see Vuong, Brown-Welty and Tracz, 2010) and motivation (see McKavanagh and Purnell, 2007). While valuable, such research can be based on the assumption that university success is primarily the responsibility of individual students and can presuppose a level playing field in relation to socio-cultural and background characteristics (Devlin, 2011). As Devlin notes (ibid.), it can be seductive to think that if non-traditional students are clever enough, or try hard enough, or persevere enough, or believe enough in their own ability, they can succeed at university. After all, many have done so. Devlin (ibid.) cautions, however, that if seduced by this thinking, it follows then that any failure to succeed at university is the fault of the student, who is assumed to be in deficit. Unfortunately, such thinking prevails in higher education.

Greenbank (2006) argues that 'victim blaming' can result from the absence of social class being considered as a key influence on the university experiences of students from low SES backgrounds. If the tacit expectations inherent in university practices are within a socio-cultural subset that is peculiar to the upper SES levels, Devlin (2011) suggests this may exclude students from low SES backgrounds who are not familiar with the norms and discourses of these groups. These students can become victims of discrimination that impedes their success (ibid.).

The second deficit conception: institutions are 'the problem'

Another possible frame is to problematise the institutions that are responsible for the success and progress of students from low SES backgrounds. Zepke and Leach (2005) examine the literature on how institutions might improve student retention and other outcomes and identify two different discourses on this issue. One discourse, which dominates the literature, centres on what institutions do to fit students into their existing cultures. Zepke and Leach suggest that the second discourse challenges the dominant one and is still emerging. Rather than requiring students to fit the existing institutional culture, it suggests that institutional cultures be adapted to better fit the needs of an increasingly diverse student body.

According to Bamber and Tett (2001), it is unfair to expect the burden of change to fall solely on the students and to suggest that institutions should make changes. Summarising the most influential research in widening participation in the UK, Billingham (2009) argues that the focus on barriers for non-traditional students needs to expand from situational and dispositional barriers to those created by institutional inflexibility. Tett states that 'the role of the educational institution itself in creating and perpetuating inequalities' (2004: 252) should be taken into account. Recent Australian research suggests that universities should make changes in terms of better heralding the expectations they have of students (James, Krause and Jennings, 2010). This suggestion is underpinned by an assumption that the deficit lies with the student in not understanding existing structures and expectations and with the institutions in not being clear enough about how they expect students to fit into these existing structures and expectations (Devlin, 2011). As Devlin notes,

> [w]hile explicitly informing students of their responsibilities is critical, this alone would constitute an inadequate response in terms of assisting them to meet these responsibilities and demonstrate their learning in a higher education culture. (Ibid.: 6)

Devlin points to the persuasive arguments of Collier and Morgan (2008) that understanding and mastering the university student role are two different requirements. Devlin (2010) argues that to genuinely contribute to the success and achievement of non-traditional students, universities will need to do much more than to spell out their expectations for student involvement in learning. Several authors suggest the importance of teaching the discourse to students from low SES backgrounds (Hutchings, 2006; Lawrence, 2005; Kirk, 2008; Northedge, 2003a, 2003b).

The socio-cultural conception: incongruence must be bridged

According to Greenbank (2006), there is evidence suggesting that students from lower SES backgrounds may have greater difficulty adapting to university life because of incongruence between their cultural capital and the middle class culture encountered in higher education. Read, Archer and Leathwood argue that '[a]cademic culture is not uniformly accessed or experienced' (2003: 261). Devlin (2011) proposes the notion of 'socio-cultural incongruence' to describe the circumstances where students from low SES backgrounds engage with the discourses, tacit expectations and norms of higher education.

To facilitate the success of students from low SES backgrounds, Bamber and Tett (2001) suggest that a two-way process of change and development is required. They recommend that institutions think beyond the deficit model of supporting students and reform teaching and student support. Billingham (2009) proposes active engagement by institutions in a 'joint venture' with the new population of students. Murphy's UK study (2009) of factors affecting the progress, achievement and outcomes of new students to a particular degree program found a number of characteristics specific to the institution and to individual students which promote progression and achievement. They refer to these factors as 'bridges'. Devlin (2011) proposes adoption of the notion of a bridge in the conceptualisation of changes that could be made to lessen or ease socio-cultural incongruence for students from low SES backgrounds at university. She summarises this as bridging socio-cultural incongruity (ibid.).

Student agency

Both deficit conceptions outlined above negate the influence of student agency (Devlin, 2011). Luckett and Luckett (2009) note that both in traditions of learning theory that prioritise individual cognition and in those that prioritise the context in which learning occurs, 'the individual agent is dissolved' (ibid.: 469). Devlin proposes, similarly, that ways of thinking about the facilitation of the success of students from low SES backgrounds

> are divided into those that prioritise individual input to that process on one hand and those that prioritise the role of the institution in which the process takes place on the other. In both of these conceptualisations ... the individual agent is considered less important. (2011: 7)

However, as Devlin notes, research by Luckett and Luckett (2009) indicates that 'the development of agency, as the student forges an identity and career path, is of critical importance in higher education' (2011: 476).

Devlin argues that '[s]tudents from low socio-economic backgrounds are not necessarily passive recipients of the middle and upper class culture and discourse of university' (ibid.: 7). While students from non-traditional backgrounds are disadvantaged by institutional cultures that place them as 'other', Read,

Archer and Leathwood (2003) maintain that individuals do not passively receive these cultural discourses but instead actively engage with them and attempt to challenge them. Indeed, Grant describes examples of students challenging the discourse of 'the independent learner' by deliberately studying with someone else as an 'interdependent learner' (1997: 112). In their research, Read, Archer, and Leathwood found non-traditional students refusing to accept a position of marginality in the academy and instead working '…to adopt the pragmatic practice of "adapting" to this culture in order to achieve' (2003: 272). They argue that non-traditional students understand the need to act in certain ways in order to be successful and give the example of a young, black, Caribbean university student in a UK institution deliberately acting confident in the '"intimidating" competitive atmosphere' (ibid.: 273) of a seminar and advising a fellow student to do the same.

Devlin (2011) notes that there is also research to support the notion of non-traditional students participating knowingly in more than one culture concurrently. Exploring this issue, Priest (2009) refers to thinking in the US around 'code switching' — where black students are encouraged not to passively adopt an alternative discourse or code but instead to understand the value of the discourse or code they already possess as well as to understand the value of the alternative one associated with, for example, academic writing.

Knowing the students

It can be argued that to enable, facilitate and support student agency, university teachers and other staff should know their students. This means knowing students' names, backgrounds, learning styles and preferences, needs, difficulties, strengths and/or weaknesses. It also means understanding the unique abilities and experiences which students from low SES backgrounds and other non-traditional students bring with them to university. In staff interviews conducted as part of the OLT-funded study exploring effective teaching and support of students from low SES backgrounds, 22 of 26 staff interviewees (85 per cent) identified knowing the make-up of the student cohort as central to facilitating student success. Some of the typical comments made by staff included:

> I think that the best advice I could say to anybody is talk to your students, find out about them, make them feel valued, make them feel important, that their knowledge and skills are as important as anybody else's, and to

> utilise those skills in particular areas. Nothing de-values somebody more than being made to feel like their skills aren't important … (COL_011)

> [Y]ou'll never know how to teach anybody anything unless you understand that person. You absolutely have to understand that, and I mean, I'm not necessarily saying you have to fully and totally understand a person, but you need to understand them in terms of the context of that knowledge you're trying to teach them … and that applies I think pre-eminently to … [those] from diverse backgrounds. (COL_016)

While agreeing with Kift's argument (2009) that it is necessary to apply caution to making assumptions about particular cohorts of students, this chapter also argues that it is helpful to know some of the characteristics commonly associated with students from low SES backgrounds in order to contribute successfully to bridging socio-cultural incongruence. As staff experienced and successful in teaching and supporting students from low SES backgrounds said in interviews conducted as part of the OLT study:

> [O]f course, you can't be inclusive unless you know your students, and I think you need to know your students; that is the most important thing. (COL_001)

> [I]t goes back to that very simplistic mantra, but the idea that you really do need to know your learner to be able to make a good judgment of where it is they want to go and where you can help them to go, so I think that's absolutely fundamental. (COL_016)

The factors identified in the literature as pertinent to students from low SES backgrounds include: financial strain; time pressures; competing priorities; unclear expectations of university; low confidence; academic preparedness; family support; and aspirations.

Financial strain

Somewhat unsurprisingly, the predominant characteristic associated with students from low SES backgrounds in the literature is that of finances. Students from low SES backgrounds often experience financial strain that can become a barrier to access and success in higher education (Lynch and O'Riordan, 1998), impacting both the choices they make (for example, mode of study, choice of institution) as well as their everyday experiences as students (Simister, 2011; David et al., 2010; Hayden and Long, 2006; Perna, 2000). On account of financial pressures, education can also become a secondary priority for students who must often undertake paid employment (Greenbank, 2006). Data from student interviews in the recent national OLT study support these findings, testifying to the financial pressures and issues that they face. Typical comments from students include:

> I have three jobs and I still can't manage. (STU_104)

> I wouldn't be here now this term, this semester, if I hadn't been able to borrow every textbook I need. (STU_085)

> The free parking, that would be the final straw. If I had to pay for parking then it would be 'sayonara'. It might be something like $5 a day but that would be the end of me, so the free parking is huge. (STU_085)

Time pressures

Time pressures affect many students from low SES backgrounds. With the need to balance paid employment with study, financial pressures and, often, family responsibilities, many of these students are under greater time constraints than their more 'traditional' peers (David et al., 2010; Murphy, 2009; Henderson, Noble and De George-Walker, 2009; Benson et al., 2009; Hayden and Long, 2006; Moreau and Leathwood, 2006; White, 2006; Winn, 2002; Douglass, Roebken and Thomson, 2007; Lynch and O'Riordan, 1998). One student in the recent OLT study explained the impact of the expectations of university study given their multiple commitments:

> I think sometimes, the expectations, though, from lecturers, when they say, you need to be doing five hours additional to what you're doing in class, like my first year of uni, I was doing twenty hours plus of in time class, and they were also saying, we want five hours on top of that for each year's subjects, and when you've got all these other things going on, like work, and just trying to adapt to uni life, that's a lot of time where you think, I can't do this, like you get very kind of stressed out ... (STU_057)

Competing priorities

Finances and time are closely linked to another factor commonly associated with students from low SES backgrounds: competing priorities. As a result of financial pressures and time constraints, the literature suggests that education can often be lower on the list of priorities for students from low SES backgrounds (Crozier et al., 2008). The need to prioritise finances and paid employment, for example, can result in many students seeing their studies as a mere 'means to an end' (ibid.: 175), which can impact on class attendance. The competing pressures and priorities that low SES students had to balance frequently arose in recent interviews:

> Well, having two jobs wasn't so easy. It was a bit difficult. Like I kind of took on two jobs because my father was ill and he didn't work for about six months. So I took on that extra job. (STU_097)

> It was difficult and — so I was just coming to the bare minimums — just the lectures, some tutes. I thought I could miss a few because I had to be at work, but I passed them, I don't know how. (STU_010)

Unclear expectations of university

Research also shows that students from low SES backgrounds often enter higher education with expectations that are disjunctive with the reality of university. These expectations can relate to teachers, teaching, assessment and university life and culture in general (Roberts, 2011; Brooks, 2004) and can significantly impact on their experiences in higher education. In their extensive research, Lynch and O'Riordan found that not knowing what to expect creates 'fears and anxieties which exacerbated practical difficulties' (1998: 461) for these students. This expectation-mismatch was substantiated in student interviews in the OLT study, with 36 of 89 student interviewees (40 per cent) commenting on the importance of expectations being made explicit:

> You can see what's coming, rather than just being blind. (STU_054)

> I mean, as I say it's got to be transparent, it's got to be set out so that you know exactly what they want. It's not something that you've got to guess at. (STU_082)

Low confidence

The disjunctive expectations and the lack of university-specific cultural capital held by students from low SES backgrounds can result in students entering higher education suffering from a lack of confidence. In their extensive study, which included 122 interviews, Lynch and O'Riordan found that students often 'did not believe in their own abilities' and felt that higher education was 'beyond their reach' (1998: 462). The literature suggests that a lack of self-esteem can hinder a student's overall sense of belonging and impact the choices they make, for example, about accessing support services or seeking help from academic staff (David et al., 2010; Murphy 2009; Christie et al., 2008; Charlesworth, Gilfillan and Wilkinson, 2004; Benson et al., 2009; Lawrence, 2005). Lack of confidence can also result in many students having fewer friends than their middle class peers, finding it difficult to 'settle' into university life and consequently being more likely to entertain thoughts of dropping out (Lynch and O'Riordan, 1998).

As one student in the recent OLT study suggested when asked what advice they would offer to a new student from the same background, 'as you go along you get to feel a little bit more confident maybe when, when it's safe' (STU_101).

Academic preparedness

Another factor associated with students from low SES backgrounds in the literature which is relevant to transition is level of preparedness for university study. The disjunct between the cultural capital of students from low SES and the middle class culture of higher education institutions can result in different levels of academic preparedness (Murphy, 2009; Northedge, 2003a; Berger, 2000; Greenbank, 2006; Kift, 2009). One student from a low SES status background in a recent OLT study interview alluded to this:

> [T]he mature age students … in the classroom … always had all these really intelligent questions to ask, and I didn't have the knowledge to even formulate the question. (STU_056)

In the staff interviews carried out as part of the recent OLT study, one staff member reported that high attrition rates at their institution were directly related to students being ill-prepared for the realities of university:

> I think that some of them didn't realise what the workload and commitments for the university might've been. (COL_023)

Research also suggests that the skill set of students from low SES backgrounds may not equate to the skill set of more traditional students in terms of writing and language, research, computer and overall academic 'know-how' (Kirk, 2008; Fitzgibbon and Prior, 2006). When asked what their advice to other students entering higher education would be, many students from low SES backgrounds interviewed in the recent OLT study spoke of the importance of developing these skills:

> Probably the first thing I'd suggest is make absolutely sure that you've got a reasonably good grasp of using, knowing and finding your way around a computer. ... [I]t's going to be a lot easier if you do know your way around technology to a certain extent. (STU_082)

> ... [T]he other advice I would give would be that if you haven't studied at university before to, to try and get a hand or an academic writing if there was a good study course where you could learn how to write academically and cite, and references and all that sort of thing would be in fact really take the pressure, take the stress off the first initial unit even ... (STU_101)

Family support

Another factor evident in the literature as relevant to students from low SES backgrounds is family support. Often the first in their families to attend university, students from low SES backgrounds can be without significant levels of support from family and friends (Murphy, 2009; Brooks, 2004; Hahs-Vaughn, 2004). In student interviews in the recent OLT study, which interviewed students from low SES backgrounds who were successful, family support emerged as a key determinant of student success in higher education. Of the 89 students interviewed, 78 students (88 per cent) commented on the importance of family support in their success. Typical comments included:

> I am really lucky to have such a good family to support me and yeah it's ... definitely been a huge part in my success at uni. Because if it wasn't for them, I probably wouldn't be here at all. (STU_003)

> The fact that my son thinks it's cool and he knows that mummy's doing this to get us a better life. So in the meantime, he's missed out on so much because as I said I've been doing this course for two years ... So I've lost a lot of time. But because he knows where it's going, he's let me do it. He's gone without weekends where I've been head down in an assignment, and it's just, 'It's okay mum, when you're finished we'll catch up'. (STU_084)

Aspiration

The final characteristic associated with students from low SES backgrounds in the literature is aspiration. Research shows that traditional students often have higher aspirations than students from lower SES backgrounds (Bowden and Doughney, 2010; Shallcross and Hartley, 2009; Walpole, 2008; Hahs-Vaughn, 2004; Tett, 2004;

Lynch and O'Riordan, 1998). However, this claim is somewhat challenged by the findings emerging from the recent study, which focused on successful students from low SES backgrounds, who expressed high levels of aspiration and determination to succeed in their studies:

> I want that cap and gown, and I want someone to call my name out. (STU_062)

> My desire has kept me on focus. I want that piece of paper. (STU_066)

These factors and characteristics drawn from the literature and recent research are important to informing understanding of the issues that students from low SES backgrounds may face in higher education. However, this chapter argues that these factors and characteristics also challenge deficit discourses surrounding non-traditional students. While many of these factors are barriers to student success, the literature testifies to the resilience and determination these students demonstrate in order to overcome these barriers. The OLT study further supports this argument. Results from the student interviews show that 56 of 89 students interviewed (63 per cent) believed that they were successful because they applied themselves and worked hard, 47 of 89 students interviewed (53 per cent) attributed their success to planning ahead and/or goal-setting, and 45 of 89 students interviewed (51 per cent) stated their success was a result of their attitude toward study.

In the staff interviews in the same study, similar findings about the determination and resilience of these students emerged:

> I just think it's very interesting that we often look at low SES and sort of go 'okay, alright, they're not going to have the study skill management or the time skill management, they're the first one in their family to go to university, they're not going to understand all the rigour and the words and all the rest' but then I look at them and go 'well actually a lot of these kids are determined to be here and they're determined to work harder and they're determined to finish'. And they're going to ask a question if they don't know because there's nobody else to tell them so they'll come to you and ask, whereas other kids who sort of have been spoon fed will look at it and go 'well you didn't tell me to do anything else so I didn't'. (COL_01)

> I've found that ... low SES kids ... are just very determined. They're very smart and determined people and it takes them a couple of years to nut out the system but if you are halfway welcoming, they can do it very quickly. (COL_00)

In addition to recognising this determination and 'academic grit', others interviewed in the OLT study pointed to the potential contributions students from low SES can make to higher education:

> [I]t's about acknowledging students ... And trying to tap in to some little something, you know some little strength that they might have, some little narrative that they might have that we can all sort of share in, in order to build that self worth if you like, that sense of ... why it is that they're here and their contribution is just as valuable. (COL_015)

The final section explores teaching and learning academic discourse as a contribution to bridging socio-cultural incongruity.

Cultural capital and academic discourse

In his prolific work on teaching in the context of diversity, Northedge claims that teaching challenges related to an increasingly diverse student body in higher education 'call for a more radical shift in teaching than simply incorporating remedial support within existing teaching programs' (2003b: 17). He proposes an emphasis on the socio-cultural nature of learning and teaching. This would include 'modelling learning as acquiring the capacity to participate in the discourses of an unfamiliar knowledge community, and teaching as supporting that participation' (ibid.). Based on her Australian research, Lawrence (2005) proposes the active facilitation of students' use of reflective, socio-cultural and critical practice to assist them to become enculturated into the ways of the university, while being cognisant of both the presence of more than one set of cultural assumptions and of the potential incongruence of these assumptions. In both cases, notes Devlin (2011), students would need to be prepared to take the risks and opportunities inherent in joining a new community and to persevere in order to ensure the learning required to function effectively in that community. Here the notion of both students and institutions/teachers making contributions to ensuring the success of the transition of low SES students to university is clear — the socio-cultural incongruity is bridged by the joint venture between the two parties.

While recognising the varied and many suggestions in the literature around how best to empower students from low SES backgrounds and bridge socio-cultural incongruence, this section focuses on teaching and learning the discourse. Teaching the discourse is an important process for facilitating the cultural capital required to 'code switch' and to thereby contribute to bridging socio-cultural incongruence. Without knowledge of — and eventually a proficiency in — academic discourse, students can struggle to communicate, participate and feel that they belong in higher education. Teaching and learning the discourse can facilitate an empowering transition into university culture for students from low SES backgrounds.

The research and scholarship around teaching and learning the discourse to students in higher education encompasses a broad range of viewpoints. Priest (2009) explains that some theorists view teaching the discourse as reinforcing 'an unjust social system' in which the message is propagated that some discourses are more 'valid than others' (2009: 75; see also Bruch and Marback, 1997; Rice, 2008). In contrast, others deny that there is 'any potential injustice, implicit or not, in the teaching of academic languages and literacies' (Priest, 2009: 75; see also Bloom, 1997). In this chapter, we accept the legitimacy of the argument that academic discourse is dominant and essentially middle class and therefore necessarily subverts other discourses. However, it can be equally argued that it is possible to teach academic discourse without 'blindly reinforcing messages of cultural inferiority or reinscribing unjust power relations' (Priest, 2009: 76). Further, as the current authors have elsewhere argued (McKay and Devlin, 2014), not only is it possible but it is essential that academic discourse be taught and learnt. Students from low SES backgrounds should be provided with opportunities to enable their contribution to bridge the socio-cultural incongruity that they meet on entering higher education. Teaching academic language — or what has been referred to as the language of power within the academy (Bruch and Marback, 1997) — brings to the fore issues of cultural privilege appositely delineated by Margolis (1994). However, to allow notions of cultural privilege to impede institutions from teaching academic discourse to students from low SES backgrounds is to disempower and disadvantage them further (McKay and Devlin, 2014).

Those students who are familiar with academic language and conventions are, according to Hutchings, *'immediately enabled, both in their learning and their sense of identity'* (2006: 259; emphasis added). In their research, Clark and Ivanic (1997) found that the sense of belonging that students experience in their institutions is clearly affected by the discourses that students bring with them.

Hutchings (2006) agrees, stressing that the level of acquaintance students have with academic language and practices can determine their feelings of belonging in higher education. Further, Hutchings suggests that a familiarity and prior knowledge of academic discourse can determine the speed with which complex 'concepts and readings are grasped and understanding is articulated in discussions and writing' (ibid.: 259). On the basis of their research, both Priest (2009) and Corkery (2009) conclude that a proficiency in academic discourse is more likely to translate into success at university.

McKay and Devlin (2014) explain that students from low SES backgrounds often enter university with no familiarity with academic discourse — either the language or its conventions. This lack of acquaintance can leave many students feeling vulnerable and can impact on their ability as well as their desire to communicate and participate (Hutchings, 2006). This claim is substantiated by interviews with students from low SES backgrounds in the recent national study where 37 of 89 students (42 per cent) spoke directly of, and/or alluded to, the importance to their success at university of being taught academic language, writing and discourse. Some of the typical comments made by students include:

> Even the simple things, which some may not think that valuable but someone like me, the essay — how to write an essay for instance, the correct format and what not — that sort of stuff, that basic stuff which would seem very basic to some or the seasoned university students, but to someone like me, it was invaluable in my learning process. (STU_046)
>
> [T]hat's half of the battle when you're first starting, learning how to write academically and it's still a battle. (STU_101)
>
> But yeah … [an introductory course] is very useful for people like me who have never been to an academic institution and didn't know that much about academic writing and stuff … (STU_082)

Not to help these students with academic discourse, Elbow argues, 'is simply to leave a power vacuum and thereby reward privileged students who have already academic discourse at home or in school — or at least learned the roots of propensity for academic discourse' (1991: 135). It is therefore critical that non-traditional students, particularly those from low SES backgrounds, be taught and learn academic discourse.

Socio-cultural empowerment through teaching and learning the discourse

Hutchings stresses that becoming literate in academic language entails more than just learning how to use the language. Knowledge of the wider rules, practices and conventions are essential, particularly for those students who are unfamiliar with academic discourse (Hutchings, 2006; Edelsky, 1996). As McKay and Devlin (2014) suggest, a critical component of teaching the discourse relates to teaching the rules and conventions of academic discourse. This means making explicit to those students who may not be familiar with academic discourse its implied rules, practices and conventions. To not teach students this broader knowledge of academic discourse can result in them feeling isolated, intimidated and forced into silence (Hutchings, 2006). Such feelings can then impact on students' successful transition into an unfamiliar world and their willingness to participate in a new knowledge community (Hutchings, 2006; McKay and Devlin, 2014). Lawrence (2005) refers to this first component of teaching academic discourse as engaging students in the relevant discourses, which include ways of thinking, ways of writing and the specific tone and style of essays. Formal academic discourse tutorials and academic study skills sessions may be an appropriate way to engage students in the relevant discourses, and Lawrence (ibid.) argues that these would ideally be provided when students first enter university.

According to the literature, the second component of teaching and learning the discourse is enabling participation in that discourse. It is essential that students be empowered to practice using academic discourse in order for them to become active members of the knowledge community. Drawing on the work of Etienne Wenger (1998), Matusov and Hayes explain the importance of students being enabled to participate in the knowledge community:

> Learning is always a question about membership in the community and participation in the community practices. A novice is not simply a person who lacks some entities, called 'skills', but rather a newcomer who needs to negotiate her or his participation in the community practices. (2002: 243)

Learning academic discourse, Lawrence (2005) claims, is dependent on students both mastering and demonstrating the discourse and cultural practices. To facilitate their mastering of the discourse, learning environments should encourage student participation and thereby provide the opportunity for students to demonstrate their proficiency and develop a voice within higher education (Northedge, 2002; Northedge 2003b). Northedge explains:

> Voice requires a sense of one's identity within the discourse community. For students with little experience in academic communities, the struggle to develop an effective voice ... can be long and difficult. Yet, until they do, their grades suffer, since their progress can only be registered through speaking the discourse. Support in establishing voice is a vital component of courses for students from diverse backgrounds. (2003b: 25)

According to Northedge (2002), learning environments should allow for vicarious participation, where students learn how the discourse works and how meanings are framed within it from more experienced discourse members. Such environments, Northedge (ibid.) argues, would also allow for generative participation whereby students take responsibility for framing shared meaning and practise projecting meaning to others within the knowledge community. This is when real learning takes place, in that learning is ultimately a process of becoming increasingly proficient as both 'a user of various specialist discourses' and 'a participant within the relevant knowledge communities' (2003b: 22). For students to become competent in academic discourse, they need to be provided with sufficient opportunity to practice using and participating in that discourse to ensure they feel that they belong in higher education as rightful members of the knowledge community. These ideas accord with those of Collier and Morgan (2008) and Christie et al. (2008), outlined earlier, of understanding and demonstrating capacity, and learning to become a student at university.

The final component of teaching and learning the discourse pertains to the guided navigation of students through the discourse (Northedge, 2003a, 2003b; McKay and Devlin, 2014). Guiding and actively supporting students from low SES backgrounds as they navigate their way through academic discourse empowers them to participate further in the knowledge community and thereby develop strong student identities (Northedge, 2003b). Northedge (ibid.) and Lawrence (2005) both stress the importance of guided navigation by teachers and its centrality to students successfully learning academic discourse. Northedge proposes supported participation in the knowledge communities to help those who are often struggling to 'make meaning in strange intellectual and social surroundings' (2003b: 17).

Lawrence (2005) claims that students need to be assisted in navigating their way through the various discourses and literacies that they are expected to engage with, master and demonstrate. Matusov and Hayes also argue that '[s]tudents require guided initiation into the discourse', as it 'is crucial to their becoming active members of a community of practice' (2002: 243).

Northedge suggests this is why the role of a teacher is so important: 'The teacher, as a speaker of the specialist discourse, is able to "lend" students the capacity to frame meanings they cannot yet produce independently' (2003a: 172). However, while guiding navigation, Northedge insists that teachers take into consideration 'where the student is starting from' (2003b: 31) and apply tolerance to any variances in understanding. Lawrence (2005, 2003) agrees, arguing that teachers should be willing to guide students through the process of learning academic discourse with an understanding that while these students bring with them different discourses, they should not be viewed as under-prepared or intellectually deficient.

Conclusion

This chapter has argued that deficit notions of students from low SES status backgrounds entering and succeeding at university are limited. It has also argued that deficit notions of the institutions into which the students transition are also limited. The chapter has engaged the conceptual notion of bridging socio-cultural incongruity as an alternative for 'the problem'. It has also argued that while caution in making assumptions about cohorts of students is warranted, it is also helpful to understand common characteristics of students from low SES backgrounds as part of knowing the students. Finally, the chapter has proposed teaching and learning academic discourse as a critical component of bridging socio-cultural incongruity and enabling the successful transition to university of students from low SES backgrounds.

Acknowledgements

We would like to acknowledge the Deakin University Strategic Teaching and Learning Grant Scheme, and an Office for Learning and Teaching (OLT) Strategic Priority Grant, both of which provided funding for the research. We also acknowledge the contributions to the OLT-funded research of colleagues Sally Kift, Karen Nelson, Liz Smith, Juliana Ryan and Helen O'Shea.

References

Adlaf, E.M., L. Glikisman, A. Demers and B. Newton-Taylor. 2001. 'The prevalence of elevated sychological distress among Canadian undergraduates: findings from the 1998 Canadian Campus Survey'. *Journal of American College Health*, 50: 67-72.

Aschaffenburg, K. and I. Mass. 1997. 'Cultural and educational careers: the dynamics of social reproduction'. *American Sociological Review*, 62: 573-87.

Bamber, J. and L. Tett. 2001. 'Ensuring integrative learning experiences for nontraditional students in higher education'. *Widening Participation and Lifelong Learning*, 3(1): 8-16.

Benson, R., L. Hewitt, A. Devos, G. Crosling and M. Heagney. 2009. 'Experiences of students from diverse backgrounds: the role of academic support'. Conference paper. *32nd HERDSA Annual Conference: The Student Experience*, 6-9 July, Darwin (545-50).

Berger, J.B. 2000. 'Optimizing capital, social reproduction, and undergraduate persistence: a sociological perspective', in J. Braxton (ed.), *Reworking the student departure puzzle*. Nashville: Vanderbilt University Press (95-124).

Billingham, S. 2009. 'Diversity, inclusion, and the transforming student experience'. Conference paper. *18th European Access Network Annual International Conference*, 22-24 June, York.

Bloom, L.Z. 1997. 'Teaching my class'. *JAC*, 17(2): 207-13.

Bourdieu, P. 1977. 'Cultural reproduction and social reproduction', in J. Karabel and A.H. Halsey (eds), *Power and ideology in education*. New York: Oxford University Press (487-551).

Bourdieu, P. 1984. *Distinction: a social critique of the judgment of taste*. Cambridge, Mass.: Harvard University Press.

Bourdieu, P. 1994. *Language and symbolic power*. Oxford: Polity Press.

Bowden, M.P. and J. Doughney. 2010. 'Socioeconomic status, cultural diversity and the aspirations of secondary students in the western suburbs of Melbourne, Australia'. *Higher Education*, 59(1): 115-29.

Bradley, D., P. Noonan, H. Nugent and B. Scales. 2008. *Review of Australian Higher Education: final report*. Canberra: Commonwealth of Australia.

Brooks, R. 2004. '"My mum would be as pleased as punch if I actually went, but my dad seems a bit more particular about it": paternal involvement in young people's higher education choices'. *British Educational Research Journal*, 30(4): 495-515.

Bruch, P. and R. Marback. 1997. 'Race identity, writing, and the politics of dignity: reinvigorating the ethics of "Students' right to their own language"'. *JAC*, 17(2): 267-81.

Charlesworth, S.J., P. Gilfillan and R. Wilkinson. 2004. 'Living inferiority'. *British Medical Bulletin*, 69: 49-60.

Christie, H., L. Tett, V.E. Cree, J. Hounsell and V. McCune. 2008. '"A real rollercoaster of confidence and emotions": learning to be a university student'. *Studies in Higher Education*, 33(5): 567-81.

Clark, R. and R. Ivanic. 1997. *The politics of writing*. London: Routledge.

Cole, D. and A. Espinoza. 2008. 'Examining the academic success of Latino students in Science Technology Engineering and Mathematics (STEM) majors'. *Journal of College Student Development*, 49(4): 285-300.

Collier, P.J. and D.L. Morgan. 2008. '"Is that paper really due today?": differences in first-generation and traditional college students' understandings of faculty expectations'. *Higher Education*, 55(4): 425-46.

Corkery, C. 2009. '"Who taught you like that!?" A study of communicative role models and academic literacy skills'. *Composition Forum*, 19 (Spring). http://compositionforum.com /issue/19/ [accessed 9 September 2011].

Crozier, G., D. Reay, J. Clayton, L. Colliander and J. Grinstead. 2008. 'Different strokes for different folks: diverse students in diverse institutions — experiences of higher education'. *Research Papers in Education*, 23(2): 167-77.

David, M., A.M. Bathmaker, G. Crozier, P. Davis, H. Ertl, A. Fuller, G. Hayward,

S. Heath, C. Hockings, G. Parry, D. Reay, A. Vignoles and J. Williams. 2010. *Improving learning by widening participation in higher education. Improving Learning Series.* London: Routledge.

Devlin, M. 2009. 'Low socioeconomic status and Indigenous background: implications for first year curriculum'. Keynote address. First Year Experience Curriculum Design Symposium, Queensland University of Technology, 5-6 February, Queensland. http://www.fyecd2009.qut.edu.au/program/Marcia_Devlin.jsp [accessed 28 May 2010].

Devlin, M. 2010. 'Non-traditional student achievement: theory, policy and practice in Australian higher education'. Keynote Address. *First Year in Higher Education (FYHE) International Conference,* June 27-30, Adelaide. http://www.fyhe.com.au/past_papers /papers10/content/pdf/Marcia_Devlin_keynote_4.pdf [accessed 14 April 2011].

Devlin, M. 2011. 'Bridging socio-cultural incongruity: conceptualising the success of students from low socio-economic backgrounds in Australian higher education'. *Studies in Higher Education,* 1-11. http://dx.doi.org/10.1080/03075079.2011.613991 [accessed 20 December 2011].

Devlin, M. and J. McKay. 2011. 'Inclusive teaching and support of university students from low socioeconomic status backgrounds'. Discussion paper. Higher Education Research Group, Deakin University, Melbourne: 1-8. http://www.lowses.edu.au/files/resources.htm [accessed 3 January 2012].

Devlin, M., J. McKay, S. Kift, K. Nelson and L. Smith. 2012. *Effective teaching and support of students from low socioeconomic backgrounds: resources for Australian higher education,* OLT Project. Available at http://www.lowses.edu.au.

Douglass, J.A., H. Roebken and G. Thomson. 2007. *The immigrant university: assessing the dynamics of race, major and socioeconomic characteristics at the University of California.* Berkeley: Center for Studies in Higher Education, University of California.

Edelsky, C. 1996. *With literacy and justice for all: rethinking the social in language and education.* London: Taylor and Francis.

Elbow, P. 1991. 'Reflections on academic discourse: how it relates to freshman and colleagues'. *College English,* 53(2): 135-55.

Fitzgibbon, K. and J. Prior. 2006. 'Students' early experiences and university interventions: a timeline to aid undergraduate student retention'.

Widening Participation and Lifelong Learning, 8(3): 17-27.

Gall, T.L., D.R. Evans and S. Bellerose. 2000. 'Transition to first year university: patterns of change in adjustment across life domains and time'. *Journal of Social and Clinical Psychology*, 19: 544-67.

Grant, B. 1997. 'Disciplining students: the construction of student subjectivities. *British Journal of Sociology of Education*, 18(1): 101-14.

Greenbank, P. 2006. Institutional widening participation policy in higher education: dealing with the "issue of social class"'. *Widening Participation and Lifelong Learning*, 8(1): 1-10.

Hahs-Vaughn, D. 2004. 'The impact of parents' education level on college students: an analysis using the Beginning Postsecondary Students Longitudinal Study 1990-92/94'. *Journal of College Student Development*, 45(5): 296-316.

Hayden, M. and M. Long. 2006. 'A profile of part-time undergraduates in Australian universities'. *Higher Education Research & Development*, 25(1): 37-52.

Henderson, R., K. Noble and L. De George-Walker. 2009. 'Transitioning into university: "interrupted" first year students problem-solving their way into study'. *Studies in Learning, Evaluation, Innovation and Development*, 6(1): 51-64.

Hutchings, C. 2006. 'Reaching students: lessons from a writing centre'. *Higher Education Research & Development*, 25(3): 247-61.

International Association of Universities. 2008. *Equitable access, success and quality in higher education: a policy statement by the International Association of Universities*. Adopted by IAU 13th General Conference, Utrecht, July. http://www.iau-aiu.net/access_he/access_statement.html [accessed 25 May 2010].

James, R., K. Krause and C. Jennings. 2010. *The first year experience in Australian universities: findings from 1994 to 2009*. Department of Education, Employment and Workplace Relations, Canberra, Australia.

Kift, S. 2009. 'A transition pedagogy: the first year experience curriculum design symposium 2009'. *HERDSA News*, 31(1): 1-4.

Kirk, K. 2008. 'Diversity and achievement: developing the learning of nontraditional HE students', in G. Crosling, L. Thomas and M. Heagney (eds), *Improving student retention in higher education: the role of teaching and learning*. Oxford: Routledge (150-9).

Lawrence, J. 2003. 'The "deficit-discourse" shift: university teachers and their role in helping first year students persevere and succeed in the new university culture'. Conference paper. *6th Pacific Rim First Year in Higher Education Conference*, 8-10 July 2002, Christchurch. http://eprints.usq.edu.au/5469/1/Lawrence_Ultibase_March_2003_PV.pdf.

Lawrence, J. 2005. 'Addressing diversity in higher education: two models for facilitating student engagement and mastery', in A. Brew and C. Asmar (eds), *Research and Development in Higher Education*, 28: 243-52.

Lefkowitz, E.S. 2005. '"Things have gotten better": developmental changes among emerging adults after the transition to university'. *Journal of Adolescent Research*, 20: 40-63.

Luckett, K. and T. Luckett. 2009. 'The development of agency in first generation learners in higher education: a social realist analysis'. *Teaching in Higher Education*, 14(5): 469-81.

Lynch, K. and C. O'Riordan. 1998. 'Inequality in higher education: a study of class barriers'. *British Journal of Sociology of Education*, 19(4): 445-78.

Margolis, E., M. Soldatenko, S. Acker and M. Gair. 2001. 'Peekaboo', in E. Margolis (ed.), *The hidden curriculum in higher education*. New York: Routledge.

Matusov, E. and R. Hayes. 2002. 'Building a community of educators versus effecting conceptual change', in G. Wells and G. Claxton (eds), *Learning for Life in the 21st Century: sociocultural perspectives on the future of education*. Individual Students: Multicultural Education for Pre-Service Teachers. Oxford: Blackwell Publishers (239-51).

McKavanagh, M. and K. Purnell. 2007. 'Student learning journey: supporting student success through the Student Readiness Questionnaire'. *Studies in Learning, Evaluation, Innovation and Development*, 4(2): 27-38.

McKay, J. and M. Devlin. 2014. 'Demystifying the higher education culture for students from low socioeconomic backgrounds'. *Higher Education Research & Development*.

Morales, E. 2000. 'A contextual understanding of the process of educational resilience: high achieving Dominican American students and the 'resilience cycle'. *Innovative Higher Education*, 25(1): 7-22.

Moreau, M. and C. Leathwood. 2006. 'Balancing paid work and studies: working (-class) students in higher education'. *Studies in Higher Education*, 31(1): 23-42.

Murphy, B. 2009. 'Great expectations? Progression and achievement of less traditional entrants to higher education'. *Widening Participation and Lifelong Learning*, 11(2): 4-14.

Northedge, A. 2002. 'Organizing excursions into specialist discourse communities: a sociocultural account of university teaching', in G. Wells and G. Claxton (eds), *Learning for life in the 21st Century: sociocultural perspectives on the future of education*. Oxford: Blackwell Publishers (252-64).

Northedge, A. 2003a. 'Enabling participation in academic discourse'. *Teaching in Higher Education*, 8(2): 169-80.

Northedge, A. 2003b. 'Rethinking teaching in the context of diversity'. *Teaching in Higher Education*, 8(1): 17-32.

Perna, L. 2000. 'Racial and ethnic group differences in college enrolment decisions', in A. Cabrera and S. La Nasa (eds), *Understanding the college choice of disadvantaged students*. San Francisco: Jossey-Bass (65-83).

Pittman, L. and A. Richmond. 2008. 'University belonging, friendship quality, and psychological adjustment during the transition to college'. *The Journal of Experimental Education*, 76(4): 343-62.

Priest, A. 2009. '"I have understanding as well as you": supporting the language and learning needs of students from low socioeconomic status backgrounds'. *Journal of Academic Language and Learning*, 3(3): A1-A12.

Read, B., L. Archer and C. Leathwood. 2003. 'Challenging cultures? Student conceptions of "belonging" and "isolation" at a post-1992 university'. *Studies in Higher Education*, 28(3): 261-77.

Rice, J.A. 2008. 'Politicizing critical pedagogies for the logic of late capitalism'. *Composition Forum*, 18 (Summer). http://compositionforum.com/issue/18 [accessed 30 September 2011].

Roberts, S. 2011. 'Traditional practice for non-traditional students? Examining the role of pedagogy in higher education retention'. *Journal of Further and Higher Education*, 35(2): 182-99.

Rose-Krasnor, L., G. Adams, J. Polivy, S.M. Pancer, M.W. Pratt, S. Birnie-Lefcovitch and M. Wintre. 2010. 'A Longitudinal study of breadth and intensity of activity involvement and the transition to university'. *Journal of Research on Adolescence*, 21(2): 512-18.

Shallcross, L. and J. Hartley. 2009. *A step out of poverty: aspirations, retention, and transformation*. Paper presented at the EOPHEA Conference, Sydney.

Simister, J. 2011. 'Elitism and meritocracy in UK universities: the UK needs investment in its labour force'. *Higher Education Quarterly*, 65(2): 113-44.

Tett, L. 2004. 'Mature working-class students in an "elite" university: discourses of risk, choice and exclusion'. *Studies in the Education of Adults*, 36(2): 252-64.

Vuong, M., S. Brown-Welty and S. Tracz. 2010. 'The effects of self-efficacy on academic success of first-generation college sophomore students'. *Journal of College Student Development*, 51(1): 50-64.

Walpole, M. 2008. 'Emerging from the pipeline: African American students, socioeconomic status, and college experiences and outcomes'. *Research in Higher Education*, 49(3): 237-55.

Wenger, E. 1998. *Communities of practice: learning, meaning, and identity*. New York: Cambridge University Press.

White, S. 2006. 'Who will look after the kids? The practicalities faced by a group of mothers participating in pre-service teacher education in New Zealand'. *Widening Participation and Lifelong Learning*, 8(3): 7-16.

Winn, S. 2002. 'Student motivation: a socioeconomic perspective'. *Studies in Higher Education*, 27(1): 445-57.

Wintre, M.G. and C.D. Bowers. 2007. 'Predictors of persistence to graduation: extending a model and data on the transition to university model'. *Canadian Journal of Behavioural Science*, 39: 220-34.

Wintre, M.G. and M. Yaffe. 2000. 'First year students' adjustment to university life as a function of relationships with parents'. *Journal of Adolescent Research*, 15: 9-37.

Yorke, M. and B. Longden. 2008. *The first year experience of higher education in the UK*. Final report. York, UK: The Higher Education Academy.

Zepke, N. and L. Leach. 2005. 'Integration and adaptation: approaches to the student retention and achievement puzzle'. *Active Learning in Higher Education*, 6(1): 46-59.

5 Changing social relations in higher education: the first-year international student and the 'Chinese learner' in Australia

Xianlin Song

Abstract

Throughout history, human movements beyond borders — geographical, cultural, intellectual or otherwise — have narrowed the distances between peoples and expanded their horizons. Border crossings and the physical annihilation of space enable peoples to interact and learn from one another and consequently alter the relationships between those involved (Dewey, 1993). Globalisation in higher education has created one of the most momentous border crossings in Australia's history; it has not only changed the face of students' population in Australia, but also transformed the social relations between university policymakers, academics and students. This chapter examines the effects of changing social relations in Australian higher education where first-year international students are concerned. In the context of students' diversity, the chapter seeks to question the appropriateness of essentialising and teaching a particular type of 'critical thinking' that erases the cultural borders these students have crossed. It engages with the ongoing debates on negotiating identities in the globalising university 'contact zone' (Kenway and Bullen, 2003), and attempts to demystify certain characteristics of the 'Chinese learner'. Taking up the theoretical concept of a 'social imaginary' advanced by Rizvi and Lingard (2010), this chapter argues for an alternative imaginary to conceptualise the identities of international students in higher education. It advocates a Confucian educational paradigm that regards everyone, irrespective of where they come from, as educable and having the right of equal access to quality education.

Introduction

Over the last decades, two fundamental shifts have taken place in higher education in Australia: the process of globalisation has increasingly diversified the student population and literally altered the face of one-fifth of students on campus; at the same time, market reforms have corporatised and commercialised the traditional administrative sections of tertiary institutions and in turn this has affected the nature of teaching and learning. Macro-transformations of this magnitude invariably have shaken the established structure of the education system, and large amounts of research have been published to debate the challenging issues in higher education. Values of what higher education stands for are being tested; identities of what makes an academic and a student are being reimagined; theoretical boundaries of what separates cultural heritages are being renegotiated; established concepts of pedagogy are being redefined; and conventional curricula are being modified. The cultural reconfiguration on campus involves a significant reorganisation of social order, transforming all stakeholders, educators and policymakers as well as international students and local students alike — transforming the nature of the social relationships between and among them.

This chapter investigates the interconnectedness and interdependency of the changes facing university policymakers, academics and students caught up in the torrents of globalisation. In particular it examines the effects of changing relations, where international students are concerned, in the complex and shifting communities and contexts of Australian universities. It aims to contextualise the implications for the international newcomer on campus, and interrogate the teaching of 'critical thinking' in relation to the 'Chinese learner', in an environment where there is a market-based homogenisation, affecting both teacher and learner. It is beyond the scope of this research to disentangle the web of all potentially related causes that might affect the academic performances of first-year international students. Rather, it seeks to question the appropriateness of teaching and learning practices concerning the new international students. Taking up the theoretical concept of a 'social imaginary' by Rizvi and Lingard (2010), this chapter argues for an alternative 'social imaginary' that shapes the identities of international students in higher education and frames the challenges to which policies are the solution. It advocates an educational paradigm that regards everyone, irrespective of where they come from, as — in Confucius's terms — 'educable' and having the right of equal access to quality education.

Higher education and the changing social relationship

In considering the context whereby students enter into their first year in Australian universities it is critical to consider the context of Australia's higher education system, which has become a multicultural environment where approximately one in five tertiary students (22 per cent) is from overseas (Australian Bureau of Statistics, December 2011). This globalisation of the student body is remarkable as it has propelled Australian higher education to be ranked third-highest in the world for non-resident/international students, after the US and UK, in 2010 (OECD, n.d.). With a significant financial contribution to the Australian economy (AU$16.3 billion in Australia, as compared to US$21 billion for the US during 2010-11), the consequence of increased numbers of international students in Australia, in many ways, has gone far beyond the market efficiency of a globalised economy. These human movements necessitated by international students seeking education in anglophone countries have not only literally changed the face of the Australian campus, but also altered the socio-political dynamics constitutive of higher education.

Within this context, higher education in Australia can be understood as the site where a neo-liberal 'social imaginary' is dominant, framing the discourses of educational policy, shaping the possibilities of students' identities, and determining the aspirations and expectations of the masses (Rizvi and Lingard, 2010). A 'social imaginary', as defined by Rizvi and Lingard, is 'a way of thinking shared in a society by ordinary people, the common understandings that make everyday practices possible, giving them sense and legitimacy' (ibid.: 34). Such a social imaginary carries with it certain assumptions, images, myths and narratives in mass media that flow over into the mass higher education system existing in Australia today. In the meta-narrative of this new social imaginary, the increasing presence of international students on campus is described in terms of customers of an irreversible trend of the globalising market economy, where they enter into a culture based on the assumption that Western education is by its nature 'superior', matching the supposed 'superior' Western culture. Consequently, the policies to meet the demands of market forces of international student enrolments and the massification of higher education are also prescribed as desired interpretations of, and responses to, these market-based changes. Education itself is deemed a utilitarian product, being 'instrumental to goods which lie outside the realm of knowledge and rational or critical understanding' (Heath, 2002: 38). Within the micro-fabric of this social imaginary, these international students in classrooms are imaged as inferior market products. They are 'characterised as passive, dependent, surface/rote learners prone to plagiarism and lacking critical thinking' (Ryan and Louie, 2007: 406), and the educational policies of standardisation of graduate attributes and assessment criteria are the necessary solution.

It is through this social imaginary of market relations between the ideal-type Western student and the attractiveness of English-based knowledge and the 'deficient' international student, desiring this knowledge, that the current social relations among key stakeholders of higher education are contested, questioned and renegotiated. Globalisation of higher education has heightened the sense of identities and belongings of these key stakeholders, and reconfigured the social relationships among and between them. Simon Marginson (2011) explicates that higher education institutions in Western countries have rested on 'an antinomy' since their beginning. The antinomy, according to Marginson, consists of two crucial elements: a place-bound locality and universal mobility of knowledge. The rationale of higher education institutions is grounded in the real location where the function of transmitting universal knowledge happens. Neither knowledge function nor the institutional location is, by itself, enough to constitute the attraction of such institutions. The attraction of Western education institutions to international students is anchored in their location as well as the universal nature of education. In the higher education scenario, this antinomy means that international students are first of all attracted to the place where English is spoken, and at the same time to the possibility that the knowledge they gain in their learning process is universal. In the Australian context, international students come to this country precisely because they want to learn the local language and culture, and because they wish to gain universally mobile knowledge. The dramatic increase of international students on campus involves a significant reorganisation of social order, transforming all stakeholders, educators and policymakers as well as international students and local students alike, and at the same time changing the nature of the social relationships among them.

Policymakers in the Australian higher education institution sector, in the name of quality assurance and accountability, have moved to pursue neo-liberal reforms of corporatisation and marketisation, implementing an intense managerial agenda across the higher education zone (Rizvi and Lingard, 2010; Hil, 2012; Marginson, 2009, 2011 and 2012; Saunders, 2010). Academics, under pressure to conform as well as cope with increased workloads and intensified measures of managerial accountability, have reported a dramatic decline of both professional satisfaction and educational autonomy. Within this broad trend, there have been accusations that academics have been pressured to lower standards and to pass international students and fee-paying students. This context has produced a critical backlash against what Richard Hil calls 'whackademia', where 'academics have been reduced to administrators and facilitators of formulaic, googlised, dumbed-down education' (2012: 9).

In this context of a university environment of surveillance, regulation and academic resistance, international students have enrolled with remarkable success. The geographically displaced international students have adapted themselves to their new learning environment and have learnt to understand the educational expectations of their teachers and the cultural practices of their new living surroundings. Bewildered by a new academic culture and new language environment, these students often recount negative experiences studying in a supposedly multicultural university (Song and Cadman, 2012). Their learning styles and social behaviours, derived from different cultural heritages, are often questioned, and pose significant challenges to the nature, value and quality of the academics' lives in the hosting education institutions (Gu and Maley, 2008). Consequently, the participation and presence of international students in campus life has shifted the established cultural dynamics between students and teachers and has presented Australian higher education with an 'ontological' challenge to transform itself in the process of globalisation (Barnett, 2012).

Up till 2010 this international flow of students has largely been one-way, with the exception of a very small proportion of social sciences and humanities students from Western countries making the reverse journey. China's latest ascent, however, has prompted an inverse trend led by Barack Obama's announcement of the '100,000 Strong' initiative, a national effort designed to increase the number and diversify the composition of US students studying in China (US Department of State, n.d.). The Gillard government, in its *Australia in the Asian Century White Paper* (October 2012), also takes the initiative to develop specific opportunities and funding sources for students from under-represented groups to study in Asia.

This one-sided flow of the student population has resulted in higher education in anglophone countries becoming a primary site of academic contention and investigation. Large quantities of research have come to light in the past two decades, rigorously debating the challenging issues related to the existence of higher education. To a great extent, issues being investigated in the research published in English are framed by the established educational traditions in anglophone countries. Central to the debates over changed/changing higher education are questions concerning the nature, value and quality of education (Shah, Nair and Wilson, 2011), and what Western education can offer, and is offering, to non-Western students. The performance of the newcomer is measured against the perceived ideal in the host institutions. Where non-Western cultural heritages are mentioned, they remain peripheral and complementary and in relation to the norm: explicitly, the relative lack of proficiency in English and the cultural barriers that hinder the transmission of knowledge, which constitutes the pivotal activity of higher education teaching. Where quality has to be upheld, international students, with their lower English competency and cultural otherness, pose a real threat to the well-established academic conventions of the hosting nation.

Policymakers and empirical realities of academics

Despite the large influx of international students implying the need for a nuanced policy approach, the reverse has happened. University policymakers have been on the move to implement sweeping reforms to catch up with the signs of the times in a commercialised market. Holders of academic power have increasingly leaned towards the managerial mechanisms of corporate enterprise in their administration of academia, treating all students as customers in a basically undifferentiated manner. In the name of accountability for quality assurance in Australian higher education, and under external pressure, managements have endeavoured to standardise educational activities on campus, redefine 'graduate attributes', prescribe pedagogies and curricula, and set rigid tables of performance indicators to frame educational practices for teachers (Rizvi and Lingard, 2010; Song and Cadman, 2012; Hargreaves and Shirley, 2009). All courses have to be validated within a set of generic attributes defined and mandated by policymakers and must conform to universalised and generalised assessment outcomes. In many ways these learning initiatives are meant to directly link to 'work-ready' outcomes, devoid of knowledge for knowledge's and life's sake. These 'graduate attributes' educators are required to address and show a range of invisible, non-contextual yet universalised criteria embedded within key assumptions underpinning internationalisation of higher education (Song and Cadman, 2012). Such incursion of managerialists into academics' lives to determine what happens in classrooms has become a matter of grave concern for academics (Saunders, 2010). According to Saunders, '[M]anagerialism is one of the principal ways whereby the commercialisation of our universities has been enforced' and its toxicity is detrimental to the academic workforce, whose professional goal has been reduced to how to 'make money for the institution that has employed them' (ibid.). This approach of standardising every aspect of teaching and learning activity seems to rest on the assumption that somehow student diversity can be dealt with through homogeneity (Song and Cadman, 2012). Managerial moves of homogenising graduate attributes and regulating assessments in the face of students' diversity have serious implications for equity and justice in education as they preclude alternatives in curriculum design and pedagogy for educators to explore 'the transformative potential of education' (Nagahara, 2011: 381).

Rizvi and Lingard, in their book *Globalizing Education Policy* (2010), point out that these changes and challenges brought about by globalisation are interpreted and enacted in the process of policymaking in higher education institutions that reflect fundamentally 'both an ideological formation and a social imaginary that now shapes the discourses of education policy' (ibid.: 23). These dominant ideas and practices are largely driven by a neo-liberal agenda, playing a central role in shaping the discursive framing of the current educational policies, channelling and limiting academic freedoms and limiting the social imagination of higher education practice and promise (Marginson, 2009: 87). Such neo-liberal reforms have negative consequences on academic freedom, 'as the capacity for the radical-critical break' is constrained (ibid.: 107). The externally determined processes driven by a market formula reduce the scope of arbitrary academic judgment and limit off-the-wall innovative practices on campus. Academic agency, though not eliminated, is tamed and harnessed to serve economic interests and a particular neo-liberal social order, and weakens, especially in social science disciplines, 'the capacity for critically-inspired invention' (ibid.: 87). Some forms of academic autonomy may survive in this neo-liberal climate, but 'the independence of faculty expertise is partly broken' (ibid.: 111).

Reactions to the rapid expansion of internationalisation with the visible presence of international students have been varied among academics working with these students on a daily basis. In theory, academics are open-minded people who embrace cultural and social diversities on campus. Many research publications attest that academics in general welcome international students and appreciate a vibrant and heterogeneous work environment that promotes cross-cultural encounters and plurality, and encourages multiculturalism and global citizenship. Academics' constructive motivation and positive energy have been devoted to theoretical research into transcultural understandings of students, critiques of the nature of education policy and explorations into innovative ways of teaching to bridge the transcultural divides between international students and their host institutions (Ballard and Clanchy, 1984, 1991 and 1997; Watkins and Biggs, 1996, 2001; Marginson, 2009, 2011 and 2012; Rizvi and Lingard, 2012; Shah, Nair and Wilson, 2011; Ryan and Slethaug, 2010; Foster, 2010; Song and Cadman, 2012).

However, as an empirical reality, the diversified student population has meant that government funding in proportion to the number of students on campus has fallen, in many cases dramatically. When the neo-liberal expansion into the international market was translated into less financial revenue in research and teaching, the empirical reality of academics, conflated with radical reforms and corporatisation of management (Rizvi and Lingard, 2010; Hil, 2012; Marginson, 2009, 2011 and 2012), prompted very 'antagonistic impulses' in the workforce (Papastephanou, 2005; Hil, 2012). Academics found themselves increasingly coping with higher workloads and bulging classrooms with decreased resources for research and teaching, and the ever-escalating demands for individual attention from 'poorly-prepared students' (Foster, 2010: 302).

Academics report an increasingly stressful and unhappy working environment with the increasing diversity of the student population. Many of the issues that academics are most unhappy about relate to the core activities that constitute their collective identity. Richard Hil, in his much publicised book *Whackademia: an Insider's Account of the Troubled University* (2012), paints a pejorative scenario of academia, one which many of those who have been in the workforce can identify with. As the blurb on his back cover phrases it:

> Australian universities are not happy places. Despite the shiny rhetoric of excellence, quality, innovation and creativity, universities face criticism over declining standards, decreased funding, compromised assessment, overburdened academics and never-ending reviews and restructures.

He argues that many of the negative and sometimes hostile reactions from academics are mostly directed towards management's implementation of a neo-liberal agenda that is unintelligent and laborious, akin to 'knowledge department stores' (ibid.: 9). Instead of focusing their energy on pedagogical activities to improve students' learning outcomes, academics have found themselves devoting a considerable amount of time to studying new educational policies, filling out various administrative forms and producing online technical gimmicks to cope with their work environmental changes (ibid.). According to research conducted by Gigi Foster (2011), the power of academics in higher institutions has been significantly reduced and their pedagogical freedoms eroded by institutional administrative barriers. Academics' power to pursue 'open-ended intellectual exploration' both in teaching and research is eroded by managements' demands for universal 'graduate attributes' and initiatives of 'assurance of learning' (ibid.: 569). Given the potential influence that teaching academics can have over students, these moves by institutions to prescribe what academics can or cannot do in their classrooms are having, and are likely to continue having, significant negative impacts on students (ibid., 2011: 573).

Students generally perceive that teaching academics are 'in charge' of teaching activities and academic standards and that their own efforts, ability and attitude are responsible for academic success (ibid.). Academics, however, feel that they are not trusted to manage their own working life in terms of teaching and research, and that their academic autonomy, their right to determine the nature of their work, is under threat (Hil, 2012; Marginson, 2009; Henkel, 2005). These changes in power relations on campus resulting from neo-liberal managerialism and the 'erosion of academic authority within the academy' not only lower academics' sense of ownership of pedagogical activities, but also their professional autonomy to engage in 'open-ended intellectual exploration' (Foster, 2011: 569). By losing control over curricula, evidence has shown that teaching academics have been coerced to manipulate their marking standards to cope with 'the flux of large numbers of under-prepared international and non-English-language-speaking students' (ibid.: 573).

In Australia the context is now clear. There has been the massification of higher education, the concomitant rise of managerial regulations and surveillance to control the mass student market toward market outcomes (human capital theory) and the casualisation of the workforce, where full-time academics work in unison with, but often supervising, a large casual workforce. This has led to widespread academic dissatisfaction and a palpable sense of loss for education as a public good. The extent to which academics' unhappiness is directly *linked* to the increased numbers of international students in Australia, however, remains unclear. Educationalists assert that learning does not happen totally independently of teaching, and a teacher's 'happiness', very often, is derived from 'experiencing satisfaction and self-realisation while teaching' (Shim, 2008: 516). Translated into the empirical realities of teachers on campuses, this may imply that the capacity to reach self-actualisation in teaching is seriously limited by this cohort of students whose mere presence erects considerable linguistic and cultural barriers between the teacher and the receiver of teaching. As documented by Ballard and Clancy, the sheer reality of 'wall to wall Asians' in a classroom is 'unnerving' for the teaching staff (1997: 1): 'The combination of time, pressure and confusion about how best to proceed very commonly produced frustration' and often resentment (ibid.: 3). Such frustration and resentment, conflated with consequences of macro-educational reforms, all contribute to the prevalent unhappiness demonstrated in the narrative of *Whackademia*. In a changed classroom, the gap between teachers' acts of teaching and the job satisfaction derived from knowing that their effort is rewarded by students' learning outcomes has widened.

In practice, the forces that coerce teachers to relinquish their 'quality standards' to compromise assessments include the ever-increasing presence of international students, who place more demands on academics, as well as the university policy-makers and administration, who limit their capacity to explore transformative curricula to help these demanding students. Researchers suggest that the decline of academic standards is linked directly with the presence of international students (Devos, 2003), and that 'international students are being allowed to underperform' (Trounson, 2011). Academics, it is alleged, have reportedly inflated grades in order to pass these 'poorly-prepared students' (Foster, 2010: 302). Teachers, though, are quick to add that the real problem underlying all the compromise of quality and standards is not the international students themselves but rather their inadequate level of English proficiency and the cultural hurdles that separate them from the rest of the students (Trounson, 2011). These inadequately prepared students nonetheless constitute and contribute to the unhappiness of academics' work environment. Research findings by Gigi Foster (2012) indicate that where there is a large concentration of EAL[1] students in one given course, it is likely that lecturers 'adjust' the overall standard of marking to take into account the large cohort of lower baseline marks resulting from 'so many poorly-written papers' (2012: 596).

Perhaps it is because of this awareness that researchers have focused considerable amounts of energy towards finding out the cultural differences that stand in between the teachers and their new students. Many well-intended efforts have gone into attempts to understand the cultural specificities of the new learners on campus (Ballard and Clanchy, 1984, 1991 and 1997; Watkins and Biggs, 1996, 2001). This ground-breaking research provides a systematic account of the difficulties overseas students face in the Australian learning environment and highlights an awareness of a clash of educational cultures which underpins the problems of students' adjustment to Australian campus life. In the manuals to prepare Asian students for better integration into Western higher education institutions and to ground the teachers to help Asian students, Ballard and Clancy (1984, 1997) highlight the variations in styles of thinking in different cultures. The Australian educational tradition, attitude to knowledge, learning approaches, and teaching and learning strategies are held up to mirror what 'Asian' students are deficient in. On the scales of 'conserving and extending attitude to knowledge',

---

[1] This cohort of international students is most commonly referred to as students from Non-English Speaking Backgrounds (NESB). However, I prefer to use the term English as Additional Language (EAL) students as it describes this cohort in terms of what they have, not what they are deficient in.

and 'reproductive, analytical and speculative learning approaches', Asian students are generally perceived to occupy the lower end of the range. Watkins and Biggs (1996) further argue for the need for a cross-cultural perspective from educators to improve the learning outcomes of newcomers in higher education. Juxtaposing the Confucian heritage of learning to Western culture, Biggs proposes the dichotomy of 'surface' and 'deep' to shed light on differences in approaches to learning.

Educationists like Ballard and Clancy (1991, 1997) and Watkins and Biggs (1996) have explicitly warned against a simplistic view of Asian students' learning style and the trap of stereotyping students as 'deep' and 'surface' learners, and recognise that these learners can be 'deep' learners as they seem to question and reflect in their learning process. Their research into the learning behaviours of Asian students, although hugely influential in Australia, has nonetheless produced some unintended effects, contributing to a much-quoted discursive formation of this social imaginary in the media. The image of the passive superficial learner, deficient of 'deep' approaches and lacking critical thinking skills, seems to have been synonymous with Asian students, especially the 'Chinese learner'. One explanation could be that these terms, used in the conceptual framework, match the researchers' own perceptions, values which underpin the so-called 'academic standards', and perpetuate the perception that these students are 'passive' in class regardless of the reasons behind their behaviour. These attributes of newcomers, researchers argue, largely rest on assumptions of what is the perceived norm. Those who are seen as deviant are contrasted to the ideal local students, standing 'as the antithesis of Western exemplars of academic virtue' (Ryan, 2010: 39). Much of the perception of the passive Asian learner was based on the evidence observed in anglophone classroom settings, and 'filtered through the researcher's own values, expectations and standards' (Clark and Gieve, 2006: 63). Others go so far as to suggest that the identity politics in the face of challenges denotes a cultural conservatism and purism which takes a defensive stand to protect an existing cultural tradition from contamination by 'obtrusive otherness' (Papastephanous, 2005: 545). To a certain extent the recently redefined and universalised ideal attributes of graduates in higher education institutions reflect this mindset. What matters is not whether those ideals are real but rather the essentialised mirror image of what these newcomers are deficient in.

Empirical realities of international students and their first-year experience in Australia

At the other end of the spectrum in the globalisation of higher education are the international students who cross borders to seek a Western-style education. Many of these students pay full fees. As a key stakeholder, this geographically, linguistically and culturally displaced cohort arguably sits at the lowest rung of power relations in the debates. Yet the changed lives of these students, mostly sojourners in the host country, are changing the face of their adopted places (Gu and Maley, 2008). Why do they choose a higher education institution in an anglophone country to study in the first place? Aside from the push factors of their own countries of origin, Marginson's notion of 'antinomy', as mentioned earlier, best describes their process of selecting a desired destination. Within this 'antinomy' is, first, a 'place-bound identity' of the institution, the place where it is located, and, second, 'universal-mobile knowledge', which is transferrable internationally and across cultural borders (Marginson, 2011). International students choose anglophone countries as their destination largely due to their recognition of the transcultural importance of English as an international language in a globalised world. At the same time, the type of knowledge they pursue has to be internationally mobile, has to transcend linguistic and cultural divides, and has to be appropriate for their transnational futures (Slethaug, 2010). These two mutually entailing heterogeneous elements of antinomy make education in anglophone countries so attractive to international students, worthy of pursuit 'at any cost' (Bergman, 2012: 52).

First-year experience

In general, the transition from high school to the university learning environment can be a challenging one, requiring a dynamic process of readjustments, negotiations on the part of students, and dialogues and exchanges amongst all participants of campus life. Scholars have a consensus that the first-year experience is the most crucial period that affects the academic achievements of students (McKenzie and Schweitzer, 2001; McKenzie, Gow and Schweitzer, 2004; Brinckworth et al., 2009), and that the transition from secondary to tertiary institutions can be difficult as many first-year students are 'ill-prepared' for the changes required in the new learning environment (Brinckworth et al., 2009). Studies on first-year students' experiences recommend non-specialised transitional programs to meet the special needs of these students and facilitate their transition into university (ibid.). For international students, the level of difficulty in transition is often compounded, and the issues related to their learning difficulties become more complex and multidimensional.

Dislocated geographically, culturally, socially and linguistically, new international students experience major impediments that go beyond the usual transition of educational institutions. Many research findings published in English demonstrate that international students manifest significantly higher degrees of psychological and socio-cultural stress in their new learning environment (Burns, 1991; Spencer-Oatey and Xiong, 2006; Gu and Maley, 2008; Zhou et al., 2008; Brown and Holloway, 2008), and attest that the symptoms of cultural shock associated with these students have predominantly negative impacts on their academic performance. When international students first arrive in their host country, they are expected to contend with new social, cultural and educational behaviours, and as such they often switch to a 'stress and coping' mode (Zhou et al., 2008; Brown and Holloway, 2008). Their reticence and anxiety to articulate their opinion further disassociates them from the local, critically thinking learners in a typical classroom setting (Liu and Jackson, 2011). Their academic performance, demonstrated by grade point average (GPA), negatively correlates with their psychological stress. These students' emotional and psychological well-being is strongly linked with their intellectual achievements.

For most of these international students, especially the 'Chinese learner', the journey to obtain a degree in an English-speaking country is a family one. When their families spend a large sum of savings, in many cases their life savings, to send their children to an anglophone country to study, the family expectation is that these students will gain 'universal-mobile' knowledge in English and receive a 'high quality education' (whatever that implies) that can be demonstrated with a glossy certificate and a distinguished academic transcript for their transcultural and transnational futures. This commonly assumed cultural advantage of family expectation, for some international students, has become a significant disadvantage. According to a UK-based study conducted by Gang Li, Wei Chen and Jing-Lin Duanmu, the high level of family expectation and the culturally perceived importance of education can be a liability and have an adverse effect on the academic performance of Chinese students (2010). For the student, the family's expectations of academic success often translate into additional pressure in their survival mode of coping in the new environment. Paradoxically, the family-inflated stress could perhaps partly explain why international students tend to survive their first year in the university and complete their study even if it means they graduate with a GPA as low as 3.5 (Song and Cadman, 2013). High expectations from families account for their anxiety as well as their perseverance and persistence.

While for local Australian students there has been a strong link between previous academic performance and their university performance (McKenzie and Schweitzer, 2001; McKenzie, Gow and Schweitzer, 2004), the same cannot be said for the international students. Such an affirmative correlation does not automatically extend beyond the linguistic and cultural hurdles they face. What they achieved in their home country in secondary education often has little bearing on their academic performance in Australia (Song and Cadman, 2012). Instead, academic research has consistently attributed the difficulties international students experience in their first year to their inadequacy in English as well as their cultural heritage. In terms of their linguistic ability and cultural background, these students, compared with their local counterparts, are considered 'poorly-prepared' and automatically remedial. Indicators of their 'poor' performance in classrooms include inability to communicate effectively, passivity in class participation, using ideas in their essays without proper referencing, and the absence of critical thinking skills, all of which are prerequisites for academic success in higher education within anglophone countries.

These two major hurdles are closely linked to the fact that English as Additional Language (EAL) students, most of whom are also international arrivals, perform significantly worse than their local counterparts when measured by their GPAs (Foster, 2012). According to the data collected from undergraduate programs within the business school of two Australian universities in 2008-10 (ibid.), EAL students 'earn persistently lower marks' and 'perform significantly worse' than their local counterparts. Aside from the cultural and social dislocations they face on a daily basis, they have to deal with the realities of learning outcomes measured against the established assessment criteria in the existing curricula. Similar to the situation faced by what Foster calls 'poorly-prepared' students in less-established universities in Australia (2010: 302), international students have few options other than to make up the numbers of natural attrition in the universities' assessment system, with limited opportunities for being taught up to 'a market-supportable standard' with 'value-added teaching' (ibid.: 303). At the same time, as there is no 'counter-pressure' against the initial recruitment standard set by the universities, the painful consequences of mismatches caused by students' diversity and a 'market-supportable standard' can only be borne by students and teachers alike. Measured against the established academic standards, the very educability of these students is called into question, as the 'poorly-prepared students' cannot be taught by the value-added teaching demanded by the standards of the market within the current higher institution system without a significant increase in funding (Foster, 2012).

International students in anglophone countries, many researchers note, can be very diligent and conscientious in their first year of study, demonstrating higher levels of motivation in learning than local students (Ramburuth and McCormick, 2001). For many of these students, especially those from a Chinese cultural background, who firmly believe hard work will eventually pay off[2], their academic transcript can be a constant source of agony and frustration. They frequently report negative experiences in their new university and are unhappy that their presence on campus amounts to little more than 'cash cows' for financially struggling universities (Ryan and Louie, 2007: 411). One study, which involved 67 third-year Chinese international students, suggests that once these students have survived their first year in university, they remain remedial throughout their undergraduate studies. These students, mostly from the Faculties of Commerce, Social Sciences and Humanities, had an average GPA of 3.5 on a scale from 1 to 7 (Song and Cadman, 2012), suggesting these students had completed two and half years of tertiary learning with merely 50 per cent passes. For some of these dislocated international students who are endeavouring to achieve the best grades possible, for the value of their family's investment, 'their problems are really due to racism or to victimisation by unsympathetic staff' (Ballard and Clanchy, 1997: 3). What is more agonising for them is the apparent nonchalance of their higher education

---

[2] The Chinese proverb 只要功夫深，铁杵磨成针 'If you work hard enough at it, you can grind even an iron rod down to a needle' (that is, 'Patience, persistence and perspiration make an unbeatable combination for success'), deeply entrenched in the students' psyche, is part and parcel of the Confucian educational doctrine.

institution towards their ongoing emotionally negative experiences. By holding up a mirror of ideal excellence prescribed in the essentialised 'graduate attributes' to reflect their performances, the higher education institution inadvertently relegates EAL international students to the 'antithesis' of the desired students. Some even go on to question the much promoted multiculturalism in Australian universities. One such international student, at the end of his final undergraduate degree wrote in a shaky hand, 'Multiculturalism is a big fat lie' (Cadman and Song, 2012: 3).

The myth of the 'Chinese learner' and 'critical thinking'

Much of the angst and frustration experienced by teaching academics is related to a particular perceived type of international student, namely the 'Chinese learner'. Though often confused with — and used interchangeably with — 'Asian', 'East Asian' or 'Confucian heritage learner', the construct of the 'Chinese learner' and what it stands for has emerged as a new form of discourse in the past two decades (Clark and Gieve, 2006). Just as the hosting countries of these international students are often referred to as 'anglophone countries', named Australia, the United States, Canada, New Zealand and the United Kingdom, 'the Chinese learner' often comes from a Confucian heritage cultural background, and includes people from Singapore, Hong Kong, Taiwan and sometimes even Japan and Korea (Ryan and Louie, 2007). The number of international students from the People's Republic of China has been steadily on the increase on the global scale. In Australia the situation is similar. According to the Australian Bureau of Statistics, between 2009 and 2010 'in total over one quarter (27%) of all international student enrolments came from China' (December 2011).

As part of the 'social imaginary' in the globalisation of higher education, the myth of the 'Chinese learner' appears to be carrying with it a transcultural valance. Representations of these students often reflect the ongoing negotiation of identities in the globalising university 'contact zone' (Kenway and Bullen, 2003). The 'Chinese learner' has been characterised in terms of a 'passive' learner 'lacking critical thinking skills' (Ryan, 2010: 41), and constructed as the academic other. Many binary descriptions frame these students, contrasting them to the qualities the ideal students supposedly have (ibid.: 43). Their approaches to learning are described in terms of *surface* or *deep*, their learning styles are referred to as *independent* or *dependent*, and their attitudes to academic debates are classified as '*harmonious*' or '*adversarial*' (Ryan and Louie, 2007; emphasis in original). What appears as absent in these students is allegedly characteristic of their ideal local counterparts. Such a 'large culture' approach describes the identities of international students as a 'fixed, reified, homogenous and homogenised group' (Clark and Gieve, 2006: 63), contributing to macro-discursive constructions prevalent in the academic debates in Australia, and reinforcing the discourse of remediation of international students.

Many scholars warn against the danger of over-generalisation of such a diverse group of students, and argue for a meta-cultural awareness that entails a willingness to meet the learning needs of all students irrespective of their background (Ryan and Louie, 2007; Cadman and Song, 2012). Ryan and Louie (2007) point out that the assumption of Western students as assertive, independent critical thinkers is just as problematic as the assumption of 'Chinese learners' as surface and dependent learners. In addition to supplementing a 'social imaginary' emergent in the process of globalisation of higher education, this particular discourse of 'deficiency' can have a negative psychological impact on the people who identify with them. These international students, mostly in their formative years, may experience seriously damaging psychological trauma as 'it is in education that students learn to develop their sense of self worth and acceptable modes of social communication' (Rizvi and Lingard, 2010: 160). The practice of setting up the binaries, or 'taxonomies of difference', between Western and Eastern scholarship (Ryan and Louie, 2007) serves to entrench perceptions of difference and feeds into the stereotyping of these diverse groups of students, perpetuating their 'obtrusive otherness' (Ryan, 2010: 43; Papastephanous, 2005: 545). The image of the 'Chinese learner' as socially inept, lacking creative initiative and being a passive rote-learner has become so entrenched that students have begun to internalise these descriptions of themselves, accept this construct as given and identify themselves with this 'social imaginary' (Ryan and Louie, 2007: 410). Overseas studies support this argument, indicating that first-year students fresh from China perform better academically than the ones who had prior experiences of studying overseas (Li, Chen and Duanmu, 2010).

Yet the myth remains that the decline in standards so bemoaned by academics can be attributed to the internationalisation of higher education rather than its massification or managerialist trends. Academics express concerns that the decline of educational standards can be directly attributed to the increase of non-Western students. Central to the 'deficit' construction of the 'Chinese learner' is the argument that these students lack critical thinking skills. In addition to their inadequate proficiency in English, Chinese learners are characterised as having different ways of thinking, which deviate from the 'critical thinking' established in Western academia (Ryan, 2010).

In the published 'graduate attributes' of all universities in Australia, critical thinking, independent learning and adversarial forms of argument are cited as virtues of Western education and 'seen as desirable goods available to international students' (Ryan and Louie, 2007: 413). Problem solving and critical thinking skills are regarded as essential attributes of university graduates and 'a primary goal of education' (Willingham, 2008: 12; Pratt, 1992; Greenholtz, 2003). Ironically, for many academics the definition of 'critical thinking' remains elusive — yet they somehow 'knew it when they saw it' (Ryan and Louie, 2007: 412). Some approach the term by considering what 'critical thinking' is supposed to achieve in education. Richard Paul and Linda Elder (2002), for example, believe that teaching critical thinking skills promotes learners to become more open-minded and tolerant of alternative worldviews.

Copious amounts of research have gone into defining what 'critical thinking' really means in Western academia. For example, Mark Mason summarises some of the better-known philosophical positions regarding the nature of 'critical thinking' as, principally, 'the skills of critical reasoning; a critical attitude; a moral orientation; knowledge of the concepts of critical reasoning; and knowledge of a particular discipline' (2009: 6). This chapter does not intend to examine in detail what these positions entail. Rather, it seeks to question the practice of regarding 'critical thinking' as 'higher-order thinking' and as a 'generic' skill, as applied to international students in anglophone countries, and to explore alternative approaches to thinking and rationality. Of particular interest to the current research is, first, whether critical thinking as a 'particular skill' should be considered as 'generic' and universal for all learners in higher education; and, second, whether critical thinking as it pertains to particular disciplines should be regarded as an essential assessment criterion in the classroom.

Critical thinking as a 'particular skill' is generally considered to be the ability to assess reasoning and identify fallacious arguments (Mason, 2009) and cannot be taught independent of what is being thought about. According to US-based researcher Daniel T. Willingham, this skill cannot be easily taught in classrooms because the processes involved in such activity are intertwined with the content of thought (2008). Challenging the practice of teaching a special type of 'critical thinking' in Western academia as a higher-order intellectual skill, Willingham speculates that critical thinking is not a skill like riding a bicycle, as one does not simply master a situation that is similar enough to be deployed regardless of content. One needs to be able to have adequate content knowledge, for 'thought processes are intertwined with what is being thought about', which in turn 'depends upon prior knowledge' (ibid.: 10, 17). The answer to the question 'can critical thinking actually be taught?' is not affirmative, as 'metacognition' or 'regulating one's thoughts' requires prior 'domain knowledge and practice' (ibid.: 17). A student's power of critical thinking begins 'from the earliest days of a child's school career' (Doddington, 2009: 110). The current assessment practice in Australian universities, which appears to privilege one particular type of critical thinking with no regard to what international students might have learned prior coming to the university, arguably disadvantages these students and renders them remedial, as no EAL learner could critically answer a question she/he has not encountered in their first language (Holmes, 2004).

In a UK-based study into the pedagogical discourses underlying assumptions of daily educational practices in higher education, Yvonne Turner (2006) takes up the much-debated notion of academic 'critical thinking' as the basis for analysing the performance of Chinese internationals in the UK. Turner probes how critical thinking is culturally privileged in Western academic discourse, and argues against the assumption that students from non-Anglo-European cultural backgrounds are generally 'cognitively limited' because of their lack of critical thinking skills. Higher education classrooms in the Anglo-European education system, Turner notes, are governed by 'locally-relevant intellectual styles' rather than 'substance' (2006: 3). Through an erudite discussion of the Confucian intellectual tradition and the 'pedagogical role of criticality', Turner warns against the danger of 'conceptual colonialism', which can thrive where alternative 'rich indigenous knowledge traditions' are disregarded. Drawing from a qualitative longitudinal study, Turner states that critical thinking, as well as other academic conventions, are culturally-based, more related to style, and therefore should not be used as the epistemological core to measure these students' cognitive capacity. Through a critique of the essentialised Western position, Turner concludes that university assessment methods should acknowledge the discrepancy between students' 'declarative knowledge' and their ability to 'be critical' (ibid.).

Academics in the current education debates often seem to be puzzled by what Watkins and Biggs (2001) call 'the paradox of the Chinese Learner' (2001: 3). On the one hand, Chinese learners appear to be passive rote-learners, merely memorising what they are taught. On the other hand, they display high levels of understanding, especially in science and mathematics. Literature indicates that Chinese learners are capable of a 'deep' approach to learning, and often out-perform Western students in areas like science and mathematics (Watkins and Biggs, 2001; Turner, 2006; Olsen and Burgess, 2006). According to a large-scale study of 22 Australian universities conducted in 2006, involving a range of disciplines, there are no overall performance differentials between international students and their local counterparts (Olsen and Burgess, 2006). These research findings suggest that the perceived cognitive limitations and lack of critical thinking skills characteristic of these newcomers only manifest in some sections of academia, namely social sciences, humanities and commerce, where a certain type of critical thinking is deemed as 'higher-order' thinking. While these international students excel in the domains of scientific reasoning and thinking, characterised by universal approaches, they fail in the academic disciplines that are restricted by culturally specific reasoning.

Researchers also warn against the detrimental effect of essentialising certain forms of thinking skills that cannot be easily taught in a classroom setting. The graduate attributes in Australian universities align critical thinking with 'good', 'higher-order' thinking, and place value judgements and moral purpose on a particular form of thinking which is historical, temporal, culturally specific and empirical (Peters, 2009). The educational implication of emphasising critical thinking as the main source of respect for a person's intellect may imply that only the person who has developed the capacity for critical thinking is worthy of such respect (Doddington, 2009). Thinking, asserts Evers (2009), should not be confused with rationality. Any thinking individual can demonstrate rationality in their thinking; it is rationality that transcends cultural boundaries, not any particular kind of thinking itself (ibid.). The current assessment system, which holds certain Western critical thinking skills to be 'good' and 'higher-order' thinking, automatically denigrates the capacity for rational thinking of those students who appear incapable of demonstrating particular 'critical thinking' skills. Such a system, says Harvey Siegel (2006), legitimates the criteria of dominant perspectives, and critiques alternative ways of knowing and alternative epistemologies on these bases, amounting to 'the hegemonic abuse of power' (ibid.: 9).

Cognitive scientists Day et al. (2010) have observed that education must validate an individual's need for hope, since 'hope uniquely predicts objective academic achievement above intelligence, personality, and previous academic achievement' (ibid.: 550). As a cognitive personality trait, 'hope' is positively related to academic achievement, since it is conceptualised as goal-oriented thinking, which leads to thinking around achieving those goals. The graduate attributes that demand the learning and teaching of culturally specific ways of thinking, and an assessment system that essentialises certain ways of thinking, can only be derived from a social imaginary, a mindset, which runs contrary to the great Western education tradition of educating the person not the subject, and takes away from these students the 'hope' for high academic achievements. When international students first come to Australian higher institutions they are automatically rendered cognitively inadequate by the educational system and, what is more, have no hope of escape.

In conclusion: the urgent challenge

The Australian education sector is sitting in an unfamiliar and unmarked juncture after two decades of globalisation. Entering into the third wave of internationalisation, it is now educating both Australian and international students as global citizens from whose ranks 'Asia-capable' leaders for and from Asia will emerge (Australian Government, 2012). Changes brought about by the transnational flow of students call for conceptual expansion in understanding the roles of educators and education providers and for reconfiguration of the boundaries between teachers and students. At the same time, such internationalisation serves as a platform for opening up meaningful intellectual discussion and debate on educational philosophies and their relationships to different cultural traditions (Ryan, 2010).

The increasing commercialisation and corporatisation of university management has severely eroded the capacity of academics to explore transformative educational imperatives, raising fundamental questions regarding what it means to be an academic and what role academics have in education and research (Henkel, 2005). While Australian universities are shifting from elite to mass education with an increasingly diverse student body (McKenzie and Schweitzer, 2001), the neo-liberal agenda underpinning educational policy has resulted in a new 'social imaginary', a perspective on education 'benefiting some individuals and communities while further marginalizing the poor and the socially disadvantaged' (Rizvi and Lingard, 2010: 185). It has narrowed the concept of education by overemphasising the value of market efficiency at the cost of equity and social justice. Alternative new social imaginaries are not only possible but also necessary to incorporate 'the construction of cosmopolitan citizenship that emphasizes collective well-being sutured across local, national and global dimensions' (ibid.: 202).

A globalised educational system by definition should be a heterogeneous system that embraces cultural differences of students. With over one in five students on campus from overseas, the Australian higher education sector urgently needs to address the implications of diversity in the student population and adopt a 'transcultural' perspective which no longer regards education as a single-dimensional, one-way flow of knowledge. No doubt the situation associated with newcomers' experience is complex, considering the macro-context of a globalised higher education sector. The current policies and pedagogies, in practice, are not heterogeneous but homogenised around a characteristically Western ideal-type. These policies and their underlying culturally determined social imagination cast doubt on the educability of international students, as they are automatically categorised as remedial and inferior to Western students by dint of their special cultural and linguistic backgrounds. Prescribed 'graduate attributes' are very often inappropriate to the specific needs of these international students, and fail to take into account what these students bring to their learning context.

Such homogenised learning imperatives alienate Asian international students, negatively affect their university experiences due to anxiety brought about by linguistic and cultural dislocation, and disproportionally discriminate against them in terms of the measurements of academic achievements (Tananuraksakul and Hall, 2011; Li, Chen and Duanmu, 2010; Song and Cadman, 2012; Holmes, 2004). Scholars have consistently argued that curricula must be internationalised, and have called for an examination of the appropriateness of the established pedagogical approaches in anglophone countries and the development of 'innovative and inventive curricula to meet the pressing challenges of students' diversity' (Webb, 2005; Ryan and Louie, 2007; Marginson, 2009; Song and Cadman, 2012: 3). The common 'add-on' response to include international examples to university curricula amounts to little more than a token effort. Serious endeavours should be made to integrate a global perspective into curriculum development, and such endeavours will involve engagement with 'global plurality in terms of sources of knowledge' (Webb, 2005: 110). A critical and reflexive stance is needed to interrogate the practice of essentialising critical thinking as a generic skill central to assessment criteria in higher education, and to explore alternative forms of knowledge (Yoneyama, 2012).

Educators and policymakers in Australian higher education could learn from the Confucian philosophy of education: first, that everyone equally has the *capacity* to be educated; and, second, that everyone equally has the *right* to be educated, *youjiao wulei* 有教无类. In other words, education should happen with(out) distinction (Song and Cadman, 2012). In the Australian context, this would mean that all students on campus, regardless of origin, are educable and should have equal access to quality education. Educational policies should recognise that international students are social and cultural as well as economic beings (Rizvi and Lingard, 2010). Further, educational practices should take into consideration the emotional, psychological and intellectual well-being of all students. A progressive pedagogy and curriculum should be grounded in, and should fully embrace, a new educational paradigm which takes into account the 'transcultural' flow of knowledge on campus, capitalises on international students' multilingual competencies and offers them equal access to 'quality-orientated education' (Ryan, 2010: 53).

References

Australian Bureau of Statistics, '4102.0 — Australian social trends, Dec 2011'. http://www.abs.gov.au/AUSSTATS/abs@.nsf/Lookup/4102.0Main+Features20Dec+2011#WHEREENROLMENT [accessed 23 November, 2012].

Australian Commonwealth Government. October 2012. *Australia in the Asian Century White Paper*.

Ballard, B. and J. Clanchy. 1984. *Study abroad: a manual for Asian students*. Selangor Darul Ehsan: Longman Malaysia SDN. BHD.

Ballard, B. and J. Clanchy. 1991. *Teaching students from overseas: a brief guide for lecturers and supervisors*. Melbourne: Longman Cheshire.

Ballard, B. and J. Clanchy. 1997. *Teaching international students: a brief guide for lecturers and supervisors*. Deakin, ACT: IDP Education Australia.

Barnett, R. 2012. 'Learning for an unknown future'. *Higher Education Research & Development*, 31(1): 65-77.

Bergman, J. 2012. 'A US degree at any cost'. *Time*, 27 August.

Brinkworth, R., B. McCann, C. Matthews and K. Nordström. 2009. 'First year expectations and experiences: student and teacher perspectives'. *Higher Education*, 58(2): 157-73.

Brown, L. and I. Holloway. 2008. 'The initial stage of the international sojourn: excitement or culture shock?' *British Journal of Guidance and Counselling*, 36(1): 33-49.

Burns, R.B. 1991. 'Study and stress among first year overseas students in an Australian university'. *Higher Education Research & Development*, 10(1): 61-77.

Clark, R. and S.N. Gieve. 2006. 'On the discursive construction of "The Chinese Learner"'. *Language, Culture and Curriculum*, 19(1): 54-73.

Day, L., K. Hanson, J. Maltby, C. Proctor and A. Wood. 2010. 'Hope uniquely predicts objective academic achievement above intelligence, personality, and previous academic achievement'. *Journal of Research in Personality*, 44(4): 550-3.

Devos, A. 2003. 'Academic standards, internationalisation, and the discursive construction of "the international student"'. *Higher Education Research & Development*, 22(2): 155-66.

Dewey, J. 1993. *The political writings*. Indianapolis: Hackett.

Doddington, C. 2009. 'Critical thinking as a source of respect for persons: a critique', in M. Mason (ed.), *Critical thinking and learning*. Hoboken, New Jersey: Wiley-Blackwell (109-19).

Evers, C.W. 2009. 'Culture, cognitive pluralism and rationality', in M. Mason (ed.), *Critical thinking and learning*. Hoboken, New Jersey: Wiley-Blackwell (25-43).

Foster, G. 2010. 'Teacher effects on student attrition and performance in mass-market tertiary education'. *Higher Education*, 60(3): 301-19.

Foster, G. 2011. 'Academics as educators in Australian universities: power, perceptions and institutions'. *Economic Papers: A Journal of Applied Economics and Policy*, 30(4): 568-75.

Foster, G. 2012. 'The impact of international students on measured learning and standards in Australian higher education'. *Economics of Education Review*, 31: 587-600.

Greenholtz, Joe. 2003. 'Socratic teachers and Confucian learners: examining the benefits and pitfalls of a year abroad'. *Language and Intercultural Communication*, 3(2): 122-30.

Gu, Q. and A. Maley. 2008. 'Changing places: a study of Chinese students in the UK'. *Language and Intercultural Communication*, 8(4): 224-45.

Henkel, M. 2005. 'Academic identity and autonomy in a changing policy environment'. *Higher Education*, 49(1-2): 155-76.

Hargreaves, A. and D. Shirley. 2009. *The fourth way: the inspiring future for educational change*. Thousand Oaks, CA: Corwin.

Heath, G. 2002. 'Introduction to symposium on globalisation'. *Educational Philosophy and Theory*, 32(1): 37-9.

Hil, R. 2012. *Whackademia: an insider's account of the troubled university*, Sydney: New South.

Holmes, P. 2004. 'Negotiating differences in learning and intercultural communication: ethnic Chinese students in a New Zealand university'. *Business Communication Quarterly*, 67(3): 294-307.

Kenway, J. and E. Bullen. 2003. 'Self-representations of international women postgraduate students in the global university "contact zone"'. *Gender and Education*, 15(1): 5-21.

Li, G., W. Chen and J.-L. Duanmu. 2010. 'Determinants of international students' academic performance: a comparison between Chinese and other international students'. *Journal of Studies in International Education*, 14(4): 389-405.

Liu, M. and J. Jackson. 2011. 'Reticence and anxiety in oral English lessons: a case study in China', in L. Jin and M. Cortazzi (eds), *Researching Chinese learners: skills, perceptions and intercultural adaptations*. New York: Palgrave Macmillan (119-37).

Mason, M. 2009. 'Critical thinking and learning', in M. Mason (ed.), *Critical thinking and learning*. Hoboken, New Jersey: Wiley-Blackwell (1-11).

Marginson, S. 2009. 'Hayekian neo-liberalism and academic freedom'. *Contemporary Readings in Law and Social Justice*, 1(1): 86-114.

Marginson, S. 2011. 'Higher education and public good'. *Higher Education Quarterly*, 65(4): 411-33.

Marginson, S. 2012. 'The impossibility of capitalist markets in higher education'. *Journal of Education Policy*, 28(3): 1-18.

McKenzie, K. and R. Schweitzer. 2001. 'Who succeeds at university? Factors predicting academic performance in first year Australian university students'. *Higher Education Research & Development*, 20(1): 21-33.

McKenzie, K., K. Gow and R. Schweitzer. 2004. 'Exploring first-year academic achievement through structural equation modelling'. *Higher Education Research & Development*, 23(1): 95-112.

Nagahara, M. 2011. 'Fazal Rizvi and Bob Lingard: globalizing education policy'. *Journal of Educational Change*, 12(3): 377-83.

Olsen, A. and Z. Burgess. 2006. 'The comparative academic performance of international students'. *International Higher Education*, 42(42): 11-12.

OECD (Organisation for Economic Co-operation and Development), n.d. 'Foreign/international students enrolled'. http://stats.oecd.org/Index.aspx?DatasetCode=RFOREIGN [accessed 28 November 2012].

Papastephanou, M. 2005. 'Globalisation, globalism and cosmopolitanism as an educational ideal'. *Educational Philosophy and Theory*, 37(4): 533-51.

Paul, R. and L. Elder. 2002. *Critical thinking: tools for taking charge of your professional and personal life*. New Jersey: Pearson Education Inc.

Peters, M. 2009. 'Kings of thinking, styles of reasoning', in M. Mason (ed.),

Critical thinking and learning. Hoboken, New Jersey: Wiley-Blackwell (12-24).

Pratt, D.D. 1992. 'Chinese conceptions of learning and teaching: a Westerner's attempt at understanding'. *International Journal of Lifelong Education*, 11(4): 301-19.

Ramburuth, P. and J. McCormick. 2001. 'Learning diversity in higher education: a comparative study of Asian international and Australian students'. *Higher Education*, 42(3): 333-50.

Rizvi, F. and B. Lingard. 2010. *Globalizing education policy*. London and New York: Routledge.

Ryan, J. 2010. '"Chinese learners": misconceptions and realities', in J. Ryan and G. Slethaug (eds), *International education and the Chinese learner*. Hong Kong: Hong Kong University Press (37-56).

Ryan, J. and Kam L. 2007. 'False dichotomy? "Western" and "Confucian" concepts of scholarship and learning'. *Educational Philosophy and Theory*, 39(4): 404-17.

Ryan, J. and G. Slethaug (eds). 2010. *International education and the Chinese learner*. Hong Kong: Hong Kong University Press.

Saunders, M. 2010. 'A disease killing our universities', *The Australian*, 23 June. http://www.theaustralian.com.au/higher-education/letters/a-disease-killing-our-universities/story-e6frgcox-1225882926319 [accessed 1 May 2013].

Shah, M., S. Nair and M. Wilson. 2011. 'Quality assurance in Australian higher education: historical and future development'. *Asia Pacific Education Review*, 12(3): 475-83.

Slethaug, G. 2010. 'Something happened while nobody was looking: the growth of international education and the Chinese learner', in J. Ryan and G. Slethaug (eds), *International education and the Chinese learner*. Hong Kong: Hong Kong University Press (15-36).

Shim, S.H. 2008. 'A philosophical investigation of the role of teachers: a synthesis of Plato, Confucius, Buber, and Freire'. *Teaching and Teacher Education*, 24(3): 515-35.

Siegel, H. 2006. 'Epistemological diversity and education research: much ado about nothing much?' *Educational Researcher*, 35(2): 3-12.

Song, X. and K. Cadman. 2012. 'Education with(out) distinction: beyond graduate attributes for Chinese international students'. *Higher Education Research & Development*, June: 1-14.

Spencer-Oatey, H. and Z. Xiong. 2006. 'Chinese students' psychological and sociocultural adjustments to Britain: an empirical study'. *Language, Culture and Curriculum*, 19(1): 37-53.

Tananuraksakul, N. and D. Hall. 2011. 'International students' emotional security and dignity in an Australian context: an aspect of psychological well-being'. *Journal of Research in International Education*, 10(2): 189-200.

Trounson, A. 2011. 'Free ride past language barrier'. *The Australian*, 16 March. http://www.theaustralian.com.au/higher-education/free-ride-past-language-barrier/story-e6frgcjx-1226022052413 [accessed 1 May 2013].

Turner, Y. 2006. 'Students from mainland China and critical thinking in postgraduate business and management degrees: teasing out tensions of culture, style and substance'. *International Journal of Management Education*, 5(1): 3-12.

US Department of State '100,000 Strong Initiative', n.d. http://www.state.gov/p/eap/regional/100000_strong/index.htm [accessed 23 November 2012].

Watkins, D.A. and J.A. Biggs (eds). 1996. *The Chinese learner: cultural, psychological and contextual influences*. Hong Kong and Melbourne: Comparative Education Research Centre and Australian Council for Educational Research.

Watkins, D.A. and J.A. Biggs. 2001. *Teaching the Chinese learner: psychological and pedagogical perspectives*. Hong Kong and Melbourne: Comparative Education Research Centre and Australian Council for Educational Research.

Webb, G. 2005. 'Internationalisation of curriculum: an institutional approach', in J. Carroll and Janette Ryan (eds), *Teaching international students: improving learning for all*. London: Routledge (109-18).

Willingham, D.T. 2008. 'Critical thinking: why is it so hard to teach?' *Arts Education Policy Review*, 109(4): 8-21.

Yoneyama, S. 2012. 'Critiquing critical thinking: Asia's contribution towards sociological conception', in K. Cadman and X. Song (eds), *Bridging transcultural divides: Asian languages and cultures in global higher education*. Adelaide: University of Adelaide Press (231-52).

Zhou, Y., D. Jindal-Snape, K. Topping and J. Todman. 2008. 'Theoretical models of culture shock and adaptation in international students in higher education'. *Studies in Higher Education*, 33(1): 63-75.

6 Relating experiences: Regional and Remote students in their first year at university

Michael Maeorg

Abstract

Developing positive relations with peers at university has long been recognised as a key to academic success for transitioning students. This chapter explores this issue from the perspective of Regional and Remote students in their first year at the University of Adelaide, through their experiences as related by them. While it might appear self-evident that these students would be particularly disadvantaged and 'deficient', relative to their urban peers, in terms of peer engagement and social integration, this chapter adopts a student-centred view of transition as 'becoming', and a 'strengths'-based focus, to demonstrate how students problematise such normative assumptions. Through their experiential narratives and commentaries, the students not only affirm their own competency and agency but also point to challenges faced by city school leavers in navigating the increasing diversity of peer social domains.

Introduction

Many studies have highlighted the importance of social integration and the development of positive relations and networks amongst peers as a key to academic success at — and, in particular, in the critical transition to — university. As James, Krause and Jennings (2010: 43) have reminded us:

> [t]he quality of students' engagement with peers in the university learning environment is a strong predictor of student persistence and retention. Peers play an important role in both social and academic integration in the first year.

Relating to fellow students — whether a group of supportive friends, a discipline-specific cohort of peers, or a 'significant other' — is demonstrably a key to becoming, to transitioning into, a successful university student.

This chapter explores this issue from the perspective of Regional and Remote students in their first year at the University of Adelaide.[1] In exploring this issue I draw upon the experiences, as related by them, of students participating in a project carried out in 2011-12 by LocuSAR[2] called 'Listening to Students from Regional and Remote Areas at the University of Adelaide: Experiences, Challenges and Strengths'.[3] As the name suggests the project was framed by a concern to capture the experiential dimension of the transition process; that is, to put the 'experience' — indeed 'experiences' — back in studies of the 'First Year Experience' which, ironically, are frequently based on quantitative rather than qualitative data. In this respect the project is responsive to recent calls to 'foreground students' lived reality' (Gale and Parker, 2011: 36). The project was also framed by an appreciation of students' strengths, rather than an assumption of their 'deficits', and as such contributes to a growing body of research that questions the application of a 'deficit model' to equity groups in higher education (e.g. Lawrence, 2002, 2005; Gale and Parker, 2011; Devlin, 2011). These orientations dovetail with a view of transition as 'becoming', recently articulated by Gale and Parker (2011). This student-centred approach locates transition to university in a broader framework of subjectively experienced lifelong transformation, and sees it as a complex and fluid process of identity construction and negotiation entailing multiple subjectivities and relations.

---

[1] While an important and related issue for Regional and Remote students is the development of support networks based 'in the city', external to the university and the student body, I focus here strictly on relations with fellow students both on campus and in off-campus contexts.

[2] LocuSAR, 'Locus of Social Analysis and Research', is a multi-disciplinary social research and consultancy team based in the School of Social Sciences at the University of Adelaide.

[3] This project was funded through an 'Equity and Diversity Grant' from the Gender, Equity and Diversity Committee at the University of Adelaide.

In terms of social integration and peer engagement, it might appear self-evident that Regional and Remote students transitioning to university would be particularly challenged and disadvantaged relative to the normatively constructed middle-class city student, fresh from high school. In the language of the deficit model, Regional and Remote students are assumed to be simply *lacking*. They come to university, for example, *without* the key resource of a cohort of high school friends, which most of their city peers take for granted. They also come *without* the kinds of experiences and understandings of urban-based sociality and social codes which might facilitate their engagement with city school leavers. While acknowledging the particular and very real challenges faced by Regional and Remote students on a city campus, and the value of and need for university initiatives to assist in addressing these challenges, this chapter seeks to shift the 'deficit' focus. It does so by adopting a student-centred approach which takes into account what students come with: the strengths, strategies and resources that students bring — and bring to bear — on these challenges. The approach also acknowledges students' agency in their active construction of identities and relationships in their process of 'becoming'.

This chapter demonstrates that, through their experiential narratives and commentaries, Regional and Remote students problematise the notion of 'deficit' and its application to them relative to normative 'city students'. Regional and Remote students see themselves as coming to university with 'socio-cultural competencies' (Lawrence, 2005), grounded in rural sociality and amplified by life experiences and scholarly interests, which they see as key in making connections with student peers from a variety of backgrounds. Students overwhelmingly reported establishing strong and supportive friendships with other Regional and Remote students, with students from interstate and overseas, and with local mature-age students, as a result of these competencies. By contrast, the students generally reported encountering significant difficulties in creating relations with city school leavers and in deepening these relations to a more substantial level. Significantly, the students did not see this as a reflection of inadequacies on their part. Rather, they attributed this to the socialisation and social circumstances of city school leavers, whom they characterised as having a more closed, unwelcoming and untrusting urban-based sociality, an inward-looking cohort mentality, relatively limited life experience and, often, a relative lack of commitment to their fields of study, all of which ill-equipped *them* to meet the challenge of meeting new people in this academic environment. The Regional and Remote students thus expressed continuing confidence in their own powers of relating to and befriending others, and represented themselves as having agency and choice in their selective fashioning of *their own* social circles according to *their own* emergent identities, interests, past experiences and future trajectories.

In this chapter I first provide a brief discussion of the importance of peer engagement at university, particularly in relation to studies of Regional and Remote students in transition. I then provide a brief outline of the project undertaken, focusing on its key theoretical and methodological orientations. I then present — as much as possible in their own words — accounts of students' experiences of relating to peers at university, and discuss how these narratives effectively problematise the assumption that Regional and Remote students are self-evidently 'in deficit' relative to their urban counterparts.

With a little help from my friends: engaging with peers at university

Issues surrounding the engagement of first-year students with tertiary institutions and their constituent structures, knowledges and communities have received enormous attention in studies of transition in recent years. Krause and Coates note that 'engagement is a broad phenomenon that encompasses *academic* as well as selected *non-academic* and *social* aspects of the student experience' (2008: 493; emphasis added). Within this broad phenomenon the critical importance of 'peer engagement' — students' academic and social engagement with their fellow students — has been recognised in the literature for some time. Already in 1995 McInnis and James concluded:

> Successful learning and the development of a positive view of the university experience did not occur in a social vacuum … [F]irst year students' orientation towards learning is in a formative stage and inextricably linked to the pursuit of identity and self-efficacy developed in a peer group. (1995: 119)

Krause and Coates draw upon contemporary anthropological theories of 'situated or distributed learning', whereby individuals learn by involvement in fields or communities of practice (e.g. Lave and Wenger, 1991; Hutchins, 1995), to emphasise that academic knowledge is developed in collaboration with peers (Krause and Coates, 2008: 501). In light of this they point to the need for a 'holistic view of student engagement' which includes 'academic and social dimensions' (ibid.: 500). They clarify that

> [t]he effectiveness with which students engage with the transition process is ... notably connected to their intellectual engagement and their out-of-class experiences. These include interactions with peers for reasons other than class assignments and involvement in extra-curricular activities. (Ibid.)

Establishing strong and supportive friendships which are relevant to and located in the academic learning environment but are also fostered and maintained beyond it in non-academic contexts is clearly one of the keys to successful transition. As James, Krause and Jennings note, 'peer connections such as these may help to provide a buffer against the possibilities of disengaging and dropping out' (2010: 44).

Regional and Remote students in higher education

A number of studies have drawn attention to the multiple difficulties and disadvantages confronting Regional and Remote students in terms of access to and participation in higher education, including issues surrounding peer engagement (e.g. King et al., 2011; Godden, 2008; Lewis et al., 2007; Woodlands, Makaev and Braham, 2006; Sawyer and Ellis, 2011; Drummond, Halsey and van Breda, 2011; Shanks, 2006; Alston and Kent, 2003; James et al., 2004; James et al., 1999; James, 2001, 2000). This literature tends to focus on the lack, or loss, of social networks for students transitioning to university, and the negative consequences of such a lack. Often this disadvantage is framed in terms of Regional and Remote students' general lack of the 'social and cultural capital' that their city counterparts possess. As Krause comments in relation to various equity groups,

> [s]tudents from disadvantaged backgrounds typically lack the social and cultural capital required to 'talk the talk' and 'walk the walk' at university ... They lack the social networks which provide avenues for participating in casual out-of-class conversations. (2005: 9)

King et al. note that, along with significant financial problems, 'a loss of social support and sense of community are commonly reported issues for rural students undergoing ... transition' (2011: 2). They go on to report that, in their study of relocating students, 55 per cent stated they had felt 'significant amounts of loneliness' (as compared with 6 per cent of non-relocating students) — in spite of the fact that all the students had made new friends at university and 77 per cent said that they felt part of the university community (ibid.: 4). Godden discusses, among a number of factors affecting rural participation in higher education, the 'culture shock' of transitioning alone to independent living, the city and the institution, and says that in her 2007 study 'every focus group, and 30% of the interviewees, reported that some rural young people experience homesickness and depression' (2008: 5). Likewise Lewis et al., in exploring financial difficulties for Regional and Remote students, comment on the 'social poverty' that results from moving to a new area knowing no one (2007: 540). Woodlands, Makaev and Braham report that 'anxiety' about not having a support network in the city and on campus is a key barrier, among other factors, for rural high school students considering university study (2006: 25-6).

Instructive and insightful as such studies are regarding these very concerning issues, the literature tends to ignore the strengths, strategies and resources which Regional and Remote students employ in facing and — in many cases — meeting the challenge of making connections with peers in the academic environment[4], as well as the experiential process of how this occurs. Having a student-oriented awareness of such challenges, strengths and experiences can valuably inform an understanding — for students, their families and tertiary institutions — of appropriate means of support and pathway options for Regional and Remote students in their navigation of peer social domains at university. This was one dimension of the research project undertaken.

'Listening to Students from Regional and Remote Areas': a brief outline

The project, 'Listening to Students from Regional and Remote Areas: Experiences, Challenges and Strengths', was framed, firstly, by a concern to capture the *experiences* of students transitioning to university. As noted earlier, there is a certain irony in

---

[4] It is interesting to note that, according to James, Krause and Jennings, Regional and Remote students today are not among groups 'significantly more likely to say they keep to themselves at university and avoid social contact' or 'significantly less likely to feel they belong to the university community' (2010: 41-2).

the fact that much, though by no means all, of the research conducted on the 'First Year *Experience*' has been founded on methodologies oriented to quantitative rather than qualitative data (surveys, questionnaires and so on). While such data has proven invaluable in informing our understanding of the transition process — and, for instance, is fruitfully drawn upon throughout this chapter — there is a place for more ethnographically oriented methods, such as semi-structured interviews and group discussions, in providing rich, detailed accounts of student-centred experiences, perspectives and opinions (see, for instance, Christie et al., 2008).

The project was also framed by an appreciation of the *strengths* students brought, and brought to bear, on the challenges posed by their transition to university, rather than by institution-centred assumptions of their 'deficits'. In this respect the project contributes to a growing body of research which contests 'normative accounts of student transition ... which represent variations from the norm as "deviant", "deficient"... "unruly" and "inadequate"' (Gale and Parker, 2011: 31). This ongoing scholarly work constitutes, in Lawrence's terms, the 'deficit discourse shift' (2002). A focus on students' strengths needs to be cognisant of Devlin's recent caution against research which locates students' success 'within an individual students' sphere of influence' and therefore 'can be based on the assumption that university success is primarily the responsibility of individual students'; this reproduces the 'deficit model' in that failure is seen as the fault of the 'deficient' student, and socio-cultural factors are erased from the analysis (2011: 5). In this project, we sought rather to explore how students' strengths, located in the socio-cultural worlds from which they had come, could play a role in aiding and abetting students' sense of agency in navigating university cultures. Such a sense of agency is 'of critical importance in higher education' as students forge their identities and career pathways (ibid.: 7). As Devlin suggests, an appreciation of non-traditional students' agency and strengths can lead to tertiary institutions 'thinking beyond the deficit model' of merely 'supporting students', to instead engaging in 'joint ventures' with them (ibid.).

These orientations resonate strongly with Gale and Parker's recent theorising of transition as 'becoming', a concept 'with a rich tradition in social theory and philosophy' (2011: 32). This approach draws upon the foundational work of theorists such as Deleuze and Guttari (1987) to contest notions of the 'linearity and normativity of life stages' implicit in the understanding of 'transition' as a 'transformation from one identity to another'. Instead, such processes are reconceptualised in terms of 'rhizomatic' movements involving 'multiplicities' in dynamic and heterogeneous composition (Gale and Parker, 2011: 32). Located in the broader context of subjectively experienced lifelong transformation, the transition to university is reconceived as neither 'a particular time of crisis', nor as 'part of a linear progression', nor as 'universally experienced and normalised' (ibid.: 31). Rather, in this student-centred, experience-oriented view, 'transitions' are always plural, and are fluid and complex processes of lifelong identity construction and negotiation entailing multiple subjectivities and relations. In light of this, as Gale and Parker say, 'the normative and the universal do not capture the diversity of student lives, their experiences of university or of universities themselves' (ibid.: 32). 'Transition as becoming' emphasises institutional change to accommodate difference.

Implementing the project: engaging with students

The project began with an initial survey designed to collect biographical and other information, and also to elicit students' feelings and experiences around a number of issues — related to study, finances, accommodation, friends and other matters — at the point of commencing tertiary study. Researchers engaged face-to-face with Regional and Remote students to invite their participation in the survey in a number of contexts. The first was SmoothStart Day, the first and main event of the SmoothStart program, which was held on the Friday before Orientation Week. Although the funding for the program, co-ordinated and managed by University of Adelaide staff in the Transition and Advisory Service in 2011, is at the time of writing uncertain, the program was originally specifically designed for students coming from rural, interstate and Adelaide metropolitan schools with few students going on to tertiary study. It incorporated information sessions, social networking activities and a peer mentoring system. Other contexts for engagement were at the University's 'Welcome Tent', and at the 'Humanities/Social Sciences Student Peer Mentor Transition Presentation', both during Orientation Week. The first survey, completed by 91 students, was followed by an online survey in mid-May, completed by 40 students, which sought to track students' feelings and experiences to that point.

The two surveys were used to inform the core phase of the research, which took place in September and October 2011[5], and which consisted of semi-structured interviews with 19 students (who participated individually or in pairs), eight of whom returned for further focus group discussions. While the researchers were careful to cover designated areas and issues, students were encouraged to engage in free-flowing discussions and to drive the agenda according to their interests and concerns.

The students came from a variety of socio-economic and educational backgrounds. While a number were from relatively affluent families whose members had previous educational experience of university, seven were the first in their families to come to university and had made, with their families, particular efforts and sacrifices in financial and other terms. Four of the students were commuting to university from rural areas in the vicinity of Adelaide while the remainder had relocated from various regions in South Australia, Victoria, Tasmania, New South Wales, the ACT and the Northern Territory. Three of the students were aged 18, nine were 19, three were 20, two were 21, one was 26, and one was 41.

Facing up: meeting the challenge of meeting people and making friends

The students were open and generous in their discussions of the challenges they faced in forming friendships at University, and the contexts, processes and strategies through which they met these challenges. We were careful to encourage students to distinguish between 'friends' whom they considered to be close and supportive, and more casual acquaintances. As the students' narratives mounted up, a distinctive pattern emerged: their *primary* relations tended overwhelmingly to be with 'non-traditional' students, such as other Regional and Remote students, relocating students from interstate or overseas, and local mature age students.[6]

---

[5] We acknowledged from the outset that, by conducting the core research at this time, we would most likely be listening to students who had been relatively successful in the transition process rather than those who had already dropped out or had become significantly disengaged. As indicated, this was in keeping with our concern to explore students' experiences of, and strengths in, navigating the transition process over their first year.

[6] The students did not specifically identify local low SES school leavers in their discussions. However, it is possible that many engaged with them at SmoothStart and in other contexts.

These relations were *primary* in two senses: they tended to be the first relations established, and also those that remained most central and substantial in their social networks. By contrast, the students experienced significant difficulties in making contact and forming friendships with local students fresh from high school, who often came to the university in cohorts of high school peers.

New kids in town: challenges

Arriving on campus without a ready-made network of friends created very real and particular challenges for the Regional and Remote students we listened to. As one student put it, 'at home, you start with family and friends' whereas 'here, the slate's wiped clean' and 'you have to build from the ground up' (male, 19, Music). Interestingly, even students who reported in the initial survey that they had 'no dramas' in making friends often revealed, in interviews, that they experienced some anxiety about the issue. This anxiety was amplified by the contrast with local school leavers, who evidently knew each other from day one. As one student said:

> [o]n the first day I was, like, freaking out, I'm like, Where's all the country people? ... You could see all the Adelaide people sitting and talking to each other. (Female, 19, Music Education)

Students also felt intimidated by the sheer number of students on campus and in lectures, as opposed to the small student populations and class sizes of rural schools. One student described her experience of a Maths lecture of 500 students, compared to her high school Maths class of six, in the following terms:

> Sometimes I find it hard to talk to people I don't know, when you sort of walk into a lecture and you're, like, Hey ... What else do I say? (Female, 19, Architectural Engineering)

Moreover, students described their rural high schools as institutions embedded in close-knit community ties, characterised by relations of friendship amongst students and staff extending — in fact, based — beyond the classroom. Students experienced the university environment, by contrast, as particularly impersonal, and therefore confronting in terms of creating friendships. As one student put it, the 'key issue' was 'not having a personal relationship with everyone in the room [i.e. classroom]', including students and teachers.

> At home you run into your teachers at the pub, you serve them at work on the weekend, they come over for dinner, like it's very different walking into a tute and not knowing your tutor ... (Female, 20, Development Studies)

Students experienced varying degrees of challenge in making friends. For instance, those who were staying in university accommodation, and/or doing courses with significant numbers of Regional and Remote students (such as Agricultural Science and Veterinary Science), and/or who participated in SmoothStart, made connections which deepened to supportive friendships in the first few weeks. For other students the process tended to be longer and more difficult:

> For the whole of first semester, like, I was just by myself, like, I don't really have any problems with that, I'm happy to be by myself, but it's not as good as eating your lunch with friends and that sort of thing ... (Male, 26, Development Studies)

Students in this position often expressed frustration at the lack of opportunities to build friendships in the course of the day-to-day round of lectures and tutorials. As one student said:

> [t]here are so many interesting people out there who are to me so inaccessible ... [I]t's a real shame ... [B]y the end of my semester in History we were a tight little tute group, and there were some really interesting people in there, but you don't find out who they are until you're all ready to move on. Socially it's really challenging. (Female, 41, International Studies/Arts)

Students particularly commented on how difficult it was to transform the casual interactions with peers, which took place in contexts such as tutorials, into more profound relations of friendship. As one student put it,

> [i]t's relatively easy to meet people in tutes and, like, become 'uni friends', but sometimes it can be quite hard to become 'outside uni friends', especially if you don't already have a group of friends. (Female, 20, Arts)

This comment points to the key issue underlying many of the Regional and Remote students' challenges in forming friendships: the observation that local school leavers tended to keep to their own pre-existing groups. As the student quoted above went on to elaborate,

> [e]veryone in Adelaide seems to have gone through high school together and now be doing the same tutes together, and it's kind of intimidating to approach three people as opposed to approaching one person. (Female, 20, Arts)

As another student explained:

> [t]hey've grown up together and ... they've got their little groups and cliques ... [I]t's always difficult to break into them, I guess ... whereas I think in the country, because the groups are a lot smaller, you have to be more welcoming. (Male, 26, Development Studies)

In addition, a particular challenge for some students commuting to university from surrounding rural areas was that the distance and time involved made it more difficult to establish and deepen relations with university peers through after-hours and off-campus interaction. Additionally, the fact that these students already had friendship networks at hand mitigated their sense of need to create new friendships.

Breaking the ice: making connections and forming friendships

By the time of the interviews in the second semester the students had, almost uniformly, established their own social circles at university anchored by key friendships. This was particularly the case with relocating students. Bucking this trend to some extent, as indicated above, were a couple of commuting students, both of whom had pre-existing social networks and who actually expressed satisfaction with their more limited social sphere at university. As one of these students explained,

> I'm not really, really close friends with anyone at uni, but if I run into someone in a lecture, or something, or sit down, I'll chat ... [Study is] easier, cos there's no distractions ... I like it as it is. (Male, 20, Aerospace/Engineering)

Here, I discuss the contexts, strategies and processes, both on and off campus, through which the students made connections and developed relations of friendship with fellow students.[7]

SmoothStart

Ten of the students we listened to participated in SmoothStart Day in 2011. They generally gave extremely enthusiastic responses to the event as a whole and, in particular, as an opportunity to meet peers and form friendships. The majority of

---

[7] These all involved face-to-face interactions. Students emphasised that they communicated online to maintain, rather than to establish and build, relations with peers.

participants made good friends with whom they were still in close contact at the time of the interviews. While a couple of students reported that they had made 'no close friends' through SmoothStart, they nevertheless said that it was 'comforting' and 'reassuring' to see familiar faces during Orientation Week and in the first few weeks at university as a result of the experience.

For many students, SmoothStart was the key to the development of their social worlds at university. One student said of the day:

> All of my best friends I have now are all through that — I have, like, a really good group of, I don't know, 10 of us, and we all study together and socialise together and so that just worked really well ... If I hadn't done that I would've really struggled ... It meant that during O-Week you'd sort of see someone and then spend the day with them. (Female, 19, Architectural Engineering)

According to another student, SmoothStart was the

> best thing I could have done ... I made friends and was able to get the feel of uni ... and talk to people who are like me — first years from a bit further away. (Female, 19, Psychology)

She went on to say that through SmoothStart she made her 'best friend down here [at Uni], from Victoria'.

Students talked about how their SmoothStart experiences not only gave them immediate connections and friendships but also provided the basis for further expansion of their social circles. As one student said:

> I made a friend there [at SmoothStart], who was doing the same course, and then from there it kind of accelerated, now I'm friends with, like, second years and third years, and I've made more friends now than I have in [my home town]. (Female, 19, Music Education)

Crucially, making connections and friendships through SmoothStart provided students with a sense of support and, with that, the confidence to navigate their way socially through their first few weeks at university. As the student quoted above put it,

> You had *someone there*, you didn't have no one on the first day of Uni, you had *someone there* to support you. (Female, 19, Music Education; emphases as spoken)

University accommodation

Five of the students we listened to were staying in university accommodation such as colleges and apartment complexes. Additionally, at the time of the interviews another student was in the process of moving into a university-run student lodge.[8] All the students found these institutions to be an ideal context for developing relations with peers. They reported forming good, supportive friendships with domestic students from Regional and Remote areas and various Australian capital cities, and with international students from various countries. As one student put it,

> It's awesome ... amazing, like, wow, I'm meeting so many fantastic amazing people ... [O]ne girl, her Dad's a gynaecologist from Germany and she's got a house in Hong Kong ... she's such a cool person ... [A]nother girl, her Dad's a psychiatrist and lives in Melbourne, and other people come from Darwin or, y'know, just rural South Australia ... and a couple of people from Malaysia and Singapore. (Female, 21, Health Sciences)

Students uniformly said that it was 'easy' meeting people and making friends in this environment. One student described how he made 'good friends' shortly after his arrival when some guys asked him to 'come up for a party' (male, 19, Law). Another student summed up:

> At college, you just knock on someone's door ... you have college events ...
> or you go out with a group. (Female, 19, Veterinary Science)

In addition, two of the students were in share houses with fellow Regional and Remote students. They described these circumstances as very supportive and a good base from which to expand their friendship networks.

Campus life

An important context for making friends was in the general flow of student life on campus, in the daily round of lectures, tutorials, workshops and practicals. For students without the opportunities afforded by other circumstances, this was the main avenue for making friends:

---

[8] James, Krause and Jennings found that 32 per cent of Regional and Remote students stay in university accommodation (2010: 66).

> Most of the friends I've made are from tutes or lectures or people I've just sat with and said "Hi" to … and friends of friends. (Female, 20, Development Studies)

As indicated earlier, the four students in courses with significant numbers of other Regional and Remote students tended to make friends particularly quickly and easily. A student of Veterinary Science explained that she had made virtually all her friends through her course, and that 'most of them are from rural areas far from Adelaide'. She elaborated that

> [i]t's a big group of rural people doing this course … [M]ost people you talk to have had horses or sheep or cattle. (Female, 18)

Similarly, an Agricultural Science student said:

> We're all from a rural background and we all heap shit on each other all the time … We've got a pretty good group with Ag, so it's been good being able to make friends pretty easily. (Male, 19)

For other students, the process of making friends through their course-based activities tended to be more gradual, but did eventually happen. As a Health Science student said:

> Gradually, through the tutes and practicals you'd just get to know a few people better and then you find out, wow, I really like this person, so you'd just naturally gravitate towards them. (Female, 21)

Similarly, a Development Studies student explained:

> The people I hang out with now were in my tutorials last semester … so I've kind of got to know them a little bit cos we have spent more time together, yeah, and now we've got a few of the same subjects so we hang out together. (Male, 26)

A few students claimed to find it easy to make friends through such contexts. For instance, a Law student said that he had 'no problems' making friends because he was 'so talkative in tutes' (male, 19). In similar vein an Aerospace/Civil Engineering student explained:

> I think just being around the place you're just making friends all the time, and if you're gonna hang around with new people in lectures and stuff there's always gonna be a time when you talk to someone next to you … so the social side of things is pretty easy. (Male, 18)

However, these instances tended to be the exception rather than the rule; for many students the process was quite lengthy and difficult, as indicated earlier. Students did comment on the fact that more interactive styles of pedagogic activity — team-building projects, musical ensembles, well-conducted tutorials promoting collegiality — helped greatly in breaking the ice and providing opportunities for making friends. In addition, students were able to develop friendships through various kinds of 'extra-curricular' university contexts: sporting clubs (particularly football), interest clubs (such as Science Fiction, Psychology, Film) and the University Bar.

Not really meeting the locals: patterns of friendship

In these narratives, the distinctive pattern that emerged was that the students tended to form their primary relations of friendship with students other than local school leavers. The previous discussion has already provided some indications of this general pattern, particularly with regard to contexts of interaction such as SmoothStart, university accommodation and courses attracting significant numbers of Regional and Remote students. Here I provide some more pointed examples from other contexts of campus interaction, including other courses.

One student in Marine Biology recounted how she had made some 'really good mates' on campus in first semester, explaining that

> country students all — y'know, we have similar interests and — I met them, so I met about … 7 or so girls and guys that are doing Ag[ricultural] Science and they all grew up in the regional South Australian areas as well … [N]ow this semester [through the course] I've made a couple of good friends … who are a bit older, 30 and 40, but, I guess having a bit more maturity than most 21-year-olds, we get along really well. (Female, 21)

She clarified that both were from Adelaide. Another student explained that, as well as developing friendships with students from various backgrounds in university accommodation, she had made friends through her course, thus developing

> a good network … actually a lot of mature age students, which is good — I'm the baby of the group … They say, 'You should be hanging out with younger people' — but nah, they're cool, they're fine. (Female, 21, Health Sciences)

She clarified that the students were in their 30s and 40s, from Adelaide. Another student, herself in her 40s, talked about how she had struggled to form 'relationships of substance' until she met younger, country students:

> I've started to make country kid friends who are infinitely far more sensible, far more polite, and I've really struggled cos a lot of the students in my tutorials had tended to be young, male, privately educated, vapid … I've really, really struggled … until I finally made some younger friends that were country kids. (Female, 41, International Studies/Arts)

A student studying Music, who described himself as 'socialis[ing] better with people who are a bit older', commented:

> Country bumpkins in the music course are a bit of a dying breed, so you have to make do with who's there … A few of the people in their 20s, they're really good, they're really interesting to talk to … but some of the people who are straight from high school, they're a bit more self-obsessed. (Male, 19)

A Development Studies student (male, 26) explained that he had 'struggled' to form friendships throughout first semester until befriending two fellow mature-age students, also in their 20s, while an Arts student (female, 20) had similarly 'struggled' until she befriended students from the University of Canterbury, who had been invited to study at the University of Adelaide as a consequence of the earthquake in Christchurch, New Zealand, in February 2011.

These instances, and those discussed earlier, point to the overwhelming tendency on the part of the students to form their primary relationships with students who were not local, and — amongst locals — with mature-age students, rather than school leavers. Students who had 'missed out' on particular contexts for meeting other Regional and Remote and relocating students appear to have connected particularly with local 'mature-agers'. While some students did say that they had made 'good friends' amongst local school leavers, this generally involved having a circle of friends from a variety of groups, in which the central, anchoring friendships tended to be with other non-traditional students.

Measuring up: relative strengths

In their successful navigation of university social life and formation of peer networks with the diversity of student groups indicated, the Regional and Remote students we listened to understood themselves to be drawing on strengths and resources *which they brought with them* from their rural socialisation and related experiences. Following Lawrence (2002, 2005), I characterise these strengths and resources as 'socio-cultural competencies'.[9] In the context of her reconceptualisation of 'the contemporary university' as 'an unfamiliar and dynamic culture, encompassing a multiplicity of sub-cultures, each with their own discourses and languages' (2002: 6), Lawrence draws on cross-cultural communication theory to emphasise the crucial role of 'socio-cultural competencies' in enabling transitioning students to cross sub-cultural barriers and engage with these multiple discourses. These discourses may be administrative, technological or academic (for example, faculty, department, discipline, subject and so on), and may also include a variety of 'student discourses' such as 'school leaver, mature-age, international, on-campus, external' and 'online' (2005: 247). Lawrence highlights socio-cultural competencies such as 'seeking help and information', 'participating in a group' and 'making social contact' (2002: 6), and with respect to the latter elaborates:

> The ability to make social contact and social conversation, in socially and culturally appropriate ways, across a multiplicity and diversity of cultural groups is ... an essential ability for a new student. This competency is crucial as it facilitates the development of study groups, writing groups or learning circles, as well as study partners, mentors and friends, and perhaps, the support of a 'significant other'. (2002: 8)

The students we listened to represented themselves as having an evolving mastery of competencies such as these, and as deploying them to positive effect in forming their friendship circles. They saw their competencies as grounded in their long-term experience of rural sociality — that is, their socialisation as rural people — amplified by their breadth and diversity of life experiences in rural and other contexts. They also regarded their passion and commitment to their respective fields of study as a source of their capacity to form new friendships in this academic context. They saw local school leavers, by contrast, as relatively underdeveloped in terms of such socio-cultural competencies and as 'keeping to themselves' in cohorts of peers from high school. They attributed this to urban forms of sociality and socialisation, relatively limited life experience, and — sometimes — a relative lack of scholarly interest, which tended against propelling students out of their established social comfort zones to meet new peers in their chosen fields of study.

---

[9] Lawrence also refers to these as 'interpersonal communication competencies' (2000).

Rural sociality

Above all, students saw their experience of being born and raised in rural areas and communities as the key source of their interpersonal communication competencies. They described rural social codes and etiquette as open, welcoming and friendly. By contrast, they characterised city sociality as more closed, inward-looking and untrusting. As one student explained,

> If I recognise someone I try and say hello, just try and, like, break the ice I suppose … I've just tried to say G'day to people that are in my tutes and that sort of thing … I think country people are a lot more like that, generally … People will just say G'day and that sort of thing, like if you're walking along you say G'day and have a chat, whereas here everyone's a bit more head down and, I guess, less personal. (Male, 26, Development Studies)

As another student put it:

> I'm not gonna be rude to city people, but … you're brought up when you're in a rural area that you just talk to people, that's just what you do … whereas Adelaide's kind of got more of that Stranger Danger kind of thing going on … We're brought up to talk to everyone, really, that's just part of living out in rural areas. (Female, 18, Veterinary Science)

One student described how 'awkward' it was to ask city students she'd met in tutorials to catch up socially, saying it was 'like asking someone out on a date, but a "friend-date"' (female, 20, Arts).

Students described their hometown communities as close-knit social domains in which engagement across the divides of age, occupation, class, gender and so on was part and parcel of 'talking to everyone'. Students saw themselves, as a result, as skilled in communicating respectfully and appropriately across social boundaries, and in social situations generally. As one 19-year-old student said:

> Back in [my hometown] I associated with people who were older … like, Mum and Dad would have friends over all the time … I don't believe in sitting at the table with your mobile phone … I was brought up not like that … If someone's there in front of you, you devote that time to them … otherwise it's disrespectful. (Male, Music)

Similarly, a female student compared the easy familiarity between her male and female friends in her social circle back home with her involvement in an exclusively female group of young city students. As she put it:

> I miss my boys! … [H]ere I've got all girl friends, and that's a big difference for me … [H]aving, like, feminine company all the time is very different for me. (Female, 20, Development Studies)

Students described rural styles of social engagement as collaborative and communal, as opposed to the more individualistic, self-focused, competitive styles of engagement in the city, which they saw as discouraging the formation of new friendships. As one student said, 'there's more of a sense of community in towns … you watch everyone's back', whereas 'for city people, life's a competition — they'll have to one-up you' (male, 19, Music). Similarly, another student commented:

> Everyone's trying to be the smart kid … not jumping on top of each other or anything, but everyone's trying to impress everyone else in the room. That's very odd for us cos we just sort of dag around in our gum boots. (Female, 20, Development Studies)

Life experiences

The Regional and Remote students we listened to generally saw themselves as having considerable 'life experience' — particularly relative to most urban school leavers — and saw this as augmenting their capabilities to meet and engage effectively with others. This was often linked to the fact that they tended to be older than their urban peers: seven of the 19 students were no longer teenagers.[10] Even students who had come to university directly from high school generally talked about having had a significant degree and diversity of life experience: for instance, they had completed their final year over two years, and/or been involved in considerable part-time work (often to raise money for their university and relocation costs), and/or been engaged in overseas student exchange programs, and/or moved school or home frequently in rural areas as well as to and from capital cities.

The students overall had worked and/or undergone training in a great variety of occupations and fields, including farming, shearing, nursing, the navy, tourism, hospitality and retail. Some had volunteered for development and charity

---

[10] James, Krause and Jennings note that Regional and Remote students are more likely to be older than urban students; this is partly related to taking a gap year, which 26 per cent of the students surveyed had done (2010: 66).

organisations in Australia and overseas. Many had worked, studied or holidayed extensively throughout Australia and in various parts of the world, including South America, South Asia, South-East Asia, Europe, Japan and the Pacific. For three of the students, too, this was their second attempt at university study. In short, while students' experiences varied according to multiple factors, including their socio-economic backgrounds, their biographies as they related them to us were all interwoven with complex patterns of movement and transition across diverse geographical and social domains, which they understood as characteristic of their lived reality as people in and from regional and remote areas.

The students saw these kinds of experiences as a useful 'training ground' for developing, or extending, the maturity, confidence and skills required to engage with others. For instance, one student commented:

> [Because of] my experience in tourism, I've always been confident in approaching people and talking to them. (Female, 21, Marine Biology)

Another student who had spent a year as an exchange student in Argentina commented:

> Moving … to Argentina is a lot more of a change than moving to Adelaide, so … it makes meeting people and stuff a bit easier, cos I'm sort of comfortable with not really knowing people and walking up to a bunch. (Female, 20, Development Studies)

As another student said:

> I've moved house like a zillion times … and been to like five different schools … so, yeah, it was kind of easy to come to Uni and start talking to people. (Female, 19, Veterinary Science)

Scholarly interests

The students overwhelmingly expressed a strong passion and commitment to their chosen fields of study, typically making comments such as 'I know I'm in the right degree', 'I'm studying what I love', and so on. This scholarly commitment was linked, in part, with life experiences; as one student said, a gap of two years 'gave me a chance to grow up a bit more and have more of a focus about where I want to end up in my career' (female, 21, Marine Biology). More particularly, however, this commitment was directly linked to students' social and geographical circumstances as people living in and coming from regional and remote areas. The sheer enormity of the emotional and financial investment that the students, with the support of their families, had to make in relocating (or commuting) to the city and studying at university, meant that they tended to be particularly clear, committed and passionate about their chosen studies. This relative clarity of academic purpose in comparison with their urban counterparts has been noted for Regional and Remote students generally (e.g. James, Krause and Jennings, 2010: 19, 38).

Students found that their academic passions, in many cases, augmented their capacities for interpersonal communication with fellow students by providing a shared interest and discourse which facilitated the crossing of the social divides between them. As one student said of her course:

> [t]here's more people with the same interests as me and we all have the same focus of music. (Female, 19, Music Education)

Another student commented:

> Studying science, everyone's got that similar interest ... so it's quite easy to break the ice and talk to people. (Female, 21, Marine Biology)

While this was an asset in making connections with select peers — with academic 'kindred spirits' — students reported that it did not necessarily facilitate relationship-building with many urban school leavers, who were often characterised as relatively less committed to their fields of study.[11] In the words of one student:

> I'm interested in what we're learning about ... I noticed that ... a lot of the young crew [city school leavers] generally don't want to do the readings and that, whereas a lot of the readings I find pretty interesting. (Male, 26, Development Studies)

Notwithstanding this, he had made 'good friends' through the course as he had found 'a lot of like-mindedness' — 'social awareness' and 'caringness' — amongst students of 'a mix of ages and ethnicities'.

Problematising deficit: competency, agency and identity

One of the students in our study, who had been brought up in Adelaide and had attended university for a short time after high school before spending the bulk of

---

[11] James, Krause and Jennings report that, on average, Regional and Remote students spend 11.5 hours on private study compared with 9.9 hours for urban students (2010: 38).

her adult life living and working in regional and remote areas, was able to offer an interesting comparative viewpoint:

> I'm so used to country kids — how respectful they are, how independent they are, how resourceful they are, how grown-up they are, and the different manners in the country and how people behave, and the strong community networks and all that sort of stuff, and you come into the city — I mean, people are rude, they are incredibly rude … and I guess … a lot of [young city students] are coming from — fed from — private schools, who are incredibly vapid and who have been, I think, babied to a degree. (Female, 41, International Studies/Arts)

While this is a singularly strident criticism of normative, middle-class city school leavers, it does reflect the views shared by Regional and Remote students more broadly regarding the multiple competencies which they bring to bear on the challenges of relating with peers at university, and the sources of these competencies in their rural socialisation and related experiences. It also highlights their perception of local school leavers as having their own challenges to meet, lessons to learn and competencies to master in this domain. Through this discourse, the Regional and Remote students effectively confound and problematise the notion that they are the students who are self-evidently 'in deficit' relative to their city counterparts.

The students, in consequence, and in spite of the difficulties that they had often encountered, expressed continuing confidence in themselves and in their powers of relating to and befriending others. They represented themselves as having agency and choice in their fashioning of their social worlds according to the kinds of people with whom they wished to relate, and the kinds of people they themselves sought to become. Their emergent identities and relational worlds were reflections of the diverse roads they had travelled to come to university and the pathways they envisaged into the future in an ongoing process of 'becoming' (Gale and Parker, 2011). If there was little or no room in these worlds for local school leavers, who — in the view of the Regional and Remote students — often had a lot to learn about meeting people and making friends, then so be it; the loss, ultimately, was not theirs. As one student said:

> I associate with people who I want to associate with, and who want to associate with me, rather than chasing down people … [L]et them come to me and if not, I'll just do my own thing. (Male, 19, Music)

Concluding remarks

The Regional and Remote students we listened to had all drawn upon and used significant strengths and competencies in actively creating their own distinctive social worlds at university. However, it was noteworthy that students who had not had the advantage of SmoothStart, university accommodation or courses with significant numbers of other Regional and Remote students in them had struggled for long periods to form friendships. This underscores the importance of tertiary institutions providing appropriate contexts for peer interaction and engagement for students in this equity group. This should not be seen as catering to the 'deficits' of students but as providing contexts in which students' strengths — their socio-cultural competencies — can be deployed and expressed. SmoothStart has proven to be one such context. As the co-ordinating university staff have progressively taken more of a 'back seat' role and encouraged previous participants — now experienced university students — to conceive, structure and deliver sessions and activities, SmoothStart has evolved as an exemplary instance of a 'joint venture' (Devlin, 2011) between the institution and non-traditional student groups.

This study also points to the need for universities to go further in addressing issues of 'social inclusion' for all students, and suggests that local school leavers may be the ones particularly challenged in 'opening out' to the increasing diversity of the student population. This calls for 'joint ventures' between universities and both their traditional and non-traditional student bodies.

References

Alston, M. and J. Kent. 2003. 'Educational access for Australia's rural young people: a case of social exclusion'. *Australian Journal of Education*, 47(1): 5-17.

Christie, H., L. Tett, V.E. Cree, J. Hounsell and V. McCune. 2008. '"A real rollercoaster of confidence and emotions": learning to be a university student'. *Studies in Higher Education*, 33(5): 567-81.

Deleuze, G. and F. Guattari. 1987. *A thousand plateaus: capitalism and schizophrenia*. Minneapolis and London: University of Minnesota Press.

Devlin, M. 2011. 'Bridging socio-cultural incongruity: conceptualizing the success of students from low socio-economic backgrounds in Australian higher education'. *Studies in Higher Education*, 1-11. http://dx.doi.org/10.1080/03075079.2011.613991 [accessed 12 January 2012].

Drummond, A., R.J. Halsey and M. van Breda. 2011. 'The perceived importance of University presence in rural South Australia'. *Education in Rural Australia*, 21(2): 1-18.

Gale, T. and S. Parker. 2011. *Good practice report: student transition into higher education*. Surry Hills, NSW: Australian Learning and Teaching Council (Australian Government: Department of Education, Employment and Workplace Relations).

Godden, N. 2008. *The rural right to education: submission to the 2008 review of Australian higher education*. Melbourne: Monash University.

Hutchins, E. 1995. *Cognition in the wild*. Cambridge, MA: MIT Press.

James, R. 2000. 'Non-traditional students in Australian higher education: persistent inequities and the new ideology of "student choice"'. *Tertiary Education and Management*, 6: 105-18.

James, R. 2001. 'Participation disadvantage in Australian higher education: an analysis of some effects of geographical isolation and socioeconomic status'. *Higher Education*, 42(4): 455-72.

James, R., G. Baldwin, H. Coates, K.-L. Krause and C. McInnis. 2004. *Analysis of equity groups in higher education, 1991-2002*. Melbourne: Centre for the Study of Higher Education, University of Melbourne.

James, R., K.-L. Krause and C. Jennings. 2010. *The first year experience in Australian universities: findings from 1994-2009*. Melbourne: Centre for the Study of Higher Education, University of Melbourne.

James, R., J. Wyn, G. Baldwin, G. Hepworth, C. McInnis and A. Stephanou. 1999. *Rural and isolated school students and their higher education choices: a re-examination of student location, socioeconomic background and educational advantage and disadvantage*. Melbourne: Centre for the Study of Higher Education and Youth Research Centre, University of Melbourne.

King, S., R. Garrett, A. Wrench and N. Lewis. 2011. 'The loneliness of relocating: does the transition to university pose a significant health risk for rural and isolated students?' Conference paper. *First Year in Higher Education Conference*, Queensland University of Technology,

29 June-1 July, Brisbane.

Krause, K.-E. 2005. 'Understanding and promoting student engagement in university learning communities'. Keynote address. *Sharing scholarship in learning and teaching: engaging students*, James Cook University Symposium, 21-2 September, Townsville/Cairns.

Krause, K.-L. and H. Coates. 2008. 'Students' engagement in first year university', *Assessment & Evaluation in Higher Education*, 33(5): 493-505.

Lave, J. and E. Wenger. 1991. *Situated learning: legitimate peripheral participation*. Cambridge: Cambridge University Press.

Lawrence, J. 2000. 'Rethinking diversity: re-theorising transition as a process of engaging, negotiating and mastering the discourses and multiliteracies of an unfamiliar culture rather than as a problem of deficit'. Conference paper. *4th Pacific Rim First Year in Higher Education Conference: Creating Futures for a New Millennium*, 5-7 July, Brisbane.

Lawrence, J. 2002. 'The "Deficit-Discourse Shift": university teachers and their role in helping first year students persevere and succeed in the new university culture'. Conference paper. *6th Pacific Rim First Year in Higher Education Conference: Changing Agendas 'Te Ao Hurihuri'*, 8-10 July, Christchurch, New Zealand.

Lawrence, J. 2005. 'Addressing diversity in higher education: two models for facilitating student engagement and mastery', in A. Brew and C. Asmar (eds), *Higher education in a changing world: annual conference proceedings of the Higher Education Research and Development Society of Australia, 3-6 July 2005*, Sydney, Australia: HERDSA (243-52).

Lewis, C., V. Dickson-Smith, L. Talbot and P. Snow. 2007. 'Regional tertiary students and living away from home: a priceless experience that costs too much?' *The Australian Journal of Social Issues*, 42 (4): 531-47.

McInnis, C. and R. James. 1995. *First year on campus — diversity in the initial experiences of Australian undergraduates*. Melbourne: Centre for the Study of Higher Education, University of Melbourne.

Sawyer, J. and B. Ellis. 2011. 'An Investigation into why students from regional South Australia choose to study business programs in the capital city'. *Education in Rural Australia*, 21(2): 125-48.

Shanks, P.-A. 2006. 'A critical policy analysis of the Crossroads Review:

implications for higher education in regional Western Australia'. Master of Education Thesis, Murdoch University.

Woodlands, J., L. Makaev and K. Braham. 2006. *Going to university: rural and regional students' perceptions of studying in Adelaide*. Report prepared for the Cowan Grant. Adelaide: Online Media Unit, South Australian Policy Online, The University of Adelaide.

Part 3

Realising: transformations on campus

7 The University of Adelaide Student Learning Hub: a case study of education co-creation

Pascale Quester, Kendra Backstrom and Slavka Kovacevic

Abstract

In 2009, the University of Adelaide embarked on a co-creation process, with the aim of providing the best on-campus experience within the Australian national tertiary sector for all our students. Completed in September 2011, on time and on budget, the project involved more than 9,000 individual student hours of consultation and over 3,000 hours of staff participation and discussion, and acted as a catalyst for a profound change in the relationship between the university and its students.

The construction of a $41.8 million student learning hub (the Hub) enabled the university to develop and implement an innovative method for consulting with its student population. By involving the university-wide student cohort, via a number of mechanisms throughout the life of the project, the university has given ownership of the Hub's final outcome to those for whom it is intended, the students.

Located in the 'heart' of the university's main campus on North Terrace, the new dedicated learning space now supports up to 25,000 undergraduate and postgraduate students enrolled at the University of Adelaide. It brings together informal learning and social spaces with student information services and food and service retail outlets. It integrates with the Barr Smith Library and provides new connections through to existing lecture theatres and across campus.

Background

In the past five to ten years, significant changes made within the Australian higher education sector have impacted on the University of Adelaide. Considerable growth in student numbers, including international student numbers, has placed increased pressure on aging facilities. There has also been a generational change in terms of attitudes, expectations and learning behaviours. The Learning Hub Project aimed to accommodate this modern, diverse student cohort and update the campus environment with a facility dedicated to support their learning activities and requirements.

In September 2008, the University of Adelaide Council approved the allocation of the Better Universities Renewal Fund (B.U.R.F.) money, received from the Federal Government, towards the redevelopment of Hughes Plaza as a student learning hub. The concept of the Learning Hub was to construct a purpose-built 'informal learning' space for students, enabling them to remain on campus to study. Informal learning being the self-directed learning activities that students undertake outside their formal or teacher-led classes (Marsick and Watkins, 2011), the Learning Hub would provide a flexible space that would accommodate various ways in which students could undertake their learning activities.

Although in the past the University had provided many different spaces for students to study outside their class contact times, these spaces (such as student common rooms) were gradually being re-purposed as staff offices or teaching spaces, in order to accommodate the expediential growth in student and staff numbers which the University had experienced in the past five to seven years. With the loss of these informal spaces, more and more pressure was placed on the Barr Smith Library to provide study facilities, as students struggled to find places to study either individually or in groups whilst on campus.

The introduction of Voluntary Student Unionism (V.S.U.)[1] also had a

---

[1] Until 1 July 2006, Australian universities required that students become a member of a student organisation that charged a fee for services provided by that organisation on campus — for example, cheap food outlets. The Federal Liberal Government passed legislation on 9 December 2005 to abolish these 'Compulsory Up-front Student Union Fees' because the Government regarded it as a form of forced unionisation. While the Federal Labor Government in 2012 legislated for universities to again be able to collect fees from students for on-campus services — fees that are not able to be

significant impact on campus life, with many social activities disappearing for lack of funding and students retreating off campus as soon as their formal classes were finished. Consequently, this resulted in a perceived loss of community within the student population.

The University was noticing changes in the learning behaviours of its students as well. When two experimental informal study spaces were established within the Faculty of Professions and the Barr Smith Library, it became clear that students partook in their study activities using methods quite different from the traditional methods of study that the University was accustomed to supporting. Furthermore, the introduction of new technologies and social media contributed to twenty-first century students favouring spaces that enabled them to study both independently and collaboratively on projects, without having to change their work environment (Somerville and Harlan, 2008). An increase in peer-to-peer learning, whereby friends or classmates assist each other as they work through their course materials meant that the University needed to build spaces that could accommodate these changes in the way students study (ibid.).

As a dedicated learning facility, the Learning Hub would provide 10,500 square meters of space for students. To ensure that this significant investment of space in the heart of the campus was fit for purpose, the idea of co-creating the space with the student population emerged, and the University embarked upon significant research of other tertiary institutions. Through this research it discovered that student consultative processes had been implemented in other universities, such as the University of South Australia and Swinburne University, although not to the same scale and breadth planned for the Learning Hub Project.

There were also examples where co-creation consultation processes had been implemented in the private sector (M.L.C. Campus and N.A.B. at Docklands). However, a key factor in determining the University of Adelaide's consultation process was the need to shift the paradigm away from an autocratic mode, where a project controlled from the Project Delivery Unit (or the University to students) was imposed on the student population. In-depth discussions with key staff within the University had also highlighted concerns about the low-level of consultation

---

used for political activity — the intervening years had seen a significant diminution of student life on campus because of a lack of funding.

during the construction process. As part of this research into ways of engaging key stakeholders with the project, the lead in the redevelopment of M.L.C. Campus and N.A.B. at Docklands (Rosemary Kirkby) was invited to the University to share her experience. In meeting with the Learning Hub Champions in October 2009, Rosemary explained that the main benefit of stakeholder involvement is the ownership that stakeholders — in this case students — feel over the end result.

From this interaction and review of examples of consultative processes, a truly co-creative process emerged. The term co-creation (or co-production as it is sometimes also referred to) is derived from an emerging discourse in the marketing and consumer behaviour literature, identifying the need for brand managers to shift the paradigm away from dictating brand attributes to consumers, to jointly building brand meaning with them (Edgar, 2008; Cova and Salle, 2008; Lush and Vargo, 2006a; Pralahad and Ramaswamy, 2004; Vargo and Lush, 2004). Consequently, according to marketing scholars, to respond to the increasing power that consumers have gained through consumer-to-consumer communication via social networks and the internet, brand managers should surrender their previous unilateral control over brands and products (Lee and Allaway, 2002; Fisher and Smith, 2011), and allow consumers to have a voice and to share in the design and positioning of brands (Lush and Vargo, 2006b).

Given the increasingly demand-driven nature of the education sector, and the University's strategic decision to become more student-centric in its decision-making, the adoption of a co-creation approach seemed not only desirable but indeed necessary. According to the project's Academic Champion, a marketing academic herself, the Learning Hub Project had not only the potential to transform the relationship the University had with its students, but it could also serve as a pilot project to demonstrate the merit of this approach as a modus operandi for future large-scale projects.

The key guiding principle was that the various stakeholders who would use the facilities would be fully involved at all stages of the process, from design to construction, ensuring that the Learning Hub was genuinely co-created. Involving the student population and other key stakeholders throughout all stages of the project in a transparent and inclusive way resulted in a greater degree of engagement from students, a better understanding of their needs and more ownership over the final result.

Introduction

Prior to the commencement of the Project, the relationship between the University and its student population was stilted. Although the University has an active student union, there were reservations as to whether the Union truly represented the diversity of the student population. Over the years, the relationship built between the University and students had been that of mistrust: each party was sceptical, or had no understanding of the other's true motivations and intentions. The University also had a history of being somewhat authoritarian in its dealings with the student population, expecting students to learn, access services and utilise facilities however and whenever the University wanted to provide them.

By 2009, however, it was clear that to remain competitive in what the Bradley Review had suggested should be a demand-driven and student-centric sector, the University needed to re-connect with the student population and gain a clearer understanding of what students required.

Vision and objectives of the Project

The University of Adelaide therefore embarked upon an innovative co-creation process aimed at engaging its diverse student population. The vision of the Project was 'to provide the best on-campus experience within the Australian tertiary education sector for all students, by providing the most dynamic Hub'. It was determined that to realise this vision, three key objectives had to be fulfilled:

1. to transform student experience through the provision of suitable facilities and seamless services to support their academic activities
2. to improve attraction and retention rates, securing the University's position within the Go8[2], by placing a specific emphasis on the undergraduate experience within the Project
3. to actively engage with the community at large to support lifelong learning.

Early in the Project, a framework was established which categorised student experience into four main components; learning, teaching, support and social.

---

[2] The Go8 (Group of 8) is a coalition of what are considered to be leading Australian universities, distinguished from other Australian universities in a number of ways. For more details, see https://go8.edu.au.

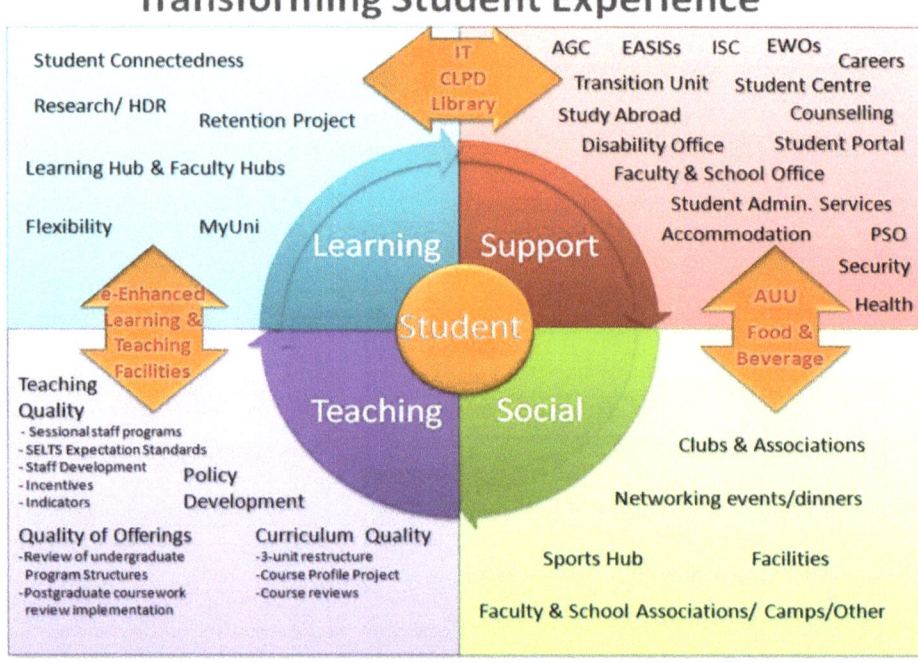

Figure 7.1. Student experience as defined by the Learning Hub Project

The Project acknowledged that the four components do not exist in isolation and that experience in one component can affect perception of experience in other components (see Figure 7.1). Key to the success of the Learning Hub Project was addressing each of these components holistically through the ability of stakeholders to have input into the component(s) relating to themselves.

Methodology

From the outset of the Learning Hub Project, the consultation process had to deliver two key objectives, which would distinguish it from any other construction project ever undertaken on campus:

1. to engage fully with the University's student population throughout the duration of the project
2. to enable adequate opportunity for key stakeholder groups to have input into the project.

As the first student-centric project undertaken on campus, it was important for the University not to be seen as determining the needs and wants of its student population in isolation. Similarly, as a project that incorporated a number of business areas within the University, it was equally important for University management not to be seen as dictating the final outcomes in regards to scope, priorities and budget allocation. Therefore a unique project organisational structure was established. This project governance ensured that the Learning Hub was the result of a co-creation process, as it sought to bring many different and disparate groups within the University together to work as one team and deliver one of the most significant projects under the banner of Student Experience.

Project structure

The overall Project needed to be governed by a group where every member was committed to listening to stakeholders and balancing that against time and cost pressures. In this case, the Executive Control Group (E.C.G.) provided that direction and advice on key project deliverables, as well as receiving, reviewing and providing feedback on reports, project scope, plans, timetable and budgets.

The establishment of the Transforming Student Experience Committee (T.S.E.) as a group that was separate to, and equally influential with, the Project Construction Control Group (P.C.G.) was a definitive step away from traditional project delivery methods. The T.S.E. Committee was dedicated to ensuring that the student voice was heard and to promoting the student experience ideal, whilst the P.C.G. maintained responsibility for delivery of project to budget, time and scope. Both groups held equal standing in authority and enabled the University to determine and define the Hub without a construction emphasis. Ultimately responsible for the consultation process with the student population, the T.S.E. was the linchpin for embedding the student population within the Project's organisational structure. Chaired by the Academic Champion, who was then an Executive Dean of the largest faculty of the University in terms of student numbers, the T.S.E. provided an innovative and transparent conduit for the input of many reference groups, of which the Student Reference Group was one of the most important.

The other key role of the T.S.E. in this Project was to act as a change agent on behalf of the University. By upholding its mandate of listening to the

	MEMBERSHIP	SELF DEFINED ROLE
Student Reference Group	• One undergraduate student for each Faculty (nominated by Executive Dean) • One postgraduate student for each Faculty (nominated by Executive Dean) • Three International Students • Eight representatives from the AUU • Two students who participated in previous Student Focus Groups	• Provide input into the development of the Hub • Act as project ambassadors and communicate to friends and social networks • Provide feedback from friends and networks • Keep the project honest
Learning & Teaching Reference Group	• Associate Dean Learning & Teaching (Faculty of Health Sciences) • Associate Dean Learning & Teaching (Faculty of Sciences) • Associate Dean Learning & Teaching (Faculty of Professions) • Associate Dean Learning & Teaching (Faculty of Humanities and Social Sciences) • Associate Dean Learning & Teaching (Faculty of Engineering, Computer and Mathematical Science) • Teaching award winning staff	• Identify how the Learning Hub can assist current and future Learning and Teaching • To provide an academic and staff perspective to the Learning Hub development • Assist staff in how they can get students to use the Hub • Act as a conduit for staff input into and from the Learning Hub and assist with communications. • Presentations to Faculty Board, open forum etc. • Explore inter-campus connectivity and industry linkages • Identify a network of champions
Services for Students Reference Group	Representatives from: • Student Services • Adelaide Graduate Centre • Each Faculty (5 x Faculties) • Library • IT • AUU • Centre for Learning & Professional Development • Campus Services	• To develop principles that determine which services should be provided in the Hub • To develop a list of services to be provided in the Hub • To develop a set of recommendations on the mechanisms by which the services will be provided on the Hub

Library Reference Group	• University Librarian
	• Senior Library staff including:
	  ○ Research Librarians
	  ○ Heads of Departments
	  ○ Library Technical Officer
	  ○ Senior Management Staff
		• Provide a Library perspective and feedback on the impact of the Learning Hub
		• Determine Library responsibilities to improving student experience.

Table 7.1: Membership and roles of the T.S.E. reference groups

student voice, the T.S.E. were able to instil change within the University's business areas. The needs of students were communicated to the T.S.E. Committee via a stakeholder Communications and Engagement process set up within the Learning Hub Project Team. One of the key engagement mechanisms was the formulation of four key stakeholder groups, whose membership and responsibilities are shown in Table 7.1.

These Reference Groups formed a crucial part of the consultation process. They were instrumental in developing the aspirational, functional and design briefs for the Project. Unlike traditional project establishments, these groups were involved extensively in the project, in a similar capacity as a client representative. They had input into key decisions such as priority setting during value management sessions, and the expenditure of contingencies during the construction process.

Finally, the role of Programme Director was pivotal in ensuring that the everyday running of the Project was maintained, and information from each of the above-named Reference Groups was communicated up through the organisational structure. The Programme Director managed the stakeholder engagement on behalf of the T.S.E. and embedded the consultation methodology within the construction process. It was essential to have adequate cross-over of membership on the T.S.E., P.C.G. and E.C.G. (or all of the decision/recommending bodies). Therefore the Programme Director occupied a role on the T.S.E., ensuring that critical timelines were met, recommendations were made to the E.C.G. in a timely manner and that the consultation process was implemented. The Director also sat on the P.C.G. to ensure transparency, and on the E.C.G. to provide insight into student feedback.

Project process

The key documents that provided clear definition for the project were the Aspirational Brief and the Major Benefits Framework (M.B.F.). Through numerous in-depth discussions with the various reference and governance groups, including several workshops over the summer break where students were paid to attend and contribute, and by using the University of Adelaide's Strategic Plan as a guide, an Aspirational Brief for the Project was completed in February 2010. The Aspirational Brief set out the University's vision and goals for the Learning Hub and what it ultimately wanted to achieve in the undertaking of this Project.

Midway through the Project, workshop sessions with the E.C.G. resulted in the development of the M.B.F. The M.B.F. clearly outlined the business objectives considered as critical for the Hub to be considered successful. The framework allowed the University to identify the eight key benefits that the Project needed to achieve. These benefits were derived from consultation with students and staff as part of the development of the Aspirational Brief. They span four overarching areas of business which the University wished to focus on:

1. learning
2. services
3. community
4. process/engagement.

The M.B.F. now forms the basis of the K.P.I.s for staff working in the Hub and gives the University a steady reference point for future evaluation of the facility.

Student engagement initiatives

The development of a project governance structure that enabled ample opportunity for students to provide input into the project was crucial. Embedding students in the Project structure and being transparent and honest with them throughout the process meant that students and co-creation became the epicentre of development of the new Learning Hub, which is summarised by Figure 7.2.

The Learning Hub Project was as much about changing from a supply-driven organisation towards a student-centric organisation, as it was about the new physical facility that was being constructed. Therefore engagement with the students was pivotal in determining not only what facilities they wanted, but also what services and resources are required by today's students to undertake their learning activities. Through the T.S.E., several key consultation initiatives and mechanisms were established to ensure that ongoing interaction with the student population was maximised. This was a move away from traditional approaches of conducting student focus groups only at key times during the project.

One of the key student engagement initiatives was the recruitment of a Student Communications Intern, in recognition of the fact that communication to the student cohort should be written in student language. A student internship opportunity was initially workshopped in November 2009, and received strong

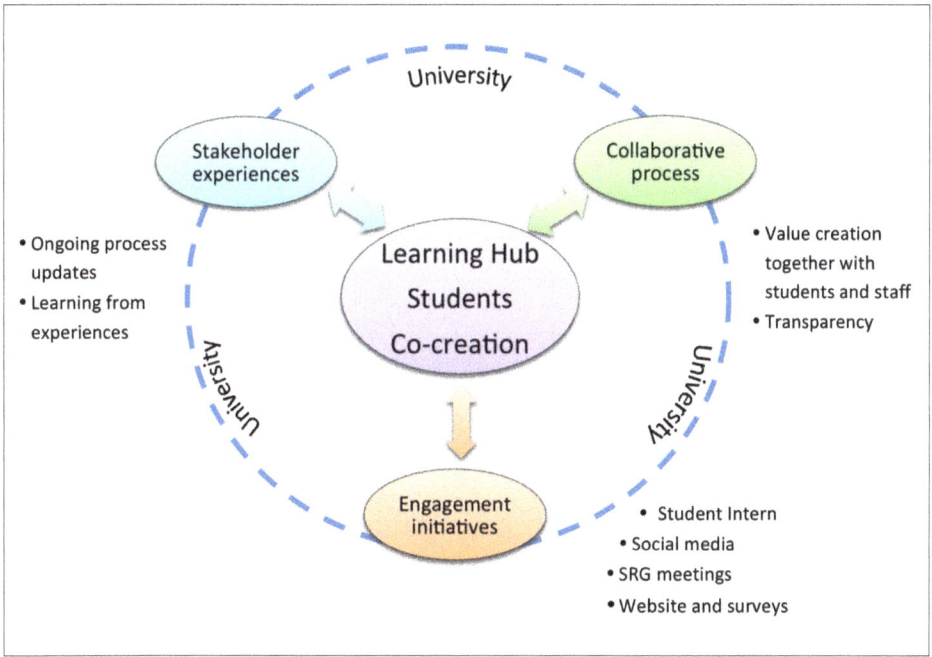

Figure 7.2: The co-creation process

support. The Internship was implemented with two students commencing on 9 March 2010. Their responsibilities covered a number of student engagement activities including:

- *Set-up and updating of the Learning Hub blog*

    The blog was launched in March 2010, and received approximately 5,220 unique page visits, with an average of 120 unique visits per week, for the duration of the Project.

- *Development and use of Facebook as a key communication tool*

    Within two months of the Interns starting, the Facebook fan base increased to 200 fans with the final number of fans rising to more than 980. Active participation throughout the project by both students and staff and regular posts on the Facebook wall attracted an average of 6,500 views per week, in the final few months of the Project, with a significant amount of constructive feedback.

- *Recording feedback from the Student Consultation ('What?') Wall*

    The Student Consultation Wall developed by three students from the University's School of Architecture, Landscape and Urban Design was a great success. It was designed to enable students to provide anonymous comments in response to changing questions relating to different issues at various stages of the Project. Located in the Barr Smith Library, it received more than 1,000 constructive feedback messages on it throughout the Project.

Student engagement was further sought via the Learning Hub Project website and four student surveys, relating to service provision, learning spaces and support, as well as retail services in the Hub.

By adopting this co-creation process, the University became receptive to student ideas and suggestions it would not have otherwise thought of, and was therefore able to capture the interests and demands of the student cohort. For example, early in the Project students indicated that feeling a part of the University and having a sense of belonging to its community contributes significantly to their on-campus experience. Without this feedback the University would never have known of this sentiment and would have delivered a very different facility.

Another example of the impact of student feedback on University processes related to students indicating that they wanted more choice regarding how and when they access their services but not at the expense of face-to-face delivery of services. They also wanted a place to go to receive advice and assistance without having to visit numerous areas across the campus to resolve their issues.

In addition, spaces such as the student kitchen and the serenity zone were only designed and integrated into the Hub as a result of student consultation. The process of naming the space, based on a student and staff competition and online vote, reflected the co-creation ethos, as did the Hub's opening on 12 September, which was held with little fanfare, because that was what the students wanted. A formal opening in October saw the facilities already well-established and very much in use by students as they prepared for their Semester Two exams, populating naturally the space they had so directly contributed towards designing.

It is through continuing dialogue with the students that we can ensure that the spaces and services the Hub and the University provide remain relevant to the needs and wants of future generations of students.

Outcomes

Since the Hub's opening in September 2011, the University has been committed to the task of seeking user feedback and feeding this into a continuous improvement cycle. It has conducted surveys of both students and staff to understand their experiences with the new facility and hear their views on the success of the innovative co-creation process. The University has also collated real-time traffic and usage data relating to the Hub and its services.

The results have demonstrated the unequivocal success of the Learning Hub Project (see Figure 7.3):

- 83 per cent of students believe that the Hub makes a positive contribution to their on-campus experience. This is a 20 per cent improvement over the number of students who *expected* it to contribute positively prior to the Hub opening.
- 70 per cent of staff believe that co-creating the Hub with students has been beneficial.
- 59 per cent of students spend at least one extra hour per day on campus as a result of the Hub. During peak study periods, 22 per cent of students spend up to five more hours on campus than they did before it opened.
- The Hub is heavily used by students. On average, 500-600 students are using the Hub at any one time up until 10.00 pm each day; 50-150 students are using it at any one time between midnight and 7.00 am.
- There are eleven group study project rooms in the Hub which are hugely popular. In general, they are fully booked until 10.00 pm each day.
- Computer usage is at capacity from 9.00 am-6.00 pm; then at 60 per cent until midnight.

These statistics are reinforced by the positive qualitative feedback received from both students and staff:

> Great idea!! At first I didn't really see the point, but after using it for study with my friends, I am definitely a fan! Nice to have somewhere out of the weather with natural light, but not 'stuffy' like the library ... (2nd Year domestic student)

> Very good work from the University. Students can experience more of the student life as they can spend after-hours in the Uni. Good way to socialize, have fun and study at the same time. (1st Year international student)

Universities in Transition

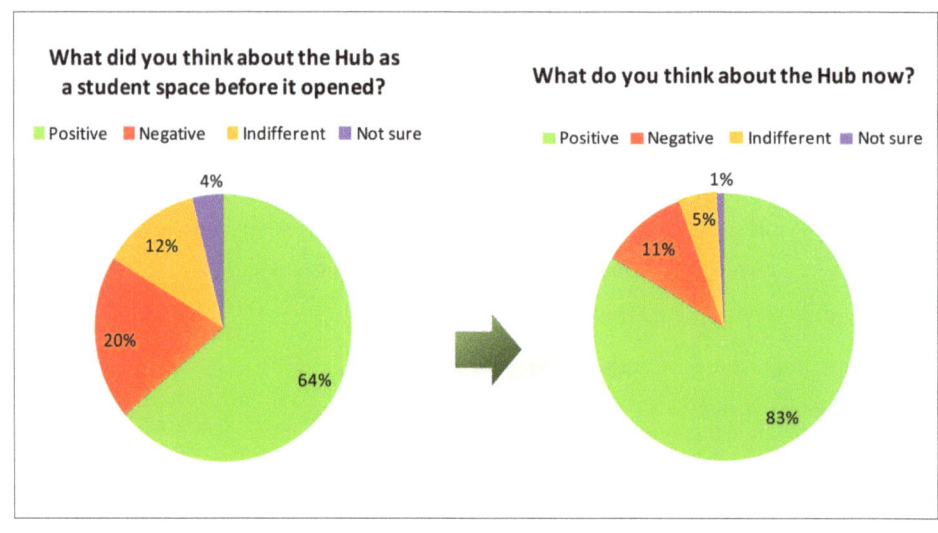

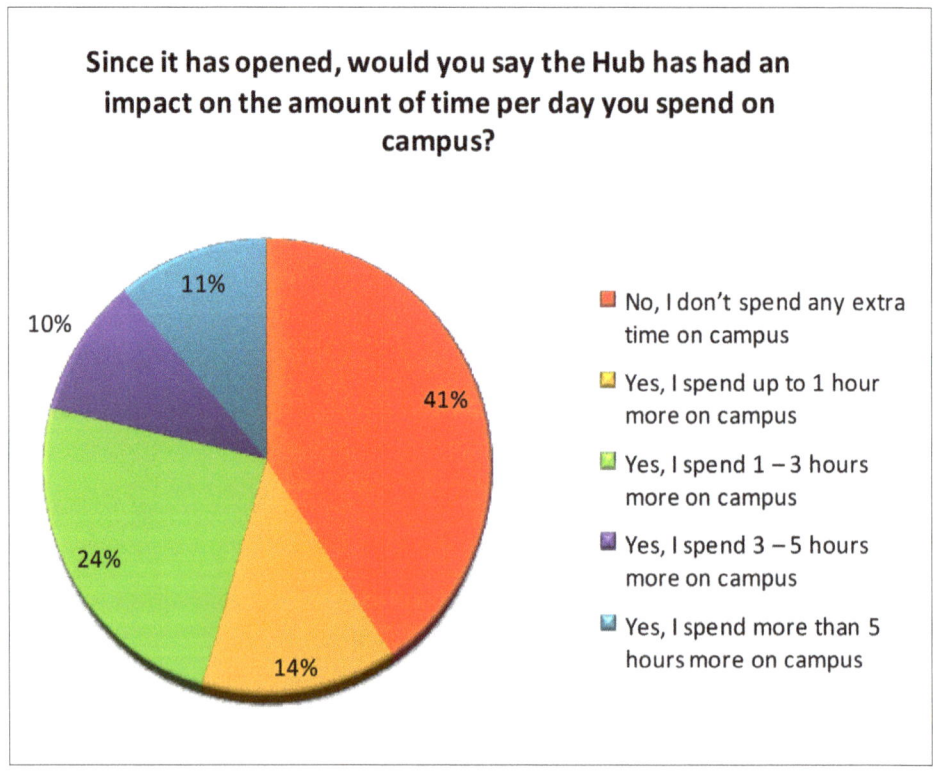

Figure 7.3: Impact of the Hub on student time spent on campus

> The planning for this project reflects in the really useful and creative end product. These sorts of facilities are more necessary, particularly for self-directed learning activities involving small groups … (2nd Year postgraduate student)
>
> I think the Hub is a brilliant space for students with a mix of areas to suit different activities e.g. bookable study rooms, computers, comfy places to chat, etc. I wish I had a space like that when I was a student! (Professional staff member)
>
> The various meeting spaces are great for students. There is so much collaboration going on and it is fantastic to see. I suspect students will be seeking more facilities like this … [M]y early impression is it's just what our students need. (Academic staff member)
>
> This should happen for almost every project in the University. Students are a major stakeholder group and the insights we can provide can prove to be very valuable. Also, this will lead to more ownership and buy-in. (Member of the Student Reference Group)

While the Hub is a student space, staff are strongly encouraged to use the space for interaction with students, other staff and guests of the University. This interaction between staff and students helps to build a vibrant and energising campus life on the North Terrace campus, making the Hub the heart of the university community.

Conclusion and implications

The co-creation process adopted with the student population delivered immediate benefits for students through access to facilities, services and resources that were nominated by the students as important to them. Moreover the University achieved a number of other benefits through development and implementation of the co-creation process:

- *A revitalised relationship between the University and its students*

    The most significant outcome has been the change in the relationship between the University and its students. The co-creation process has allowed us to break down the barriers, build trust and diminish the 'us and them' mentality that has previously divided the students from the University administration. The relationship between the students and the University is now viewed as a partnership, and is becoming the expected norm by the student cohort.

- *A best-practice contemporary facility and service delivery model which meets student needs and exceeds student expectations*

    From a change perspective, co-creation gave the University insight into what students deemed important to them. Providing services that students wanted (not what the University thought students wanted) through implementation of a new service delivery model has resulted in significant staff structural changes. As a result, students can now receive advice and assistance without having to visit numerous areas across the campus to resolve their issue/s.

- *An unprecedented sense of student ownership over the facility and the advent of self-regulation*

    Involving the student population and key stakeholders throughout all stages of the project in a transparent and inclusive way has resulted in greater engagement of our student body and more ownership over the final result by all involved. Students respect and see the Hub as their space: a space they helped create and, as such, want to protect. This is demonstrated by the low levels of theft of provided equipment and consumables, as well as by the space being kept relatively clean, including the student kitchen area.

- *A model to build on in the future*

    The co-creation process undertaken for the development of the Student Learning Hub has set a precedent for future improvements and projects at the University of Adelaide. The Project's co-creation process established a benchmark for the way the University should work, working in partnership with students and as one team for the common goal of better learning outcomes.

Spurred on by the construction of a new dedicated student learning space (now named Hub Central) within the centre of its North Terrace Campus, the co-creation process has redefined the relationship between the University and its students. Through discussion with reference groups, online surveys and social media, students expressed a desire for an immersive learning environment where they could study at their own pace, either in groups or individually, whilst also having access to the resources and services they require, when they require them. By involving the University students via a number of mechanisms, throughout the life of the Project, the University has given ownership of the Hub's final outcome to those for whom it is intended — the students.

What is more, the real value of the co-creation process is to the University at large. It has allowed the University to break down the barriers and diminish the 'us and them' mentality that had previously characterised the relationship between the students and University management, as well as that between University Divisions. The Learning Hub Project radically changed the University's interaction with the student body, allowed the University to build trust with the students and provided a platform, as well as the tangible evidence, for a deep cultural change whereby the University and its students become partners in the learning endeavour.

References

Cova B. and R. Salle. 2008. 'Marketing solutions in accordance with the S-D Logic: co-creating value with customer network actors'. *Industrial Marketing Management*, 27(3): 270-7.

Edgar, M. 2008. 'A descriptive model of the consumer co-production process'. *Journal of the Academy of Marketing Sciences*, 36: 97-108.

Fisher, D. and S. Smith. 2011. 'Co-creation is chaotic: What it means for marketing when no one has control'. *Marketing Theory*, 11(3): 325-60.

Lee, J. and A. Allaway. 2002. 'Effects of personal control on adoption of self-service technology innovations'. *Journal of Services Marketing*, 16 (Nov): 553-752.

Lush, R.F. and S. Vargo. 2006a. 'Service dominant logic: reactions, reflections and refinements'. *Marketing Theory*, 6: 281-8.

Lush, R.F. and S. Vargo. 2006b. *The service-dominant logic of marketing: dialog, debate and directions.* New York: M.S. Sharpe.

Marsick, V.J. and K.E. Watkins. 2011. 'Informal and incidental learning', *New directions for adult and continuing education*, 89: 25-34.

Somerville, M.M. and S. Harlan. 2008. 'From information commons to learning commons and learning spaces: an evolutionary context', in B. Schader (ed.), *Learning commons — evaluation and collaborative essentials*. Oxford: Chandos Publishing (1-36).

Pralahad, C.K. and V. Ramaswamy. 2004. *The future of competition: co-creating unique value with consumers*. Boston: Harvard Business School Press.

Vargo, S. and R.F. Lush. 2004. 'Evolving a new dominant logic for marketing'. *Journal of Marketing*, 68: 1-17.

8 Thinking critically about critical thinking in the First-Year Experience

Chris Beasley and Benito Cao

Abstract

This chapter reflects on the current emphasis placed by government and universities on graduate skills, in the face of considerable uncertainties about what these might involve and how they might be developed. One of the key areas of graduate skill development which tertiary students are meant to experience during their university degrees is their transformation into critical thinkers (Rigby, n.d.; ACER, n.d.; Moore and Hough, 2007; DEEWR, 2011; Chan et al., 2002). We note that accounts of critical thinking as a desirable skill for these students are inclined to constitute critical thinking as having an indeterminate meaning. The literature on critical thinking and university education further suggests that this inexactitude leads students to not understand or be unclear about critical thinking. The 'problem' in terms of graduate skill development is deemed to lie in students' failure to grasp its meaning, which results in their failure to develop this important graduate skill in spite of its value to them. We wish to provide an alternative approach that is rather at odds with the 'student deficit' approach employed in much of the literature. In order to outline this alternative approach we draw upon the findings of a survey and focus groups carried out in 2011 amongst transition students at the University of Adelaide — specifically, students of first-year Politics courses.

Introduction

This chapter reflects on the current emphasis placed by government and universities on graduate skills, in the face of considerable uncertainties about what these might involve and how they might be developed. Over the last ten years or so, Australian universities have found themselves increasingly required to demonstrate their capacity to improve graduate outcomes and to develop teaching excellence with regard to advancing graduate skills development (Chanock et al., 2004). However, there remains little agreement about what this might mean (Barrie, 2004). Moreover, as Barrie notes (2005), Australian universities remain rather unclear about teaching and learning strategies which might assist in producing improvements in graduate skills development in particular disciplinary/interdisciplinary content contexts. In the absence of either conceptual or teaching practice agreement, it is to be expected that gaps may be found in the literature with regard to graduate skills and how such skills might be generated.

In this context, a large body of work exists worldwide concerning the teaching of transition students and how this may have an impact on student progression and eventually graduate outcomes (Green, Hammer and Star, 2009; Green, Hammer and Stephens, 2006). One of the key areas of graduate skill development which all tertiary students, including transition students, are meant to experience during their university degrees is their transformation into critical thinkers (DEEWR, 2011). The increasing emphasis upon the generic employability of students which is associated with graduate skill development is by no means straightforwardly supported by academic staff and indeed forms 'part of a bigger, as yet unresolved, debate about the purpose of university education' (B-HERT as cited in James, Lefoe and Hadi, 2004: 175; see also B-HERT, 2003; see also Nussbaum, 2010; and for a USA-based view of this debate, Brooks, 2011: 11). Yet certain skills, including critical thinking, can be seen as part of the way in which universities may challenge elite and established conceptions of knowledge, opening up knowledge cultures to diversity and difference, including to a diverse population of students. Access to higher education can be seen as a means to challenge social hierarchies, engage with the wider community and provide students with the skills necessary to ongoing learning and critical evaluation of one's society. These are possibilities which many Political Science academics are likely to find admirable. For our purposes as academics teaching within the discipline of Political Science, critical thinking constitutes a particular element of graduate skill development which is arguably of special interest given the discipline's particular focus upon the ongoing quandary of how we human beings might govern ourselves, as well as the conditions in which we participate in or refuse such governance.

While a substantial body of work exists in relation to the teaching of transition students and graduate skill development, we concentrate here upon transition students and critical thinking because the focus of our study was on first-year Politics students at the University of Adelaide, a setting which involves academic teachers who are likely to be favourable to this element of graduate skill development. In other words, we chose to consider the situation of transition students with regard to the recent enthusiastic embrace of graduate skill development at the level of policy and management but, within this, also chose to foreground critical thinking. Critical thinking, unlike many other graduate skills, cannot necessarily be deemed complicit in challenging an academic knowledge-content orientation or complicit in any unreflective acceptance of existing social relations, the market or utility-oriented vocationalism. On this basis, critical thinking is a skill with which Political Science teachers might be expected to have some sympathy. We aimed, in short, to consider graduate skill development for transition students in a location where the teaching aim regarding graduate attributes (specifically, critical thinking) was likely to be in keeping with the concerns of the academic teachers (Political Science academics). We focused upon the development of critical thinking amongst transition students in the discipline of Political Science in order to provide a kind of 'best case scenario' for investigating what we mentioned at the start of this chapter — that is, the existing uncertainties in the literature regarding what graduate skills might involve and how they might be developed. We suggest, indeed, that these conceptual and teaching practice uncertainties may well be linked but, in the instance of critical thinking and teaching directions for transition students' skill development, not in the way the literature typically suggests.

Critical thinking: conceptual deficit?

Government and university management emphasis upon graduate skills and, in particular, upon the value of critical thinking, is supported by a range of writers who propose that it is central to learning and to the core role of higher education, as well as having a crucial importance for society more generally (Lederer, 2007;

Davies, 2006; Facione, Facione and Giancarlo, 2000; Beyer, 1987). In this context, it is no surprise to find that there exists a considerable body of literature on defining and quantifying critical thinking. Very often in such writings critical thinking is conceived as something that can be tied down to a singular meaning, if not to a singular set of internal elements (Paul and Elder, 2006), and is sufficiently capable of definition/characterisation that it can be measured and tested (on the *California Critical Thinking Disposition Inventory*, Facione, Facione and Giancarlo, 2000; on the *OCR AS Critical Thinking Examination*, Wells, Burton and Burton, 2005; on the *Reflective Judgement Interview*, Wood 1997; on the *Cornell Critical Thinking Test*, Ennis and Millman, 1985; on the *Watson-Glaser CT Appraisal*, Watson and Glaser, 1964). However, we note that this degree of certainty is by no means unanimous and that many experts in the field wrestle with the seeming difficulty of reaching a clear or concise definition (Barnett, 1997). Accounts of critical thinking within the university education setting are certainly inclined to offer rather more nuanced discussions. These discussions may involve assessing critical thinking as having decided content associations (Garside, 1996) and/or disciplinary specificity (Yanchar, Slife and Warne, 2008; Liu, Long and Simpson, 2001; King, Wood and Mines, 1990) and hence conceive it as heterogeneous and conditional. On a rather different note, some accounts depict it as engaging certain generic qualities which nevertheless are necessarily approached differently in different disciplines (Jones, 2009). Alternatively, such discussions sometimes assert that critical thinking is indeed generic and has certain universal characteristics that can be applied across the disciplines (Sá, Stanovich and West, 1999; Bensley, 1997). Consequently, in scholarship which attends to critical thinking in universities, there seems to be little certainty — let alone agreement — as to whether it should be taught in extra-disciplinary designated orientation programs, subjects or sections of subjects or, on the other hand, implanted within the disciplinary curriculum (Abrami et al., 2008). This evident lack of consensus in the context of the university setting suggests a degree of caution in relation to those approaches that assume definitional and quantifiable certainty with regard to critical thinking.

When we consider the more specific pedagogical scholarship, which concentrates upon critical thinking as a desirable skill for tertiary students, this scholarship seems to provide further evidence for caution. Writings that deal with critical thinking for tertiary students are inclined to constitute critical thinking as either lacking sufficient meaning or as too rich in meaning. For example, Vandermensbrugghe (2004) refers to the 'unbearable vagueness' of the concept and McPeck (1981) describes it as verging on a platitude, as both 'overworked and under-analysed', while Halonen (1995) describes it as a 'mystified concept'. In other words, the scholarship assumes that lack of a singular set meaning or the existence of heterogeneous meanings is a problem. Critical thinking is deemed to suffer from a 'conceptual deficit', which has untoward consequences for university students who consequently struggle to understand it, let alone acquire or demonstrate it, despite its potential value to them (Abrami et al., 2008; Harrington et al., 2006a).

We wish to suggest that this mode of analysis which conceives the 'problem' as the uncertainty of critical thinking as a concept may be subject to challenge and, relatedly, that the question of critical thinking for university students, including transition students, may be constituted in other terms which foreground the social context of their experience. We note that the view of concepts like critical thinking as having a singular and set meaning has been strongly challenged in a range of disciplines and that there exists a long standing critique of views which presume that some external and pre-existent meaning for concepts exists. In this context, we draw attention to the disciplinary example of the work of William Connelly in *Political Science* (1993). Connelly's thesis of 'contested concepts' offers a profound challenge to the prevailing positivist approach to political knowledges, an approach which takes as given the 'objective' character of concepts. In Connelly's work, the vocabulary of politics is decidedly not a value-free medium; it rather expresses particular meanings in forms and directions which arise out of socio-political contests, while similarly silencing other competing meanings. Note that Connelly is not suggesting that the meaning of concepts is incapable of characterisation or floats freely. Concepts are socially constituted, not meaningless.

In similar fashion we wish to point out that critical thinking can and does mean a variety of things and that the attempt to find the meaning of this term in order that students do not take in the 'wrong' meaning or become confused by its ambiguities or complexities involves an anxiety about being unable to pin down a set determinate meaning that is, in our assessment, unhelpful and misplaced. As Kathy Davis has pointed out, there may well be advantages in the contested character of concepts. For example, she suggests in relation to the term 'intertextuality' that, 'paradoxically, it is precisely the concept's alleged weaknesses

— its ambiguity and open-endedness — that were the secrets to its success' (2008: 67). We argue that precisely the same may be asserted in relation to critical thinking: that at least in Political Science its range of meanings may enable a wide-ranging gamut of socio-political contestation about particular common concepts in political discourse such as sovereignty, security, human rights and so on.

Student deficit? Graduate skill deficit?

The literature on critical thinking and university education is inclined to perceive a lack of a decided definition of it or, alternatively, a superfluity of different definitions which lead students to not understand or be unclear about the meaning of critical thinking. The problem in pedagogical terms is then deemed to lie in the students' failure to understand the concept, which results in their failure to develop this important graduate skill. The solution frequently advanced is therefore to recommend the development of a more specific definition of critical thinking and explicitly *instruct* students in this definition, such that there is a shared and common account of critical thinking available to both academic teachers and university students (see Harrington et al., 2006a and 2006b). The aim here is to ensure that transition and other university students can consequently understand it and presumably develop and apply it more effectively. The further implication of such a clarification is that students' understanding of critical thinking can then be tested and measured, including in graduate skills assessments. Once again we wish to provide an alternative approach that is rather at odds with the 'student deficit' approach employed in much of this literature.

There are four points we wish to raise in this setting. First, the literature assumes that students' concern that they do not have a clear idea of the meaning of critical thinking is evidence that they need to be given one, such that they can reproduce it (Jones, 2009; Garside, 1996; Halonen, 1995). Our earlier discussion of the problems attached to the 'conceptual deficit' thesis leads us to question the basis of this assumption and suggest rather that students' supposed lack of a clear, set meaning may perhaps reflect the contested and necessarily heterogeneous character of the concept. The solution is not therefore to provide a singular meaning but to clarify its possible range of meanings. This leads to the second point. If the initial problem is not a conceptual deficit, then any assumption concerning the consequent problem of a 'student deficit' becomes problematic also. In relation to this second point, we suggest that students may not lack understanding of critical thinking. Indeed, as we point out in more detail later in the chapter, it is possible that students do have some existing accounts of it, which have been effectively silenced by the emphasis in the literature upon developing a singular, articulated and shared definition of it.

Third, the literature is inclined, because of its emphasis upon student deficit, to assume that enhancing students' understandings of critical thinking is to be achieved by reducing what is perceived as problematic ambiguity in the concept. Ambiguity is accordingly banished, or at least reduced, by explicit articulation of a specific, singular meaning of critical thinking, which is bedded down by instruction in that meaning, such that it becomes shared by all contributors in the educational process. By contrast, since we do not accept the line of reasoning which regards conceptual and student deficit as the problems to be solved, we wish to decouple these elements. While critical thinking may be enhanced through explicit instructional interventions, we reject the association in the literature of these interventions with a set and convergent understanding of it and instead suggest interventions that highlight the variability and contested character of this concept. Indeed, we would argue that if governments, universities and academics value critical thinking and its associations with producing active, analytical thinkers, then there is something decidedly paradoxical about shutting down in advance for students their active analytical decision-making about the concept of critical thinking itself. We see this paradox as largely unrecognised in the existing literature on critical thinking in tertiary education.

Our fourth point is one that will be clarified further in the later section on the study. We suggest that, in the effort to locate a deficit in the concept itself and in students, the literature underestimates or even ignores the social context in which critical thinking arises — beyond some mention of the ways in which social interaction in class is important to students (Tinto, 1997). We argue shortly that other elements of the first-year experience for transition students may well be more crucial for the development of critical thinking than any presumed problems in the concept or in student understandings.

We now turn to the findings of a study carried out in 2011 amongst students of first-year Politics courses, at the University of Adelaide, to explore these points.

The study: project rationale and methodology

As noted at the beginning of this chapter, we considered that it was highly useful to undertake a project in which research on graduate skills development in a discipline-specific site was precisely undertaken by discipline-based scholars themselves, focused around a skill that is likely to be viewed by such academics as one which is not at odds with disciplinary knowledges and may even enhance them. Our research project, in keeping with the work of Green, Hammer and Star (2009) and Green, Hammer and Stephens (2006), focused on one of the skills — namely, critical thinking — because it is apposite in the context of the discipline of Political Science. This component of graduate skills development is likely to be one that is broadly upheld by Political Science academics, even if it is not explicitly taught in their courses. Within the University of Adelaide this broad skill is most strongly correlated with the graduate attribute that refers to 'the ability to locate, analyse, evaluate and synthesise information from a wide variety of sources' (University of Adelaide Graduate Attributes). We took this as a general operational guide to characterising how critical thinking may be understood in this particular university context, though by no means as an exclusive or comprehensive account. However, we did not restrict our investigations to this account. Instead, we undertook a broader investigation that included research of student expectations, in order to obtain a contextual insight into the students' experience of critical thinking in their first-year Politics courses.

The primary objective of this study was to investigate what students understood by critical thinking and how they were experiencing the development of critical thinking — as they understood it — in their first-year experience of the study of Politics at the University of Adelaide. Importantly, our concern in this project was to consider student views and thus, beyond noting the broad characterisation outlined in the University of Adelaide Graduate Attributes, we did not presume in advance any detailed or specific definition of critical thinking.

The study consisted of two components. The first component involved a short survey of students in nine tutorial groups drawn from the two first-year Politics courses taught in Semester 1, 2011 (five tutorials in *Introduction to Comparative Politics* and four in *Introduction to Australian Politics*). In total, 90 students completed the survey. The survey consisted of four questions. The first two were of a general nature and designed to find out the most important things and skills students would like to gain from studying at university in general, and from studying Politics in particular. The other two questions focused on the understanding of critical thinking amongst the students surveyed and their thoughts on how first-year Politics courses are helping them to develop that particular skill.

The second component involved two focus groups with students drawn from the two first-year Politics courses taught in Semester 2, 2011 (*Introduction to International Politics* and *Justice, Liberty and Democracy*). In total, nine students participated in the focus groups. The focus groups were conducted following the same four questions used for the survey, but these groups concentrated more upon the students' understanding of critical thinking, exploring some specific issues noted during our analysis of the survey, and they included a final question asking students for suggestions for improving the teaching of critical thinking. In other words, the discussion in the focus groups placed greater emphasis on understandings/meanings of critical thinking and on how teaching of critical thinking could be improved.

Most of the findings were more or less expected, especially in the surveys, but some were somewhat surprising. The following section provides a brief account and analysis of responses to the questions in the survey and the focus groups — for a more detailed breakdown of the survey answers see Beasley and Cao (2012: 45-50 and 2011).

The study: questions, findings and reflections

Question 1: *What are the 3 most important things/skills you would like to gain from studying at university?*

This question was designed to provide an unchallenging entry into the questionnaire, but also to get a sense of whether general student expectations from studying at university match up with the way the University presents itself to prospective students. The most popular expected responses were: get a degree (25 students), get a job (28 students) and gain knowledge (43 students). Students also mentioned several professional skills, such as research, writing and organisational skills, amongst others (25 students).

Interestingly, a significant number of students mentioned 'critical thinking skills' in the context of this question (34 students). This label is used here to encompass explicit mentions of 'critical thinking' (22 students) and responses that are reflective of critical thinking, such as: 'analytical skills', 'logical thinking', 'critical writing', the 'ability to question, analyse problems', the 'ability to analyse a political situation', the 'ability to develop arguments' and the 'ability to analyse decisions and make informed choices'. These responses indicate a predisposition amongst these Politics students towards critical thinking. Moreover, these responses already suggest some of their understandings of the term, something that we will explore in more depth in the discussion of Question 3.

The engagement with Question 1 in the focus groups produced two dominant themes: a) skills and knowledge; and b) status and success. Whilst different aspects were more important to some individual students than to others, the two dominant themes were clear and closely related in their discussion. Thus, whilst the skills and knowledge students expected to gain from studying at university were valued in and of themselves, these (and the corresponding degree) were consistently related to obtaining certain jobs or positions and gaining status and acceptance amongst their peers. Their responses reflect the social nature of getting a university education and how that relates both to a specific job/career, but also how society in general and their peers in particular perceive people with and without university degrees. The social context of a tertiary education was also reflected in references to the university as a place to establish 'contacts', 'connections', 'social networks' and 'social university groups'. However, interestingly, discussion in the focus groups, unlike the responses to the survey, did not explicitly note critical thinking as one of the crucial skills students would like to gain from studying at university. This might suggest that critical thinking does not have a particularly high profile in the *overall* university experience.

Question 2: *What are the 3 most important things/skills you would like to gain from studying Politics?*

This question was designed to establish whether there was any significant difference between what first-year Politics students would like to gain from studying at university in general and from studying Politics in particular. The responses concentrated very heavily around the notion of 'knowledge' or 'understanding'. In total, there were 149 responses to that effect. Most students wrote at least two responses that fit under this general label, including 'knowledge' (13 students); 'understanding' (6 students); 'understanding politics' and 'political systems'

(25 students); 'understanding the Australian political system' (15 students); a 'better understanding of current affairs' (7 students); a 'better understanding of local and foreign affairs' (7 students); and 'knowledge of other countries' (8 students).

Importantly, for our purposes in this chapter, the other significant concentration of responses to this question arose with regard to the notion of 'critical thinking'. In total, there were 45 responses covered under this rubric. The most popular responses encompassed under this label were: 'critical thinking' (16 students); analytical abilities — that is, the ability to think critically, to carry out objective analysis and so on (11 students); and argumentation abilities — that is, the ability to develop an argument, to argue with evidence, to think through both sides of an argument and so on (7 students).

The engagement with this question in the focus groups was along similar lines. In both the survey and focus groups, the most significant finding to emerge from Question 2 was the emphasis on knowledge and understanding, which defines what students expect to gain from studying Politics in contrast with the wider range of expectations they have about studying at university. In the context of this study, it is intriguing that critical thinking was so prominent in the student responses to this question.

However, the discussion in the focus groups centred upon the applicability of the knowledge, understanding and critical thinking skills associated with a degree in Politics. Thus, whilst some students noted their interest in theory 'in and of itself', all the participants emphasised that the value of the knowledge and critical thinking skills they expected to gain from their degree was, first and foremost, in their application to 'everyday life'. Some students showed a degree of frustration regarding work with concepts and theories in some courses, on the basis that 'at the moment, it's very all up in the air'. Others concurred but took this as an instance in a larger process that 'prepares you for what's to come ahead'.

Question 3: *Politics teachers believe critical thinking is an essential skill for Politics students/graduates. Do you agree? If yes, why? If not, why not? What does critical thinking mean to you?*

This question was designed to establish whether Politics students share with Politics teachers the view that critical thinking is an essential skill when it comes to studying Politics, and thus whether they also see it as an essential skill for

Politics graduates. The second part of this question asks students to express their views of the meaning of critical thinking. Responses to this part of the question would enable us to test, albeit in this relatively limited sample, the claim that critical thinking is often not understood by students, and the extent to which the 'unbearable vagueness' (Vandermensbrugghe, 2004) of critical thinking is responsible for that supposed lack of understanding.

The responses revealed an almost unanimous agreement with the statement that 'critical thinking in an essential skill for Politics students/graduates'. The total number of students who answered in the affirmative was 86 (out of 90). Not surprisingly, the definitions of critical thinking were many and varied, and included the following: to analyse, reason, seek evidence (23 students); question, avoid gullibility, find truth (15 students); come to own conclusion (14 students); and to understand and think deeply and fully (10 students).

The focus groups yielded similar results. There was consensus on the importance of critical thinking for Politics students/graduates. For example, one student stated that, for her, critical thinking is 'the most important factor'. The students' conception of critical thinking covered, once again, a wide range of aspects/meanings, including: evaluation (for example, 'the ability to evaluate'); assessment (for example, 'assess the merits of something'); reasoning (for example, 'to pick out the flaws', 'testing assumptions', 'finding the premises and testing whether or not they're true and then looking at their relationship'); reflection (for example, 'self-reflectiveness'); argumentation (for example, 'formulate your own arguments'); objectivity (for example, 'the ability to look at things objectively'); scepticism (for example, 'not taking [things] at face value'); and understanding (for example, 'comprehensive understanding'). However, the most popular and elaborate responses associated critical thinking with deconstruction: for example, 'pulling [something] apart and then building it back together, so you know the ins and outs' and 'pulling things apart, seeing how they work, why they work, why they fit together'.

The definitions of critical thinking provided by these students are arguably no more or less vague than those of most academics (Barrie, 2004; Kirkpatrick and Mulligan, 2002). In fact, the range of responses comprised definitions that related to the two main categories in which existing definitions of critical thinking can be broadly divided: the ability to reason logically and cohesively (for example, the capacity to apply theory to practice) and the ability to question and challenge existing knowledge and social order (for example, the capacity to identify and challenge assumptions and explore and imagine alternatives) (Vandermensbrugghe, 2004: 419). However, more important here is the fact that this diversity of meanings never posed a problem for the participants — not even when it transpired, in one of the groups, that there was no consensus on whether critical thinking meant the same thing across all disciplines. Some students viewed critical thinking as a general skill, transferable across disciplines, whereas others thought the meaning would vary according to the discipline. These contrasting views are, as is outlined earlier in the chapter, in keeping with the extensive literature on the nature of critical thinking, with some arguing the generic view (Sá, Stanovich and West, 1999; Siegel, 1988) and others the discipline-specific position (Garside, 1996; McPeck, 1981). This complexity did not raise any issues for the participants' understanding of critical thinking. In other words, the vagueness of critical thinking appeared to be perfectly bearable for this group of first-year students.

Overall, these findings support the assumption that critical thinking has several meanings for students, but do not support the view that students do not understand the term or find that diversity of meaning unbearable. This is not to say that the teaching and learning of critical thinking might not benefit from some explicit instruction. Indeed, there is solid research that indicates that some explicit instruction and/or engagement with critical thinking has positive outcomes (Marin and Halpern, 2011); but, as noted earlier, this does not necessitate a set or shared definition. Instead, as we will see in the engagement with the next two questions, the real problems with the teaching and learning of critical thinking lie somewhere else.

Question 4: *Do you think your first year Politics courses are helping you develop critical thinking skills? If not, can you explain why not? If yes, please provide specific example/s.*

The final question was designed to get a sense of how well (or not so well) first-year Politics courses are contributing to the development of students' critical thinking skills at the University of Adelaide. The aggregate responses to this question were as follows: 67 students replied 'Yes' (representing 74 per cent of the student cohort). The rest of the responses were: qualified yes (7 students); don't know or not sure (3 students); no answer (2 students); and 'No' (11 students). The latter represent 12 per cent of the student cohort.

The reasons and examples given to justify and illustrate overall responses regarding whether Politics courses were viewed as helping students to develop critical thinking varied, but some responses were much more common than others. The most common response by far made reference to 'debates' and forming arguments (24 students). In this setting, one student noted that '[d]ebating every week or at least listening to a debate helps students to see how others approach the same problem and think about issues in different ways', while another reiterated the value of debating by drawing attention to the critical analytical aspects of this activity, pointing out that debates compelled students 'to sift through several articles and sort what is relevant and what is not'. Such comments are largely reflective of the fact that in one of the first-year courses surveyed in Semester I, *Introduction to Comparative Politics*, structured weekly debates are central to the tutorial activities. The evidence from the surveys clearly indicates that students regard this pedagogical approach to tutorial work as very effective in terms of helping them develop their critical thinking skills.

The second most common response — one that can somewhat overlap with the support for structured debates — arose in relation to hearing challenging views and hearing other views than one's own (12 students). This aspect was explored specifically in the focus groups, and the overall consensus was that being presented with challenging and discomforting views was useful and important, but not necessary or essential to develop critical thinking skills. That said, most participants valued this approach, because challenging views compels students to test assumptions, to consider 'why you feel that way about it', to 'justify your own beliefs' and to 'see why that [alternative view] might have merit to someone'.

The third most common response to the question of examples of developing critical thinking made reference to written work (9 students). The most illuminating comments on this included the following: '[t]he essays we have been assigned encouraged us to explore different angles and points of view' and '[t]he tutorial papers require research, sometimes independent, from a range of sources with independent critical thinking'. Participants in the focus groups also reflected on the value of written assignments, especially weekly tutorial papers, noting that 'when you actually wrote them you became more interested in the topic and you began to actually more critically think about what was happening'. The link between essays and tutorial papers and critical thinking is encouraging, insofar as written work is the foremost method of assessment in Politics courses at the University of Adelaide. However, the fact that only 10 per cent of the respondents mentioned written exercises in relation to critical thinking suggests that more can be done to explore the link between critical thinking and essay writing to first-year Politics students.

The engagement with this question in the focus groups reiterated the reference to debates and discussion in general. In particular, the participants highlighted the value of tutorials in the development of their critical thinking skills. In the words of one participant: '[t]he analysis comes more in the tutorials, where you're challenged by something and then you have to evaluate a proposition or argument'. This statement found instant agreement by another participant: '[t]hat's the critical thinking in the course, during the tutorial and discussion rather than when you're actually reading through the coursework'. One student described the experience of debating and, in particular, disagreeing with other students as 'awesome'. Students valued the exploration and discussion of issues in tutorials, no matter the subject, but they also noted that the quality of tutorials varied (presumably depending of the group and the tutor). Similarly, they noted that participation varies from tutorial to tutorial, but valued the fact that '[e]ven if you don't say anything, as long as you're taking it in, you're still forming opinions'. In short, tutorials emerged from the discussion as the key site for the development of critical thinking skills.

Students also reflected on how critical thinking was aided or hindered by other aspects of the teaching and learning process, namely lectures, readings and essays. They found lectures helpful when these provided them with the general context and understanding of a theme. The value of readings was associated with the exposure to a range of different arguments. Essays were seen as useful to enable deeper engagement with themes and arguments. Thus, students understand the purpose and use of each of the four main components of the teaching and learning of Politics at the University of Adelaide (lectures, tutorials, readings and essays) and their relation with the development of critical thinking. This is not to say they did not identify any problems or areas where they felt more could be done to improve the teaching and learning of critical thinking (as we shall see in the final question), but it does indicate that the problems with the teaching and learning of critical thinking would seem to lie somewhere else, not in the students' understanding of critical thinking.

Question 5 [*only in the focus groups*]: *How might critical thinking be taught better?*

This question, asked only of the participants in the focus groups, was designed to get some suggestions from the students regarding how the teaching of critical thinking could be improved. Student responses to the previous question already provided some indication as to what they considered was effective (for example, structured debates, tutorial papers) and what could be improved in the teaching of critical thinking. In this question, the focus groups explored those aspects further. Once again, there was no reference whatsoever to the need to clarify or define critical thinking. In other words, there was no evidence that the supposed vagueness and diversity of meanings associated with critical thinking posed obstacles to its development. Instead, students focused consistently on *how* the teaching of critical thinking could be improved. In a nutshell, their main suggestions were: a) lectures should provide context and examples; b) tutorials should focus on debate and discussion (for example, 'based around arguments'); c) readings should provide a range of arguments (for example, 'cover different angles') and be manageable and consistent in volume; and d) essays should be dispersed rather than concentrated at the end of the semester. Such suggestions show that these first-year students have reasonably developed ideas about what to expect and how each component can potentially assist the development of their graduate skills, in particular critical thinking.

  The discussion also indicated that the problem lies not in students being ignorant of the value of critical thinking and of what critical thinking entails. Instead, the discussion suggested that the problem — such that there may be said to be a problem — was located elsewhere. For the students themselves the problem lies in two areas: a) in the quality of the teaching components, such as the quality of the lectures/lecturers and tutorials/tutors, and the quality and quantity of readings, and; b) the quantity of time students spend on their education. Leaving aside the specific choices individual students may make in terms of the time they allocate to read, study, research and so on, these students noted that many of them work part-time, on holidays and on weekends, amongst other times. This translates into their inability to handle academic commitments effectively, especially when the volume of readings is unmanageable and when several assignments are due close to each other at the end of the semester. The most powerful articulation of the detrimental impact the time factor has upon their potential to develop critical thinking skills was expressed by a student who offered a reflection on her experience of writing an essay early in the semester, when time was not bearing down on her:

> It was nice to be able to sit down and go through it and then actually go back and edit it, and then I noticed, again, a huge change in my thinking. From right at the beginning of the essay to the end my idea on the subject developed and changed.

The problem, in the words of other participants, is that, in general, 'there are not enough hours in the day' and that 'life gets in the way, especially when you get to the end of the semester'.

The social constraints that produce time-poor students are arguably beyond the capacity of universities and academics to correct. However, improving the quality of the pedagogical components (lectures, tutorials, readings) is certainly within our reach. Whatever the case, the crucial point for this chapter is that it is in the social context of knowledge production in the first year, and not in the development of more uniform and shared definitions of critical thinking, that we find the key to improving the teaching and learning of critical thinking.

Concluding remarks

The findings of our study indicate that, first, students understand the value and the meaning(s) of critical thinking (at least to the same degree that academics do). Indeed, first-year Politics students at the University of Adelaide seem to understand critical thinking more than many or most academics might think. Moreover, to the degree that these findings indicate that any problem associated with critical thinking is not necessarily[1] located in a conceptual deficit or student

---

[1] The students' focus on the significance of teachers in relation to the development of critical thinking is entirely in keeping with a significant body of existing educational research, including, for example, much-quoted research undertaken by John Hattie on how important teachers are to the learning process (Hattie, 2003). If universities and academics aim to advance critical thinking, reassessment of the value and requirements of teachers and teaching would seem to be a crucial element.

deficit, then the solution is not necessarily to develop explicit instruction aimed at fixing a shared homogeneous meaning of the concept. Indeed, we wish to challenge the assumption that a fixed definition is required or that heterogeneity of meaning is an issue. We propose instead that the pejorative assessment of vagueness or mystified complexity in relation to critical thinking, and of students' knowledge of it, might be reconsidered. Indeterminacy and/or heterogeneity of meaning may actually be intimately linked with critical thinking. On this basis we have suggested other issues of relevance to improving critical thinking associated with the social context of the first-year experience, and relatedly other possible strategies for enhancing the development of this important skill.

References

Abrami, P.C., R.M. Bernard, E. Borokhovski, A. Wade, M.A. Surkes, R. Tamim and D. Zhang. 2008. 'Instructional interventions affecting critical thinking skills and dispositions: a Stage 1 Meta-Analysis'. *Review of Educational Research*, 78(4): 1102-34.

ACER (Australian Council for Educational Research), n.d. 'Graduate skills assessment'. http://www.acer.edu.au/gsa [accessed July 2014].

Barnett, R. 1997. *Higher education: a critical business*. Buckingham: Open University Press.

Barrie, S. 2004. 'A research-based approach to generic graduate attributes policy'. *Higher Education Research & Development*, 23(3): 261-75.

Barrie, S. 2005. 'Rethinking generic graduate attributes'. *HERDSA News*, 27(1): 1-6.

Beasley, C. and B. Cao. 2011. 'Transforming first-year university Politics students into critical thinkers'. Conference Paper. *6th Annual Conference of Education Research Group of Adelaide (ERGA): Transformations*, 28-30 September, Adelaide.

Beasley, C. and B. Cao. 2012. 'Transforming first-year university Politics students into critical thinkers'. *ergo: The Journal of the Education Research Group of Adelaide*, 2(3): 41-52.

Bensley, D.A. 1997. *Critical thinking in psychology: a unified skills approach*. Pacific Grove, CA: Brooks/Cole.

Beyer, B.K. 1987. *Practical strategies for the teaching of thinking*. Boston: Allyn and Bacon.

B-HERT. 2003. 'Developing generic skills: examples of best practice'. *B-HERT News* (16): 1-21. http://www.bhert.com/documents/B-HERTNEWSNo.16_001.pdf [accessed December 2011].

Biggs, J. 2003. *Teaching for quality learning at university*, 2nd edn. Maidenhead, Berkshire: The Society for Research into Higher Education and Open University Press.

Brooks, P. 2011. 'Our universities: How bad? How good?' *The New York Review of Books*, 24 March. http://www.nybooks.com/articles/archives/2011/mar/24/our-universities-how-bad-how-good [accessed July 2011].

Chan, C.C., M.S. Tsui, M.Y. Chan and J.H. Hong. 2002. 'Applying the structure of the Observed Learning Outcomes (SOLO) Taxonomy on students' learning outcomes: an empirical study'. *Assessment & Evaluation in Higher Education*, 27(6): 511-27.

Chanock, K., R. Clerehan, T. Moore and A. Prince. 2004. 'Shaping university teaching towards measurement for accountability: problems of the Graduate Skills Assessment Test'. *Australian Universities Review*, 47(1): 22-9.

Connolly, W.E. 1993. *The terms of political discourse*. Princeton: Princeton University Press.

Course Experience Questionnaire, The Role of the Australian Government. http://www.deewr.gov.au/HigherEducation/Programs/Quality/QualityAssurance/Pages/TheAusGov.aspx [accessed December 2011].

Davies, T. 2006. 'Creative teaching and learning in Europe: promoting a new paradigm'. *The Curriculum Journal*, 17(1): 37-57.

Davis, K. 2008. 'Intersectionality as buzzword: a sociology of science perspective on what makes a feminist theory successful'. *Feminist Theory*, 9(1): 67-85.

DEEWR (Australian Government, Department of Education, Employment and Workplace Relations). 2011. 'Executive Summary, Graduate Skills Assessment'. http://www.deewr.gov.au/HigherEducation/Publications/Pages/GraduateSkillsAssessment.aspx#summary [accessed December 2011].

Ennis, R.H. and J. Millman. 1985. *Cornell critical thinking test, level X*. Pacific Grove, CA: Midwest Publications.

Facione, P.A., N.C. Facione and C. Giancarlo. 2000. 'The disposition toward critical thinking: its character, measurement, and relationship to critical thinking skill'. *Informal Logic*, 20(1): 61-84.

Garside, C. 1996. 'Look who's talking: a comparison of lecture and group discussion teaching strategies in developing critical thinking skills'. *Communication Education*, 45: 212-27.

Gordon, K. and A. Lee. 1998. 'Exploring co-production in academic literacy'. *Literacy and Numeracy Studies*, 8(2): 5-23.

Graduate Qualities, Flinders University. http://www.flinders.edu.au/teaching-strategies/graduate-qualities [accessed December 2011].

Green, W., S. Hammer and C. Star. 2009. 'Facing up to the challenge: Why is it so hard to develop graduate attributes?' *Higher Education Research & Development*, 28(1): 17-29.

Green, W., S. Hammer and R. Stephens. 2006. 'Embedding graduate skills into a first year management course: theory, practice and reflection'. *Critical visions: thinking, learning and researching in higher education. Proceedings of the 29th HERDSA Annual Conference*, 10-12 July, Perth.

Halonen, J.S. 1995. 'Demystifying critical thinking'. *Teaching of Psychology*, 22(1): 75-81.

Harrington, K., J. Elander, L. Norton, P. Reddy, O. Aiyegbayo and E. Pitt. 2006a. 'A qualitative analysis of staff-student differences in understandings of assessment criteria', in C. Rust (ed.), *Improving student learning through assessment*. Oxford: Oxford Centre for Staff and Learning Development (235-47).

Harrington, K., L. Norton, J. Elander, J. Lusher, O. Aiyegbayo, E. Pitt, H. Robinson and P. Reddy. 2006b. 'Using core assessment criteria to improve essay writing', in C. Bryan and K. Clegg (eds), *Innovative assessment in higher education*. London: Routledge (110-19).

Hattie, J. 2003. 'Teachers make a difference: What is the research evidence?' Australian Council for Educational Research, October. http://www.acer.edu.au/documents/RC2003HattieTeachersMakeADifference.pdf [accessed July 2014].

James, B., G. Lefoe and M. Hadi. 2004. 'Working "through" graduate attributes:

a bottom-up approach'. *Transforming knowledge into wisdom: holistic approaches to teaching and learning. Proceedings of the HERDSA 2004 International Conference*, Miri, Sarawak. Milperra, NSW: HERDSA (174-84).

Jones, A. 2009. 'Redisciplining generic attributes: the disciplinary context in focus'. *Studies in Higher Education*, 34(1): 85-100.

King, P.M., P.K. Wood and R.A. Mines. 1990. 'Critical thinking among college and graduate students'. *The Review of Higher Education*, 13(2): 167-86.

Kirkpatrick, A. and D. Mulligan. 2002. 'Cultures of learning: critical reading in the social and applied sciences'. *Australian Review of Applied Linguistics*, 25(2): 73-99.

Leaman, D. 2005a. 'Politics across the curriculum: teaching introductory political science courses in learning communities'. 101st annual meeting of the American Political Science Association, 1-4 September, Washington, DC.

Leaman, D. 2005b. 'Diversifying the study of politics: non-traditional texts as supplements and challengers in political science courses'. Conference paper. *2nd Annual APSA Conference on Teaching and Learning in Political Science*, 19-21 February, Washington, DC.

Lederer, D.A. 2007. 'Disposition towards critical thinking among occupational therapy students'. *American Journal of Occupational Therapy*, 61(5): 519-26.

Liu, G., S. Long and M.E. Simpson. 2001. 'Self-perceived gains in critical thinking and communication skills: are there disciplinary differences?' *Research in Higher Education*, 40(1): 43-60.

Marginson, S. and M. Considine. 2000. *The Enterprise University: power, governance and reinvention in Australia*. Cambridge: Cambridge University Press.

Marin, L.M. and D.F. Halpern. 2011. 'Pedagogy for developing critical thinking in adolescents: explicit instruction produces greatest gains'. *Thinking Skills and Creativity*, 6: 1-13.

McPeck, J.E. 1981. *Critical thinking and education*. New York: St Martin's Press.

Moon, J. 2008. *Critical thinking: an exploration of theory and practice*. Abingdon, Oxon and New York: Routledge.

Moore, T. and B. Hough. 2007. 'The perils of skills: towards a model of integrating graduate attributes into the disciplines', in H. Marriott, T. Moore and R. Spence-Brown (eds), *Learning Discourses and the Discourses of Learning*. Melbourne: Monash University Press.

Nussbaum, M. 2010. *Not for profit: why democracy needs the humanities*. Princeton: Princeton University Press.

Paul, R. and L. Elder. 2006. *The miniature guide to critical thinking: concepts and tools*, 4th edn. Foundation for Critical Thinking. http://www.criticalthinking.org.

Paul, R., L. Elder and T. Bartell. 1997. 'Research findings and policy recommendations: study of 38 public universities and 28 private universities to determine faculty emphasis on critical thinking in instruction — executive summary'. *Critical Thinking Community*. http://www.criticalthinking.org/pages/study-of-38-public-universities-and-28-private-universities-/598 [accessed July 2011].

Research in Critical Thinking. http://webshares.northseattle.edu/IS/Assessment/research_in_critical_thinking.htm [accessed July 2011].

Rigby, B. 'The Assessment of Graduate skills: orienting students and standards for an uncertain future'. Australian Learning and Teaching Council. http://graduateskills.edu.au/assessing-skills [accessed July 2014].

Sá, W.C., K E. Stanovich and R.F. West. 1999. 'The domain specificity and generality of belief bias: searching for a generalizable critical thinking skill'. *Journal of Educational Psychology*, 91(3): 497-510.

Tinto, V. 1997. 'Classrooms as communities: exploring the educational character of student persistence'. *Journal of Higher Education*, 68(6): 599-623.

University of Adelaide Graduate Attributes. http://www.adelaide.edu.au/dvca/gradattributes [accessed July 2011].

Van Gelder, T. 2005. 'Teaching critical thinking: some lessons from cognitive science'. *College Teaching*, 53(1): 41-6.

Vandermensbrugghe, J. 2004. 'The unbearable vagueness of critical thinking in the context of the Anglosaxonisation of education'. *International Education Journal*, 5(3): 417-22.

Wade, C. 1995. 'Using writing to develop and assess critical thinking'. *Teaching of Psychology*, 22(1): 24-7.

Watson, G. and E.M. Glaser. 1964. *Watson-Glaser critical thinking appraisal manual*. New York: Harcourt, Brace and World.

Wells, I., A. Burton and E. Burton. 2005. 'The OCR AS level examination as a means of assessing the critical thinking skills of undergraduate students: a pilot study'. *Psychology Learning and Teaching*, 5(1): 32-6.

Wood, P.K. 1997. 'A secondary analysis of claims regarding the reflective judgement interview: Internal consistency, sequentiality and intra-individual differences in ill-structured problem solving', in J.C. Smart (ed.), *Higher Education: Handbook of Research and Theory*, Volume XII. New York: Agathon Press.

Yanchar, S.C., B.D. Slife and R. Warne. 2008. Critical thinking as disciplinary practice'. *Review of General Psychology*, 12(3): 265-81.

9 Knowing students

Heather Brook and Dee Michell

Abstract

In 2010 we taught a large first-year class of Women's Studies students. The previous year we had reviewed the literature amassing in support of the Federal Government's push to increase the representation of Indigenous, low socio-economic status (SES) and rural students at university in the wake of what is known as the Bradley Review (2008). This reading had sensitised us to the situation that some students were at risk of dropping out, particularly those who were first in their family at university, a category of students which overlaps with those who are Indigenous, rural or from low SES backgrounds, as well as some who are refugees. Not wanting to put students on the spot, but wanting to identify those who might need some extra support, we designed a 'getting to know you' questionnaire for students to complete in the first tutorial. While we both had a keen intellectual interest in the information we gathered, and while we both would have characterised ourselves as committed and conscientious teachers, we were unprepared for the transformative effect the exercise had on us.

Introduction

Marcia Devlin and Jade McKay (Chapter 4, this book) assert that 'to enable, facilitate and support student agency, university teachers and other staff should know their students' (106). According to Rose Zimbardo (1993), a US academic, knowing something about our students is crucial to effective teaching because a student's personal history is bound to affect their experience of the classroom. US educationalist Parker Palmer agrees. He tells a story in his 1998 book *The Courage to Teach* about a 'student from hell'. With some 25 years' teaching experience under his belt and invitations coming to lead workshops on improving university-level pedagogy, he was asked after one such workshop to run a political science class for 30 students on a campus in the mid-west of the US. Palmer describes how, during that lecture, he became increasingly fixated on a student whose posture and demeanour suggested disinterest. Try as he might for the full hour, and despite his successful workshops on teaching earlier in the day, Palmer was unable to engage the student in the material and left feeling sorry for himself, a fraud, and enraged at the student for ruining his class. Later in the evening Palmer was driven to the airport in the university van by this same young man. Reluctant as he was initially to listen, Palmer discovered in the ensuing conversation that the young man lived with his father who was unemployed and unhappy that his son was at university. Berated by his father on a regular basis for even thinking he could get a university degree, the student was at the point where his motivation was so low he was considering dropping out. By the time the young man dropped Palmer off at the airport Palmer was transformed; he had been forced 'into a deeper understanding of the student condition' which in turn was transformative for the way in which he taught.

In this chapter, we recount a similar experience of transformation. In 2010 we were teaching a large first-year class of Women's Studies students. In the previous year we had reviewed the literature amassing in support of the Federal Government's push to increase the representation of Indigenous, low SES and rural students at university in the wake of what is known as the Bradley Review (Bradley et al., 2008). This reading had sensitised us to the situation that some students were at risk of dropping out, particularly those who were first in their family at university, a category of students which overlaps with those who are Indigenous, rural or from low SES backgrounds, as well as some who are refugees. We devised, partly in response to an administrative directive, a 'getting to know you' questionnaire for students to complete in the first tutorial. While we both had a keen intellectual interest in the information we gathered, and while we both would have characterised ourselves as committed and conscientious teachers, we were unprepared for the transformative effect the exercise had on us. Our aim, in this chapter, is to share this modest but effective initiative, and to consider some of its expected and unanticipated consequences. The double meaning in our title is deliberate: our contention is that in knowing something about our students — even if what we know is insufficient or partial — we are better able to position students as knowing, and to begin unsettling the line dividing teaching and learning.

What we did and why we did it

Our university, like most, is keen not just to attract and enrol students but also to retain them. Universities, after all, are in the business of producing graduates. To this end, our university asks lecturers co-ordinating first-year topics to report measures they have implemented to identify and support students 'at risk' of dropping out. There is no prescribed way of doing this: precisely how 'at risk' students are to be recognised is not specified, and it is up to each of us to devise our own strategies. It is appropriate, in our view, to allow topic co-ordinators to approach such a task in autonomous and even idiosyncratic ways. In our sizeable Faculty of Social and Behavioural Sciences, different strategies are implemented according to a host of factors — not the least of which is whether lecturers could care less about how their students fare. Our anecdotally informed view is that most lecturers do care deeply about their students but may nevertheless interpret the task of identifying and supporting 'at risk' students as an administrative exercise. In our faculty — which includes disciplines as diverse as Psychology, History and Women's Studies — most lecturers tackle the task of identifying 'at risk' students by setting an early assessment task in order to 'follow up' those who do not submit or otherwise fail the assignment.

We took a different approach for several reasons. Setting an early assessment component in order to 'catch' those who perform poorly wrongly assumes that 'at risk' students are less capable than others. Too often difficulties with the middle-class university culture are interpreted as a deficit on the part of low SES or working class students (Kadi, 1993; Ball and Vincent, 2001). The reality is somewhat different: Australian figures suggest that students from low SES backgrounds are not significantly different from others in terms of their rates of completion and level of achievement (Gale, 2010). Secondly — and here we rely on our own experience as erstwhile 'at risk' students — it seems to us that being unable to complete or otherwise failing an early assignment constitutes a reasonably sound reason to quit. In this way, paradoxically, such a strategy might accomplish precisely that which it aims to prevent. We worried, then, that what many of our colleagues perceived as a safety net with which to 'catch' students at risk might in fact be more like a highwire.

We did not envision, however, that the alternative strategy we developed would form the subject of any individual or collaborative research. Our combined expertise lies in areas other than educational equity, but is thoroughly informed by discourses of social justice and equality. In this sense, the substance of this chapter is a kind of accidental action research. Action research, in its broadest sense, encompasses 'the whole family of approaches to inquiry which are participative, grounded in experience, and action-oriented' (Reason and Bradbury, 2001a: xxiv). Its methods are defined more precisely in many and various ways, not all of which are consistent with each other (Reason and Bradbury, 2001b: 1-3). It includes, in many instances, a reflective element — a bringing-into-consciousness of our own part in research processes (Tobert, 2001: 250). For some researchers, the reflective aspect is planned and deliberate: for Coghlan and Brannick (2005), for example, action research involves a high level of planning and intention. Our experience, however, is much more in keeping with Judith Newman's description: 'Action research isn't like [traditional research] at all. The research activity begins in the middle of whatever it is you're doing — something happens you don't expect' (as cited in Zeichner, 2011: 273). Our action research occurred in exactly this way. We did not set out to think about the ways our own practices inadvertently contribute to processes of domination, but this was one effect of our initiative. The 'interruption' to our practice has since prompted many more questions, some of which we will consider here.

We began by considering what constitutes risk for first-year students. Using our combined experience (as learners and teachers) we compiled a list of factors we assumed to be significant in our students' risk of dropping out. Our list included the following items:

- Substantial paid work commitments (e.g. studying full-time and undertaking paid work for more than 25 hours per week)
- Limited familiarity with the university habitus (e.g. being 'first in family' or coming to a city university from a rural/remote location)
- Limited access to computing and/or library resources

- Parenting or other care responsibilities
- Excessive daily travel time (e.g. where travelling to university takes more than 1.5 hours each way)
- Language/culture issues (being subject to ethnocentrism; growing up in a home where a language other than English was spoken)
- Class background (being subject to classism; being of or from a low socio-economic status)
- Aboriginal or Torres Strait Islander (being subject to racism)
- Disability (being subject to ableism and/or having a condition affecting study).

There is a considerable scholarly literature on every one of these items, as well as on risk factors in general. For example, Pearce, Down and Moore's (2008) critical ethnography of working class students attending Murdoch University (in Western Australia) shows that poor and working-class students come from a very different cultural background, or habitus, to that of middle- and upper-class students, even though it is usually assumed that Australian-born non-Indigenous people are monocultural (Branson and Miller, 1979). The Pearce, Down and Moore study confirms findings from Australia, the UK and the US demonstrating that students from poor and working-class backgrounds have distinctly different cultural backgrounds to that of their middle- and upper-class peers (Jackson and Marsden, 1962; Willis, 1977; Branson and Miller, 1979; Dwyer, Wilson, and Woock, 1984; Tokarczyk, 2004; Zandy, 1995; Lucey and Walkerdine, 2000; Livingstone, 2006). However, at the time, we referred to this literature only in passing, and only in order to confirm our intuitions.

Having confirmed what constitutes risk, we packaged the list of risk factors as a questionnaire, and distributed it in tutorials. We did not flag the purpose of the questionnaire as identifying those students at risk of failing or dropping out. Our intention was to avoid intimidating or humiliating those students negotiating multiple risk factors, and to offer information and resources to those who might need them. We were aware, however, that our students might perceive an association with even the label of disadvantage as risky in itself. As 'first in family' graduates from working-class backgrounds ourselves, we remembered being very careful with our own such identifications and disclosures (Brook and Michell, 2010;

Brook, 2011; Michell, 2011). Consistent with our aims, then, we presented the questionnaire to our students as an entirely voluntary exercise in ensuring that we could direct *all* of our students to as much advice and assistance as the university was able to provide.

We were somewhat blasé in our implementation of this strategy. We did not think very carefully about how we would use the information gleaned in the exercise or how we might respond to students' concerns. Our detachment stemmed partly from the questionnaire's genesis as an administrative initiative, and partly from our somewhat smug confidence that we were already well-attuned and responding adequately to structural disadvantage in our classrooms. We thought of ourselves as academics who avoid the '"banking" concept of education' (Freire, 1993 [1970]), who know and care about our students, care about how we teach, and have some personal understanding of at least some of the experiences and situations which constitute risk. For example, we were already aware that for those from poor and working-class backgrounds the internalising of oppression can generate doubt about their ability to succeed in higher education, producing a lack of self-confidence generated and perpetuated by class bias (Kadi, 1993). What we failed to think about — and what turned out to be very important — was what it meant to our students to have the opportunity to disclose their situation to us, and what it meant for us to witness that disclosure.

The largest part of the questionnaire consisted of a list of checkable boxes — one for each risk factor we had identified. A second, smaller part took the form of an open-ended invitation with some blank space. Over many years teaching first-year classes, we are continually reminded that in the first semester, first-year students are often very anxious. That anxiety, in our experience, could infect entire classes, but pinpointing its source and addressing it is no easy matter. It seems to manifest most obviously as anxiety about assessment. We have responded to this anxiety by varying the types of assignment set and by breaking down assessment tasks into smaller, more detailed components. This did not seem to work: many students still wanted to know precisely what to do, or what to write. More instruction, and more detailed rubrics about exactly what we were looking for, did not seem to allay students' fears. For this reason, the final, open-ended question invited students to tell us anything else they wanted us to know about their fears, study plan or situation. Specifically, we asked:

> Is there anything at all about your life, study plans etc. that you want us to know? Is there anything you're worried about? Are you worried about speaking up in class, or your ability to use grammar correctly? Are you worried about missing classes, or keeping up with the reading? (Don't wait until it is too late; tell us now so that we can offer advice or tailor your learning.)

In this way we hoped to shed some light on that diffuse and elusive anxiety, while taking account of *all* our students' needs and ensuring that existing resources were directed appropriately. As noted earlier, completing the questionnaire was in no way compulsory. We invited students to include their name only if they wanted to, and/or if they were happy for us to pass on relevant information to them. We affirmed that it was fine to return an entirely blank questionnaire. However, nearly everyone completed the questionnaire: some did not give their name, and some completed it just by writing their name (that is, without checking any boxes — letting us know that they were not negotiating any immediate risks, perhaps). But most of our students ticked at least one box, and many ticked multiple boxes. Nearly half of all the completed questionnaires included a response to the final, open-ended question, raising issues such as their lack of confidence in their ability to cope or persist with study, fears about keeping up with the reading load, and hard-to-categorise experiences (such as being victims of crime or having complicated personal relationships) which affected their ability to attend and study. Because we were not expecting much more from doing this exercise other than to identify those students most at risk of dropping out, we were surprised by the changes that seemed to follow, first to tutorials, and, second, to our own teaching practice.

What happened

The tutorials changed immediately after the questionnaires were completed. Where usually it would take several weeks for students to settle down, and for some to open up and actively engage in discussions, tutorials instead quickly became settings of camaraderie, familiarity and friendliness. It was as if we had all gotten to know each other a bit better and could get down to doing the work of learning in a more settled, constructive manner. There was less anxiety and trepidation in the atmosphere. It seemed as if by giving students an opportunity to disclose what was important for them, or worrying them, they felt better, relieved of burdens which may have obstructed participation in class, perhaps because they no longer needed to control what they revealed of their backgrounds (Granfield, 1991; Jensen, 2004). It may also be that we had found a way to show students that we cared about them beyond their immediate scholarly capacity, were interested in their success and wanted to get to know them, all factors which have been demonstrated by research to help to cultivate more productive learners (O'Brien, 2010).

However, it was not only the students who changed. As the two of us debriefed and discussed the changed situation in tutorials — which we discovered had occurred similarly across all groups led individually by each of us — we realised that we had been deeply affected by what students had said to us via the questionnaire. We noted the shift that had taken place in each of us as we collated the results of the questionnaire. From a keen intellectual interest in the information we had gathered — which was primarily concerned with quantifying the number of first-generation students, for example — at some point in the collation process our relationship with the students changed. No longer metaphorically sitting out the front in the role of university teacher, we had each switched to standing beside them, in solidarity with them. The identification may have been brief, but it had enduring effects. It was as if the previously rigid adherence to the categories of 'teacher' and 'student' had separated us from the students, and now we were connected in a manner that highlighted our common humanity (Chawla and Rodriguez, 2007). We remembered and recognised, in our students' responses to that questionnaire, our own frailties as beginner students. In other words, as we learned a snippet more about each student, sometimes only conveyed through several ticks on a form, we realised it made a difference to us to know more about the students in our class.

Suddenly catapulted into a reflection on whether we were 'doing the right things' rather than 'doing things right' (Hunt, 2007), we began to question our teaching practice. For example, where students had ticked multiple boxes of possible barriers to their study, we began to wonder what it was *we* needed to learn in order to be of any use to them. Through the simple but sudden realisation that a number of students were not only first-generation but also caring for at least one dependent child, travelling more than 1.5 hours to get to class, coming from low SES backgrounds and, in some cases, also using English as their second language, we became suddenly aware of our own experiential ignorance. We were the ones suddenly transformed into teachers who needed to learn how to change our teaching practices in order to serve these students better.

We also learned something about the students — and ourselves — through the expression of a few heartfelt concerns. For example, when a number of students spoke of being scared to speak up in class in case they said something stupid or wrong, we realised we needed to take extra care in our responses to them, to ensure we were not dismissive, but instead reassuring and encouraging. We also tried to demonstrate that making a fool of oneself is not necessarily a sign of stupidity. In one lecture, we recounted the experience one of us had as a first-year political science student:

> When I first started at uni, there was a Politics professor (who had a softly musical American accent) who often referred to a group I dutifully noted down as the 'Priests of Craddox'. In time, as references to the Priests of Craddox continued, I wondered why the lecturer had never explained who these people were, or even where Craddox was. So I put aside my nerves, and spoke up: who were these Priests, and where is Craddox? Shortly thereafter, I learned that thinkers who lived in Ancient Greece, prior to Socrates, are sometimes referred to en masse as the *pre-Socratics*.

As we wrote 'pre-Socratics' underneath 'Priests of Craddox' on the whiteboard, the whole class burst out laughing. They laughed at (or even with) us; in becoming comical we could hardly be intimidating, and students did then start to ask questions (even those they believed might be 'stupid' ones) — confident, perhaps, that their lecturer had already asked a stupider one.

Understanding students' anxieties about appearing stupid or ignorant also made a difference to the way we gave feedback on assignments to students. A case in point is that in the past we had used shorthand comments like 'so?' and 'says who'? The intention of the former was to encourage students to elaborate on the implications of a particular comment/observation they had made, while the intention of the latter was to elicit evidentiary support of statements and positions. However, as Richard Warner (2012) says, sending a message does not necessarily equate to the message being received or understood. Without a glossary, students were left to guess what we meant by our shorthand comments, which could perhaps be interpreted as sarcastic or confrontational, or as a negative judgement on the student, rather than a suggested improvement of the work. Consequently, we began to take more care in giving more specific feedback so there was less chance for comments to be misinterpreted and more chance they would actually be helpful and encourage change (Thomas, 2000).

We also realised that we had been harbouring negative attitudes towards some students. For example, several students alerted us to their concerns about getting to class on time, particularly the anxiety it caused them if they were not punctual. Some students needed to catch two buses across town and if they missed one connection, because one bus was late or another too early, they risked being late. Another student had a less-than-sympathetic employer who would not always release the student in good time. Our 'default' position had been to be intolerant of lateness, seeing it as a sign of personal disorganisation, poor planning and disrespect. Simply acknowledging the real difficulties some students faced in getting to class on time caused us to question and soften that default position. Similarly, we had long shared a kind of cynical amusement about some of the reasons students proffered when seeking extensions on assignments. Our scepticism has not entirely disappeared, but it made a big difference knowing in advance that a student was (say) caring for a parent with cancer, when that student later requested an extension. The timing is crucial: knowing at the start of semester that students are dealing with such circumstances sets a context for their work rather than offering an excuse for failure (to complete an assignment or meet our expectations). What we realised was that sometimes in the past we had assumed laziness, carelessness and disrespect for others in these students' actions. We were open to correction — that is, students could disabuse us of these assumptions — but, again, our 'default' position assumed the worst of them.

There is some irony in this. Working in Women's Studies and Gender Studies, we know that in all likelihood any number of our students have experienced domestic violence and/or sexual assaults as children or adults. The figures suggest that as many as one in five Australian women will experience sexual violence in their lifetime (Morrison, 2006: 10). Again, knowing this intellectually was very different to reading this information on a form, written by a student who was sitting quietly in front of us and with whom we would be in class for a semester discussing these and other difficult topics. It reminded us to be less perfunctory about on-campus counselling services, and to review course material for its potential to cause distress.

Several students who identified as low SES students expressed a concern about being judged as different, as not belonging at university. We remembered from our own experience (Brook, 2011), in addition to comments by other working-class academics, that while it is important for students to make friends, for some students trying to make friends is fraught with difficulties and often well-grounded fears (Stuart, 2006; Walker, 2007; Mora and Escardibul, 2008). This became a trigger for us to address the issue of class difference at university by modifiying an existing lecture (on preparing essays) to incorporate strategies for dealing with anxiety about belonging and not belonging at university. During this lecture we stressed that while some students begin their tertiary studies particularly well prepared thanks to their family and/or school backgrounds, not having a privileged background was not necessarily a barrier to success. We stressed that while less well-prepared students might need to put in extra work, initially, in order to make the most of their abilities, the University was well equipped to provide advice and assistance for all students, regardless of their preparedness for tertiary studies. We also disclosed how we had made use of such services in our own undergraduate degrees.

Knowing better

Even small, faltering steps can transform how we 'walk the walk' as teachers. Our findings from this exercise were not the result of a research project. Instead, a well-intentioned desire to locate and assist those students who were most at risk of dropping out in their first year at university, informed by previous research and our own experiences as erstwhile low SES students, resulted in us developing a deeper sense of ourselves as 'teacher-students', wherein we were being educated by the students (Freire, 1993 [1970]). It also turns out that the intervention accidentally implements several recommendations drawn from Sandra Griffiths's (2010) study. According to Griffiths, there are 23 factors that inhibit learning in higher education, particularly for those students not part of the middle-/upper-class majority. (In Australia, students from high SES backgrounds continue to be three times more likely to attend university compared to those from low SES backgrounds — see Tsolidis, 2009.) First on the list of factors inhibiting learning are 'lecturers who are not aware of our previous background or experience'. On Griffiths's second list of 19 factors that encourage 'Learner Engagement and

Inclusion', the factor ranked second in importance for students is lecturers who provide 'evidence of a genuine and sincere interest in students and their needs' — evidence that manifests itself in lecturers knowing something about students' backgrounds and socio-cultural location. Inadvertently, then, we had designed an intervention which, in one study at least, appears to be what students at risk most want: that their lecturers get to know them as people.

Thus, an intervention initially designed with a focus on what help students might need to avoid dropping out had expected and unexpected consequences. First, as expected, it helped us gain some insights into what our students need and caused us to review what we could offer and how we directed students' attention to a range of on-campus services and resources. Second, and unexpectedly, the intervention changed our interactions with students and how we thought about them, both individually and as a whole. We especially did not expect it to be so important to students to have the opportunity to disclose something about their circumstances and worries to us; and we did not expect to feel so differently about them, to be so immediately reconnected to those circumstances and anxieties which students experience. Ultimately, we chanced upon a tactic, or strategy, that involved almost no effort but which seemed to reduce students' anxiety and increase our pleasure in teaching. It also introduced us to the broad field of action research, which in turn has prompted us to consider and reflect on our own teaching practices in more considered, deliberate ways. In sum, inviting students to disclose to us whatever they felt we needed to know resulted in better tutorials, a more compassionate attitude (on our part), more effective communication about various student services and resources available, and a better experience for both ourselves and — we hope — our students.

Acknowledgements

A first draft of this chapter was presented at *Transformations*, the 6th *Annual Conference of Education Research Group of Adelaide* (ERGA) held in Adelaide during September 2011. We are very appreciative of the comments and questions from colleagues at the Conference, which enabled us to think more deeply about the long-term impact of this intervention. We are particularly grateful to the Conference participant who suggested that our work resonated with the 'Action Research' umbrella of methodologies.

References

Ball, S., and C. Vincent. 2001. 'New class relations in education: the strategies of the "fearful" middle classes', in J. Demaine (ed.), *Sociology of Education Today*. Houndmills, Basingstoke: Palgrave.

Branson, J. and D. Miller. 1979. *Class, sex and education in capitalist society: culture, ideology and the reproduction of inequality in Australia*. Malvern, Victoria: Sorrett Publishing.

Brook, H. 2011. 'Preparation and aspiration: access to higher education for working class students'. *Australian Universities' Review*, 53(1): 84-8.

Brook, H. and D. Michell. 2010. 'Working-class intellectuals'. *Administration and Society*, 42(3): 368-72.

Bradley, D., P. Noonan, H. Nugent and B. Scales. 2008. *Review of Australian higher education: final report*. Canberra: Commonwealth of Australia.

Chawla, D. and A. Rodriguez. 2007. 'New imaginations of difference: on teaching, writing, and culturing'. *Teaching in Higher Education*, 12(5): 697-708.

Coghlan, D. and T. Brannick. 2005. *Doing action research in your own organization*. London: Sage.

Dwyer, P., B. Wilson and R. Woock. 1984. *Confronting school and work: youth and class cultures in Australia*. Sydney: Allen & Unwin.

Freire, P. 1993 [1970]. *Pedagogy of the oppressed*. London: Penguin.

Gale, T. 2010. 'Let them eat cake: mobilising appetites for higher education'. *Professorial lecture*. University of South Australia, 3 June, Adelaide. http://www.equity101.info/files/Gale_Final.pdf [accessed 26 June 2010].

Granfield, R. 1991. 'Making it by faking it: working-class students in an elite academic environment'. *Journal of Contemporary Ethnography*, 20(3): 331-51.

Griffiths, S. 2010. *Teaching for inclusion in higher education: a guide to practice*. Kildare: All Ireland Society for Higher Education (AISHE).

Hunt, C. 2007. 'Diversity and pedagogic practice: reflections on the role of an adult educator in higher education'. *Teaching in Higher Education*, 12(5): 765-79.

Jackson, B. and D. Marsden. 1962. *Education and the working class*. London: Routledge & Kegan Paul.

Jensen, B. 2004. 'Across the great divide: crossing classes and clashing cultures', in M. Zweig (ed.), *What's class got to do with it? American society in the twenty-first century*. Ithaca and London: ILR Press.

Kadi, J. 1993. 'A question of belonging', in M. Tokarczyk and E. Fay (eds), *Working-class women in the academy*. Amherst: The University of Massachusetts Press.

Livingstone, D.W. 2006. 'Contradictory class relations in work and learning: some resources for hope', in P. Sawchuk, N. Duarte and M. Elhammoumi (eds), *Critical perspectives on activity: explorations across education, work and everyday life*. Cambridge: Cambridge University Press.

Lucey, H. and V. Walkerdine. 2000. 'Boys' underachievement: social class and changing masculinities', in T. Cox (ed.), *Combating educational disadvantage: meeting the needs of vulnerable children*. London: Falmer Press.

Michell, D. 2011. 'An interrupted pathway'. *Australian Universities Review*, 53(1): 89-93.

Mora, T. and J. Escardibul. 2008. 'Schooling effects on undergraduate performance: evidence from the University of Barcelona'. *Higher Education*, 56: 519-32.

Morrison, Z. 2006. 'Results of the Personal Safety Survey 2005'. *ACSSA Aware*, 13: 9-14.

O'Brien, L.M. 2010. 'Caring in the Ivory Tower'. *Teaching in Higher Education*, 15(1): 109-15.

Palmer, P.J. 1998. *The courage to teach: exploring the inner landscape of a teacher's life*. San Francisco: John Wiley & Sons.

Pearce, S., B. Down and E. Moore. 2008. 'Social class, identity and the "good" student: negotiating university culture'. *Australian Journal of Education*, 52(3): 257-71.

Reason, P. and H. Bradbury. 2001a. 'Preface', in P. Reason and H. Bradbury (eds),

Reason, P. and H. Bradbury. 2001b. 'Introduction: inquiry and participation in search of a world worthy of human aspiration', in P. Reason and H. Bradbury (eds), *Handbook of action research: participative inquiry and practice*. London: Sage (1-14).

Stuart, M. 2006. '"My friends made all the difference": getting into and succeeding at university for first-generation entrants'. *Journal of Access Policy & Practice*, 3(2): 162-84.

Thomas, L. 2000. '"Bums on seats" or "listening to voices": evaluating widening participation initiatives using participatory action research'. *Studies in Continuing Education*, 22(1): 95-113.

Tobert, N. 2001. 'The polarities of consciousness', in I. Clarke (ed.), *Psychosis & spirituality: consolidating the new paradigm*, 2nd edn. Chichester, UK: Wiley-Blackwell.

Tokarczyk, M. 2004. 'Promises to keep: working class students and higher education', in M. Zweig (ed.), *What's class got to do with it: American society in the twenty-first century*. Ithaca and London: ILR Press.

Tsolidis, G. 2009. 'University fodder: understanding the place of select entry and high performing government schools'. *Australian Universities Review*, 51(2): 4-8.

Walker, Lynn. 2007. 'Wider access premium students at the University of Glasgow: Why do they need support?' *Journal of Access Policy & Practice*, 5: 22-40.

Warner, R. 2012. 'Giving feedback on assignment writing to international students — the integration of voice and writing tools', in Chan, W.M., K.N. Chin, M. Nagami and T. Suthiwan (eds), *Media in Foreign Language Teaching and Learning*. Boston: DeGruyter Mouton (355-81).

Weaver-Hightower, M.B. 2010. 'Using action research to challenge stereotypes: a case study of boys' education work in Australia'. *Action Research*, 8(3): 333-56.

Willis, P. 1977. *Learning to labor: How working class kids get working class jobs*. New York: Columbia University Press.

Zandy, J. 1995. 'Introduction', in J. Zandy (ed.), *Liberating Memory: our work and our working-class consciousness*. News Brunswick: Rutgers University Press.

Zeichner, K. 2011. 'Educational Action Research', in P. Reason and H. Bradbury (eds), *Handbook of action research: participative inquiry and practice*. London: Sage (273-83).

Zimbardo, R. 1993. 'Teaching the working woman', in M. Tokarczyk and E. Fay (eds), *Working-class women in the academy*. Amherst: The University of Massachusetts Press.

This book is available as a free fully-searchable ebook from
www.adelaide.edu.au/press

www.ingramcontent.com/pod-product-compliance
Lightning Source LLC
Chambersburg PA
CBHW042033100526
44587CB00029B/4410